The Linguistics of Political Argument

The spin-doctor and the wolf-pack at the White House

How does the White House 'sell' its message to the press? How hostile or docile are political reporters? Do they really try to 'transcend the Spin to find The Truth' (*Business Week*), or do they have agendas of their own? How many roles does the spokesperson (or 'podium') enjoy and how many the journalist? How are political – and personal – arguments fought and resolved? What rules of politeness prevail? How does the podium employ 'invisible' metaphors to constrain the audience's world view? Is modern political spin really so novel or does it have any precedent in standard rhetoric?

This book examines the relationship between the White House, in the person of its press secretary, and the press corps through an analysis of the language used by both sides. A corpus was compiled of around 50 press briefings from the late Clinton years. A wide range of topics are discussed from the Kosovo crisis to the Clinton–Lewinsky affair. This was a particularly intriguing and stressful time in the White House–Press relationship.

The work is highly original in demonstrating how concordance technology and the detailed linguistic evidence available in corpora can be used to study discourse features of text and the communicative strategies of speakers. It will be of vital interest to all linguists interested in corpora, discourse and pragmatics, as well as sociolinguists and students of communications, politics and the media.

Alan Partington is Associate Professor of Linguistics in the Faculty of Political Science, Camerino University (Italy). He has published in the fields of phonetics, CALL, lexicology and corpus linguistics, and is the author of *Patterns and Meanings: Using Corpora for English Language Research and Teaching* (1998). He is currently researching ways in which corpus techniques can be used to study features of discourse.

Routledge Advances in Corpus Linguistics
Edited by Anthony McEnery
Lancaster University, UK, and
Michael Hoey
Liverpool University, UK

Corpus based linguistics is a dynamic area of linguistic research. The series aims to reflect the diversity of approaches to the subject, and thus to provide a forum for debate and detailed discussion of the various ways of building, exploiting and theorizing about the use of corpora in language studies.

The Linguistics of Political Argument

The spin-doctor and the wolf-pack
at the White House

Alan Partington

Routledge
Taylor & Francis Group

LONDON AND NEW YORK

First published 2003
by Routledge
2 Park Square, Milton Park, Abingdon, Oxfordshire OX14 4RN

Simultaneously published in the USA and Canada
by Routledge
711 Third Avenue, New York, NY 10017

First issued in paperback 2014

Routledge is an imprint of the Taylor and Francis Group, an informa company

© 2003 Alan Partington

Typeset in Baskerville by
Newgen Imaging Systems (P) Ltd, Chennai, India

British Library Cataloguing in Publication Data
A catalogue record for this book is available from the British Library

Library of Congress Cataloging in Publication Data
Partington, Alan.
  The linguistics of political argument: the spin-doctor and the wolf-pack at the White
House/Alan Partington.
    p. cm.
  Includes bibliographical references and index.
    1. Rhetoric – Political aspects. 2. Persuasion (Rhetoric). 3. Discourse analysis – Political
aspects. 4. Press and politics – United States. I. Title.

P301.5.P67P372002
808.5′1′088351–dc21   2002068183

ISBN 978-0-415-28713-5 (hbk)
ISBN 978-0-415-75389-0 (pbk)

Contents

Foreword

The spin-doctor and the wolf-pack

The players, the peculiarities and the political importance of White House press briefings

A quite remarkable variety of metaphors have been employed by commentators, many of whom are unsympathetic towards the participants, in describing the briefings held daily at the Office of the White House Press Secretary. They are 'a political chess game' (Reaves White), in which 'both sides view everything the other side does as a mere tactic' (Kamiya). Alternatively, they are 'rhetorical combat' (Kurtz), a 'war zone' in which 'combatants with a multitude of agendas […] prepared for battle' (Reaves White). They are 'a wrestling match' and a duel or 'face-off' (Reaves White) but also 'a weird formulaic dance' (Kamiya).[1]

The spokesperson (or podium)[2] is a soldier under 'hostile media fire […] on the front lines for Clinton on nearly every major battle (Baker and Kurtz) but also a sailor who must 'navigate the treacherous waters of the daily briefings' (CNN-allpolitics) and is frequently found 'desperately scrambling and bailing to keep a torrent of scandals from sinking the battered ship of state' (Jurkowitz). He[3] is both a pugilist who has 'bobbed and weaved and jabbed […] his way through all manner of Clinton scandals' but also a street thug who 'beats up on reporters' (Kurtz). He has even tried to be 'an ambassador between a president who disdained the press and reporters who didn't much trust the president' (Kurtz). Less nobly, he is 'a propagandist and a smear artist' (Irvine and Kincaid), 'a master at keeping the press in its place by doling out exclusives to reporters who will play ball with him and actually sandbagging those who will not' (Zweifel). Above all, he is a 'spinmeister extraordinaire' (Kurtz) eternally spinning the truth, whatever that might be.

There are slightly fewer metaphors to describe the journalists, probably because most of the commentators are themselves press people. Nevertheless, they are wild animals, the 'wolf-pack'[4] of my title, which 'fights over morsels' (Warren). They too can be boxers out to 'pummel' the spokesperson who has 'to stand at the podium and take whatever abuse the fourth estate wanted to dish out' (Kurtz). They are 'cynical chroniclers' (Kurtz), 'petty and manipulative [who] simply cannot put aside their "gotcha" mentality' (Zweifel). 'They like to destroy people. That's how they get their rocks off' (Dunham, supposedly quoting President Clinton). At the same time, however, they are 'a lot of dupes' (Irvine and Kincaid) and 'the White House reporter is not much more than a well-compensated stenographer' (Warren). On a more exalted note, their 'job is to transcend The Spin to find The Truth' (Dunham).

Hopefully, we will be able to judge the validity of these metaphors in the course of this book. What is beyond dispute is that these briefings comprise a particularly fascinating genre of institutional talk in which the two parties involved, the podium and the press, have very different interests and aims in life, which are in conflict on several levels. The podium wishes to project his political ideas and particular view of the world, the press to test that view – to destruction if necessary. The press hopes to uncover information, any evidence of weakness, malpractice, internal dissension and so on, the podium to give as little as possible away outside the official line. They adopt and exploit different participant roles (or *footings*, Chapters 2–4), command non-symmetrical sets of discursive resources, and employ different discourse strategies (Chapter 8), they use different metaphors to describe the world (Chapter 10) and probably even see the whole nature of the business being conducted in different ways (Section 7.8). These differences become so severe at one point – during the Clinton–Ms Lewinsky affair and the near impeachment of the President – that, as we shall see, communication between the two sides comes close to breaking down.

Despite these briefings being an instance of *conflict talk* (Chapter 8), however, and notwithstanding a recognition on both sides of their adversarial nature (Chapter 6), the protagonists know each other so well, and probably *need* each other so much,[5] that the register of the briefings is generally highly familiar. This state of affairs leads to particularly complex and intricate relations of politeness (in the Brown and Levinson sense of getting the best out of social relations) (Chapter 7).

What transpires in these briefings can also be extremely important and highly delicate from a political perspective:

> Anything McCurry (press secretary at the beginning of the Clinton administration) uttered from the podium magically attained the status of official White House policy, and if he deviated later on, the administration would be accused of the dreaded sin of flip-flopping.
>
> (Reaves White)

Not only are the podium's words often treated by the press as White House policy, but they risk interpretation by non-American bodies as official *US* policy. And since they are broadcast both on television and on the Internet, 'any misstep can be beamed instantaneously around the world' (CNN-allpolitics). A word out of place, a mistimed remark, even a simple oversight can have disastrous political or diplomatic repercussions. All this exposure, of course, means fame: 'the chief White House spokesman's face is probably as well known as any cabinet member' (CNN-allpolitics). In Galtung and Ruge's (1981) terms he is 'newsworthy', has become an 'élite person' in his own right. Many of the journalists, too, are well-known television faces or newspaper by-lines.

Acknowledgements

The corpus on which this work is based was compiled as part of the *Newspool* project of comparative research into genres of modern political English, financed by the Italian Ministry for Universities. My thanks go to the White House Library for making the briefings transcripts publicly available and to C-Span public service television for broadcasting the briefings on their website. I am especially grateful to John Morley, Peter Levy, Trudy Haarman, Linda Lombardo and Paola Corrado for their invaluable comments on the manuscript.

0 Introduction

Corpora, discourse, politics and the press

0.0 The three topics of this book

This book has three topics. It is principally a study in *corpus linguistics*, in particular, of how features of spoken discourse, including rhetorical strategies, can be analysed with the aid of corpora. It is also a study of a certain type of *institutional talk*, that of press briefings. Third, it is a case study in the relationship between *politicians and the press*. Here, we will discuss the first and last of these themes; the second will be treated in Chapter 1.

0.1 The corpus of briefings

0.1.1 Source

The research described in this work was conducted on a corpus of 48 briefings, comprising approximately 250,000 words of running text, whose transcripts were downloaded from the White House Library website, where they are openly available for inspection. The vast majority date from the period between 1996 and June 1999, that is, before and during the Kosovo crisis (although many other topics are discussed, from the budget to the Clinton–Ms Lewinsky case). This was a particularly intriguing and stressful time in the relationship between the White House and the press. Many White House briefings are also transmitted over the Internet by C-Span, a US public-service broadcaster. I was able, therefore, to watch a number of them and to check the nature and quality of the transcripts.[1]

0.1.2 Transcription

The method of transcription used is fairly broad, there being no phonetic detail. The transcriber attempts to reproduce the normal punctuation of written English texts. They are further idealized in the following ways. Brief repetitions or recapitulations are omitted so that, for example, 'I beg your pardon, beg your pardon ...' becomes simply 'I beg your pardon'. Intercalations such as *y'know, er, em* are all missing, as are some (but not all) replannings, for example, 'the US has the right to make to suggest...' becomes 'the US has the right to suggest...'. This has the unfortunate result that moments of hesitation, of tentativeness, tend to be hidden from the transcript reader. Inaudible segments are marked with long hyphens but there is no indication of their duration. When two press voices are competing for a question turn, the transcriber, when possible, includes both, one below the other. When a press voice coincides with the podium's, the latter is usually the one that gets written, largely because his is clearer – he is the one with the microphone. Laughter is indicated by [Laughter] at the end of the turn. There is no indication of voice quality, for example, regional or foreign accents, loudness–softness, speed. Although the linguist may bemoan many of these transcription choices, the intention has clearly been to make the written texts as easy as possible to read. As Cook (1995: 45) remarks, the degree of detail in transcription is analogous to mapmaking, a question of choice in regard to the need of the user. The transcripts also appear to be complete in the sense that what is broadcast is transcribed. There is no editing out of compromising or embarrassing episodes. Finally, the transcriptions are produced and published on the White House website very quickly. Occasionally, what appear to be typing errors occur, but I have made no attempt to correct what I found. I have, however, often edited examples for reasons of space.

0.1.3   *Research tools*

A number of semi-automatic computational tools were used to help analyse the corpus. The most important of these is undoubtedly the *concordancer*. This is essentially a collector and collator of examples. It will search a text or set of texts for a string of letters (keyword or phrase) and present all examples in a list with a certain amount of co-text for each one. Such a list enables the analyst to look for eventual patterns in the surrounding co-text, which may provide information about the use of the key-item. These lists can be prepared and edited in several ways. The entries can be *sorted*, that is, listed in alphabetical order, according perhaps to the first word to the left (which, if the keyword is a noun would group together the adjectives preceding it), or to the right (which, if the keyword is an adverb would group the following adjectives). Unwanted lines can be removed by a *cancel* (or *zap*) facility. Most of the concordances presented in this work are *sentence concordances*, which are often easier to read than a 'crude' concordance. The lines have been saved into a text file and subsequently manually edited so that the co-text for each key-item is more or less the whole transcript sentence it appears in.

The concordances reported in this book were prepared using either *MicroConcord* (Scott and Johns 1993) or *WordSmith Tools* (Scott 1998). This latter also provides a program to prepare frequency lists; that is, the words in a corpus can be listed in order of how frequent they are in the corpus. The following are the 30 most frequent word *types* in the briefings corpus:

N	Word	Freq. (%)	N	Word	Freq. (%)
1	THE	15.174	16	HAVE	2.289
2	TO	8.603	17	LOCKHART	2.093
3	THAT	7.400	18	IT	2.049
4	OF	5.924	19	BE	1.841
5	AND	5.813	20	FOR	1.806
6	A	4.328	21	ARE	1.745
7	IN	4.078	22	HE	1.731
8	IS	3.471	23	PRESIDENT	1.731
9	I	3.466	24	NOT	1.661
10	MR	3.454	25	WHAT	1.649
11	Q	3.399	26	THINK	1.608
12	WE	2.893	27	WITH	1.600
13	YOU	2.578	28	THERE	1.562
14	ON	2.534	29	AS	1.557
15	THIS	2.328	30	WILL	1.514

Thus, just over 15 per cent of all word *tokens* in the corpus are the word type *the*, and so on. Note the huge preponderance of grammatical words. This is the case in any corpus though the precise order of the words, their places in the table, can vary.

The frequency lists of two or more corpora can also be compared using the *Keyword* facility to show up *relative* frequency, or *key*-ness of vocabulary in a corpus; it should be noted that this is a different use of *key* from that used in concordancing. This process will be explained in more detail in Section 0.4.

A number of other corpora were utilized in the course of this research as a basis for comparison with briefings discourse. These include several corpora of journalistic texts: a collection of British news interviews (*INTS*) of similar size to the briefings corpus, a four-million word corpus of written newspaper texts (*Newspaper Corpus*), the CD-ROM of all articles in the *Times* from 1993 (*Times*). The *Brown*, *Frown* and *Flob* corpora and the Wellington spoken corpus (*WSC*) of general conversation were all used when appropriate.[2] The *British National Corpus* (BNC) on the Web was also occasionally consulted.

0.2   Corpus linguistics and discourse

This book is proposed in the first place as a contribution to the field of corpus linguistics. It attempts to show how it is possible to use concordance technology and the detailed linguistic evidence available in corpora to enhance the study of the discourse features of a particular genre of the language. It is especially an investigation of the communicative strategies used by speakers to pursue their designs.

0.2.1   *Studying discourse using corpora*

This makes it an unusual contribution to the discipline. In comparison with the impressive strides corpus linguistics has made in the fields of lexicography, grammatical description and register studies among others (see McEnery and Wilson 1996: 87–116; Kennedy 1998: 88–199; Partington 2001: 46–63), it has had relatively little to say in describing features of discourse, particularly of inter-action, that is, the rhetorical aspects of texts. Much research on (large, hetero-generic) corpora strives to make observations about 'the language' with the goal of explaining and improving human understanding of it, and has practical proj-ects in mind, such as building more accurate grammars or of generating more informative dictionaries. Language in these endeavours is treated as *product*, as a preexisting entity, deliberately and of necessity removed from its context of production, from the *processes* of its authorship and reception. The aim is to get to know the product as well as possible.

On the other hand, 'the amount of corpus-based research in pragmatics and discourse analysis has to date been relatively small' (McEnery and Wilson 1996: 98). Biber *et al.* (1998) also note that discourse studies 'are not typically corpus-based investigations'. There are a number of reasons for this. 'Pragmatics and discourse analysis rely on context – pragmatics has often been defined as "mean-ing in context" – whereas corpora strip much of the context of utterances' (McEnery and Wilson 1996: 98). Many corpora have also tended to take frag-ments of texts rather than whole texts, whereas the latter are necessary for many types of discourse analysis. There has until relatively recently been a paucity of spoken corpora to use for spoken discourse analysis.[3] Although some modern corpora like the *BNC* include socially relevant information (speaker's sex, age, geographical extraction, etc.), it is still up to the analyst to relate systematically such information to what speakers are attempting *to do* at any moment in their interaction.

The present work however, attempts to study discourse strategies by reintro-ducing as much attention to context as possible – including both the wider historical, political, mediatic context, and the more immediate local and personal contexts, especially the participants involved, the speakers and hearers. Moreover, attention to the *co-text* is maximized by having whole texts, whole briefings acces-sible in both mechanical and non-mechanical form, so that they are available for various different methods of analysis. It attempts, thus, to 'take into account both product and process: not only the text itself, but also its production and reception' (Stubbs 1996: 8). Such an approach is feasible with specialized corpora, corpora of a single text-type (monogeneric), where these processes and the contexts they take place in remain relatively constant, or at least alter in relatively predictable ways (see the discussion of specialized corpora in Chapter 13).

Questions of authorship and reception are, therefore, of central interest in this book. So too are the features of *interaction* between the 'online producers/ receivers', that is, the speakers: the strategies they adopt, the aims they have and the effect they produce on each other. The main aim of this kind of corpus research is no longer to investigate the contents of the corpus as an objective in itself but as a means, an instrument – along perhaps with others – to study what discourse participants are doing in particular circumstances. Specialized corpora are also increasingly used in this instrumental way in the field of education (Flowerdew 1993; Granger 1993), including translator training (Zanettin 1994). Corpora of scientific English, business English, computer science and many other text-types have been compiled in ESP contexts in order to teach them better (McEnery and Wilson 2000: 201–8).

In addition, this work also recognizes the need to study discourse production in its social and political context, that is, to investigate the relationship between texts, authors and the social institutions which produce them, of which they are a part and which they help to reproduce (i.e. produce anew, Fairclough 1989: 39–40). Since social institutions are always defined and supported by particular texts in this way, there is a natural link between institutional analysis and textual analysis. Nowhere is this relationship more clear than in these texts – in the briefing, the discourse *is* the institution, the use of language is the whole point of the enterprise. This book then is also meant as a contribution to the study of institutional talk, of which more later.

The present work, thus, has two main areas of concern. The first, the linguistic, 'is on lexical and grammatical patterns in texts, particularly those patterns which express the point of view of the speaker' (Stubbs 1996: 20). Beyond this, I add those patterns that reveal relationships between speakers, their strategies of persuasion, the metaphors of the world they adopt, and the divergencies between what a speaker professes and what they really seem to think. The problem remains, however, of elaborating a suitable methodology to study features of interaction in large bodies of texts, in corpora. Or put in another way, of designing ways of using corpus-analytical techniques to study aspects of discourse. Much of this book will be an attempt to devise such methodologies.

The second, the institutional concern, is the analysis of language in texts that are public and/or authoritative, that is, the emanation of institutions of power and influence. The particular institutions in this study are the government and the press, the first and fourth Estates, and White House briefings are public and authoritative in the ways outlined at the end of the Foreword. *Authoritative* can also have another sense, that of 'convincing'. An important question in any study of institutional language is 'how is discourse organized to appear factual, literal, objective, authoritative and independent of the author, rather than appearing to be expressed from a particular point of view?' (Stubbs 1996: 97). As we will see, the podiums in these briefings have to make an extraordinary effort to organize their discourse to these ends, since the 'authoritative', official point of view is constantly under attack. The process by which institutions attempt to construct, reproduce and constrain social reality is neither wholly deterministic nor conducted by a single power group. It has to be negotiated between parties and this negotiation is often highly conflictual. These briefings are an excellent example. In my view, they are worth studying precisely because of the interplay between the institutional aims of the two Estates and the discursive strategies adopted by the individuals involved to achieve these aims, together with the fact that the conflictual nature of proceedings requires participants to constantly refine their strategies of persuasion and resistance to persuasion, of evasion and pursuit.

0.2.2   *Why utilize a corpus?*

The general value of corpora has been discussed at length (McEnery and Wilson 1996; Kennedy 1998; Partington 1998) and can be summarized as follows:

> text corpora provide large databases of naturally occurring discourse, enabling empirical analyses of the actual patterns of use in a language, and, when coupled with (semi-) automatic computational tools, the corpus-based approach enables analyses of a scope not otherwise feasible.
>
> (Biber *et al.* 1994: 169)

Examples of authentic data can serve to support the researcher's argument or, perhaps even more importantly, as counter-evidence to make them think again. The use of corpora has profound philosophical implications for the kind of critical analysis of discourse we are engaged in here, as Hardt-Mautner argues: 'drawing on corpus evidence fundamentally redefines the nature of "interpretation"' (Hardt-Mauther 1995: 22), because it adds an empirical dimension to introspection and marries quantitative and qualitative research methodologies (Haarman *et al.* 2002).

Checking intuition against naturally occurring instances of language also frequently serves as a springboard for new intuitions, and can open up new and previously unexpected avenues of thought. This occurs because much of what carries meaning in texts is not open to direct observation: 'you cannot understand the world just by looking at it' [Stubbs (after Gellner 1959) 1996: 92]. One of the reasons why this occurs is that language is used semi-automatically. It is well known that even authors themselves are seldom fully aware of the meanings their texts convey (and not just verbal ones; the same is true of the visual and the musical). This is because meaning is spread out in all parts of a text, in far more tiny parcels than is usually realized. It is conveyed in all the choices the author makes at the lexical level – for example, whether to use *liberty* or *freedom* or the more religious *deliverance*. But it is conveyed in all the choices at the grammatical level too: whether to express a process as a verb or a noun; a description as an adjective or an adverb; what roles to give participants in an event [are they perhaps actor or reactor?; are they grammatical subject and/or thematic (or psychological) subject?]; when an utterance contains two ideas, whether to present them as coordinate (paratactically) or as one subordinate to the other (hypotactically); which order to present them in (i.e. which to *thematize*); how much and what kind of modality to employ, that is, to state how certain or frequent or necessary something is, or how able, willing or obliged someone is to do it. And these choices can be mutually supporting (such as when an entity is *always* made actor), or can be independent (random) or can indeed be contrasting [e.g. an entity is first of all made actor, then switches to acted on (perhaps *victim*) half way through]. In the first and last cases, of course, since the choices are *patterned*, their meaning becomes denser and more significant. However, the text receivers may be unaware that anything is going on at all. Section 0.2.3 shows how automatic text analysis tools can throw into relief the non-obvious in a single text, can shed light on what may be hidden thoughts, hidden perhaps even from the author.

0.2.3   Grammar and hidden thoughts: concordancing the Declaration of Independence

The way in which concordance technology can be used to examine a text to highlight how its authors see or project the world is illustrated in the following brief analysis of the Declaration of Independence of the United States.

Of all the grammatical choices an author makes, perhaps the most consistently important are those regarding *transitivity*. 'Transitivity is the foundation of representation: it is the way the clause is used to analyse events and situations' (Fowler 1991: 71). It is a consequence of the linear/temporal nature of language. It both *forces* authors to structure in linear fashion what they might originally have perceived as a unitary situation and also *allows* them to portray reality in a way they might wish, to construct an argument in syntax.

A number of authors suggest that a fruitful way to begin the study of transitivity in a text (i.e. to find out who is doing what to whom) is to look at the use of pronouns. The author(s) of the Declaration (mainly Thomas Jefferson)[4] claim that their argument is with the King of Great Britain (rather than the British people), and all references to *he* in the document refer to the King. The concordance of the word *he* is as follows:

1	egislate for us in all cases whatsoever: **He** has abdicated Government here, by declaring
2	ithout the Consent of our legislatures. **He** has affected to render the military independ
3	them and formidable to tyrants only. **He** has called together legislative bodies at plac
4	nt of and superior to the Civil Power. **He** has combined with others to subject us to a
5	worthy the Head of a civilized nation. **He** has constrained our fellow Citizen taken Ca
6	m into compliance with his measures. **He** has dissolved Representative Houses repeate
7	rom without, and convulsions within. **He** has endeavored to prevent the population of
8	amount and payment of their salaries. **He** has erected a multitude of New Offices, and
9	, or to fall themselves by their Hands. **He** has excited domestic insurrections amongst
10	e and necessary for the public good. **He** has forbidden his Governors to pass laws of
11	ur people, and eat out their substance. **He** has kept among us, in times of peace, Standi
12	ws for establishing Judiciary Powers. **He** has made Judges dependent on his Will alon

13   tions of new Appropriations of Lands. **He** has obstructed the Administration of Justice
14   rotection and waging War against us. **He** has plundered our seas, ravaged our Coasts,
15   s utterly neglected to attend to them. **He** has refused to pass other Laws for the accom
16   Facts be submitted to a candid world. **He** has refused his Assent to Laws, the most wh
17   s invasions on the rights of the people. **He** has refused for a long time, after such dissol
18   , and destroyed the lives of our people. **He** is at this time transporting large armies of for

There are no occurrences at all of the word *him* in the document. It is immediately clear that *he* is always sentence initial, and, of course, is indicative of subject position in the phrase. The King of Britain is, therefore, presented invariably as the active protagonist of the situation. The concordance is sorted according to the second word to the right of the keyword in order to highlight the verb following the *he* subject and *has* auxiliary. As can be seen they are generally unpleasant in connotation (*abdicated, constrained, forbidden, refused, obstructed*, etc.), occasionally violent (*excited … insurrections, plundered*).

The authors refer to themselves, or their supporters,[5] using *we*:

1   be the ruler of a free people. Nor have **we** been wanting in attention to our British brethren.
2   ir native justice and magnanimity, and **we** have conjured them by the ties of our common k
3   s. In every stage of these Oppressions **we** have Petitioned for Redress in the most humble
4   ng in attention to our British brethren. **we** have warned them from time to time of attempts
5   an unwarrantable jurisdiction over us. **We** have reminded them of the circumstances of our
6   of our emigration and settlement here. **We** have appealed to their native justice and magnan
7   ces our Separation, and hold them, as **we** hold the rest of mankind, Enemies in War, in Pea
8   s which impel them to the separation. **We** hold these truths to be self-evident, that all men
9   voice of justice and of consanguinity. **We** must, therefore, acquiesce in the necessity, whic
10   the Protection of Divine Providence, **we** mutually pledge to each other our Lives, our Fort
11   , Enemies in War, in Peace Friends. **We**, therefore, the Representatives of the United Stat

Many of the verbs following *we* are verbs from the semantic fields of warning and reminding, for example, *appealed, petitioned, reminded and warned*. *We* is projected as a thoroughly responsible group, if a little schoolmasterly. There are an equal number of occurrences of *us* (11) where the *us* is the object of the action, the doing of which is performed by the *he*. There is a consistent contraposition of these two entities, the one who does and the other who is done to. This, of course, is consonant with the view of the world the authors wish to propound of a despotic King mistreating a blameless population.

However, by far the most common form is the possessive *our*:

1   Nor have We been wanting in attention to **our** British brethren. We have warned them from
2   For taking away **our** Charters, abolishing our most valuable Laws
3   grid0 He has plundered our seas, ravaged **our** Coasts, burnt our towns, and destroyed the li
4   , and we have conjured them by the ties of **our** common kindred to disavow these usurpatio
5   rpations, which would inevitably interrupt **our** connection an d correspondence. They too h

6	For imposing taxes on us without **our** Consent:
7	ers to subject us to a jurisdiction foreign to **our** constitution, and unacknowledged by our la
8	ve reminded them of the circumstances of **our** emigration and settlement here. We have ap
9	He has constrained **our** fellow Citizen taken Captive on the high Sea
10	mutually pledge to each other our Lives, **our** Fortunes and our sacred Honor.
11	endeavored to bring on the inhabitants of **our** frontiers, the merciless Indian Savages, wh
12	and altering fundamentally, the Forms of **our** Governments:
13	me Judge of the world for the rectitude of **our** intentions, do, in the name, and by authorit
14	our constitution, and unacknowledged by **our** laws; giving his Assent to their acts of prete
15	, Standing Armies without the Consent of **our** legislatures.
16	idence, we mutually pledge to each other **our** Lives, our Fortunes and our sacred Honor.}
17	For taking away our Charters, abolishing **our** most valuable Laws, and altering fundamen
18	For suspending **our** own Legislatures, and declaring themselves
19	sent hither swarms of Officers to harass **our** people, and eat out their substance.
20	urnt our towns, and destroyed the lives of **our** people.
21	ed for Redress in the most humble terms: **Our** repeated Petitions have been answered onl
22	to each other our Lives, our Fortunes and **our** sacred Honor.
23	He has plundered **our** seas, ravaged our Coasts, burnt our towns,
24	uiesce in the necessity, which denounces **our** Separation, and hold them, as we hold the r
25	dered our seas, ravaged our Coasts, burnt **our** towns, and destroyed the lives of our peop
26	For cutting off **our** Trade with all parts of the world:

In every other corpus I have examined, *our* is only half as frequent as *we* or even less. Their proportions here are, therefore, highly marked. Once again, the author of the action and the grammatical subject is generally *he*. Among the entities affected by the action are the rights (*our laws, our Governments, our constitution*, etc.) and the possessions (*our towns, our Fortunes, our Trade*, etc.) of the group referred to with *we*. Thus, the authors of the document achieve two ends. They emphasize that *we* are already a separate group from the British; that *we* enjoy, as the document itself proclaims, a 'separate and equal station to which the Laws of Nature and Nature's God entitle them'. (On only two occasions – lines 4 and 5 – is *our* inclusive referring to the British together with the *we* group. On the other 24 occasions, it is exclusive and refers only to the latter.) They also reveal, however, the degree to which their dispute with the British government is about property, as much about claiming *our* rightful possessions as about political rights.

How consciously Jefferson made all these transitivity choices is a matter for conjecture. It seems likely that the active portrayal of the King was deliberate. Whether or not he also meant to portray his companions' motivation as quite so business-like is less certain (although eighteenth century liberal thought was much less coy than it is today about the connection between property and freedom). What we can say for sure is that concordancing can reveal patterns even within a single text that throw light on its meaning and function, and also on the conscious and unconscious strategies adopted by authors. A detailed examination of the use of pronouns in the White House briefings is contained in Chapters 3 and 4.

0.2.4   Comparing instance with system, comparing genres

We began this discussion with the observation that much of what carries meaning in texts is not open to immediate observation. If this is true of a single short text then it is true *a fortiori* of a collection of texts, or of the whole genre it belongs to, or of the collection of genres known as a 'language'. Human observation skills, attention-span and memory just cannot process the mass of data directly. And, of particular importance to the present research, only by comparing the choices being made by speakers at any point in a text with those which are normal, usual within the genre can we discover how *meaningful* those choices are. If an author/speaker does something that is normal, this carries little meaning. They have simply followed the normal dictates of the local style. But if, as we have seen in the analysis above, they do something unusual (like making one of the protagonists unvaryingly phrase subject), a special choice has been made and the analyst must search for the reason. To be able to compare the patterns found in a single text with those usual in the genre, to compare, in Halliday's terms (1992), *instance* with *system*, a corpus of texts which, at least to some small degree, *represents*[6] the genre is invaluable. Furthermore, if we are also, as here, interested in the characteristics of the genre itself, it is vital to be able to compare its particular features and patterns with those of other genres. In this way we discover *how* it is special, and can go on to consider *why*. All genre analysis is thus properly comparative. If texts are not compared to other bodies or corpora of texts it is not possible to know or to prove what is normal. Only against a known background of what is normal and expected can we detect the unusual. And, as we said, it is the unusual and unexpected which carries meaning.

0.2.5   Corpora and context

To investigate the precise meaning of a single linguistic event, then, we need to be able to study it in its context. If, moreover, we are interested in participants' strategies of interaction, we need to know a great deal about the context of that interaction. We return, for a moment, to the discussion of context of production and reception.

A number of authors, Baldry in particular, have criticized corpus linguistics in general and the concordance, its main tool of analysis, in particular, as abstracting text from its context, of failing to include 'any criteria for showing how language, in context, systematically integrates with other semiotic resources. In this sense corpus linguistics continues to treat language as a self-contained object' (Baldry 2000: 36).

The question is a complex one and involves two related phenomenological issues. The first is that all transferral of data from one medium to another will entail loss. One need only think of the reductiveness of trying to describe music in words. A videotape of a wedding is not a wedding. The second is that all description implies abstraction (the only non-abstract description of the world is the world itself) and all abstraction also means loss of detail. The greater the abstraction (i.e. the higher the level of overview), the more of the object of study can be included but the more individual contextual detail will be lost. Conversely, lowering the level of abstraction increases the contextual detail but reduces the portion of the world that can be included for the same degree of time and effort spent on the compilation. Moreover, from an analyst's point of view, too much detail means no overview, no possibility of generalization. To revive Cook's (1995) map-making metaphor, a map of the world that depicted everything in the world would have to cover the whole world. And would be of no use to anyone.

The researcher must first of all choose the level of abstraction that best serves their purposes. If we need to find our way from the Colosseum to the Trevi fountain a map of Europe is useless. Conversely, a street plan of Italian cities will tell us precious little about European national borders. To understand a podium's in-joke, we must look at a single text in all its contextual detail, the personalities involved, what has just occurred and so on. But to design a grammar of register (such as Biber *et al.* 1999), we must exploit large heterogeneric corpora and quantitive analysis.

This said, the most desirable system of all is one that offers the greatest possible flexibility of research methods and mobility between analytical levels. Baldry (2000: 30) argues that it is important to ascertain 'what linguistic corpora have left out of the picture, and how might these other factors be re-instated in the processes of data collection, transcription and analysis'. In other words, he argues that this flexibility should be built into the design of corpus compilation from the very beginning to make it feasible and simple to move between levels of analysis. For spoken texts, Baldry and his team are in the process of devising a means of transcribing some of the visual and kinetic aspects of production: movement, gesture, gaze, colour and so on.

The methodology I adopted for this research attempted, as far as was possible for me at the time, to cater for this need to move between levels of analytic detail. The corpus comprises separate files, each containing a briefing coded by date and initials of briefer. This enables easy movement from concordance line (where file names are indicated) to the individual file. A higher level of abstraction even than the concordance are the word frequency lists prepared using *WordSmith Tools* for both the briefings corpus and a number of other corpora I decided to use as comparisons (Section 0.4). At the lower levels, I was not able, at the time of compiling, to download videos of the briefings. However, I was able to watch recordings broadcast through *Realplayer* and make notes. Researchers who might wish to replicate this work on similar data can still follow the briefings on C-Span. Nevertheless, not having the recordings means I cannot, if in doubt, check back on voice quality, intonation and so on – a regrettable loss. Increasing computing speed and memory capacity is now beginning to make it possible for the analyst of a spoken corpus to move from concordance to transcript to audio or audiovisual recording of the speech event.

0.2.6   Combining methods of analysis

One highly unusual step in my methodology was that I spent a summer reading the corpus of briefings and making notes that were transferred onto disk and were thus themselves available for concordancing. This made it quick and simple to collect at a later moment all instances of any phenomena I had noted, say, oddities of collocation or instances of question avoidance. The size of the corpus was set deliberately at a quarter of a million words in order to be large enough for meaningful patterns to emerge and small enough for a sense of it to be acquired by being read in this way. These notes clearly constitute an intervention on the part of the researcher into the object of research, but this is inevitably present at all levels (including, we should not forget, concordance preparation and interpretation).

One of the objects of research was, in fact, to compare the kinds of information that can be derived from reading a set of texts with the kinds that derive from semi-automatic analyses, to determine what can be done better with 'non-automatic' procedures and what is better performed with computer assistance. In most cases, it turned out to be a question of the one reinforcing rather than replacing the other, of results being obtained by a heuristic combination of the two. Examples of this will be found throughout the book. A few immediate examples are the following. The prereading alerted me to the phenomenon of other-reformulation, but only the concordance revealed its extent and complexity, the mass of phraseology used to perform it (Chapter 9). In Chapter 7, concordancing the same modal expression (e.g. *just*) separately in the podium moves and the press moves highlights significantly different patterns of use. I then had to go on to hypothesize why – what different strategies these patterns might serve and for this it was necessary to look at the text transcripts in detail. In Chapter 10, comparing frequency word lists derived from different corpora sheds much light on the special metaphors used in briefings. Finally, I noticed during the prereading an odd use of the word *adamant*: 'President Milosevic has proved to be quite *adamant* in his campaign of atrocities'. Concordancing the word in larger corpora revealed why I felt the use was unusual (Section 0.3.3). But why the podium used it remains a matter of speculation.

Thus, at the simplest level, corpus technology helps find other examples of a phenomenon one has already noted. At the other extreme, it reveals patterns of use previously unthought of. In between, it can reinforce, refute or revise a researcher's intuition and show them why and how much their suspicions were grounded.

0.3   Concordancing for indicators of point of view

Many writers have noted that there are a number of linguistic indicators that are particularly useful in revealing an author's opinions, attitudes and ideology. Most of them draw on the ideas of Halliday (1973, 1985), who conceives of grammar itself as a 'social semiotic'. The very categories that natural language grammars encompass have arisen as a response to the need of human animals to express certain meanings to each other (i.e. socially) through the linear medium of language. The categories of language are thus *functional* in this sense.

We have already seen an example (see Section 0.2.3) of how the transitivity system can be used to express points of view, and how the concordance can, given the right circumstances, be exploited to reveal some of them. Other linguistic areas that can often usefully be studied are those of modality, the numerous vagueness or information-concealment techniques and semantic prosody.

0.3.1 *Modality*

It is a relatively simple matter to concordance modal operators such as *can*, *may*, *might*, *could*, *would*, *should* and so on. A certain amount of editing will be necessary to remove unwanted examples (such as when *May* refers to the month). It is beyond the scope of this book to launch into a full-scale analysis of modality in discourse. But one or two interesting statistical phenomena were noticed regarding these briefings

First of all, I prepared two subcorpora by separating the questioner moves from the podium response moves contained in four of the briefings (around two hours of talk) and placing them in two separate files, the Q-file and the R-file, respectively. The importance of comparison in linguistics has already been stressed and this division made it possible to compare and contrast press and podium language. These files were used for several studies in this book.

In the Q-file, the word *might* was found to be much more frequent than *may* (nine occurrences to one); in the R-file, however, the reverse was the case, *might* was far less frequent than *may* (two to eleven). If one ignores examples of the questioner's typical permission-seeking *if I may follow up on that*, these proportions seem to be regular throughout the corpus – *may* being far more frequent in the responses, *might* in the questions. The explanation for this could be that the slightly more distancing effect of *might* makes it generally more suitable for questioning, which is notoriously face-threatening (Chapter 7) for the respondent. The preponderance of *may* over *might* in the kind of defensive responses typical of these briefings could, on the other hand, express a desire to reflect control over the situation – 'we may do so if we choose' – *we* being the predominant subject of *may* in podium replies.

By using the item *Q* as a context word, it was possible to concordance modals in the first few words (set randomly at 10) of the question moves. One interesting finding was that, of the *necessity* modals, *should*, *have to* and *need* are found in this corpus to ask questions, whilst *must* and *ought to* are not.[7] All five items were common in the podium's moves, probably because they are typical of opinion-giving:

(1)   MR McCURRY: And we think the benefits of tax relief *ought* to be focused on low and middle income

(2)   MR LOCKHART: [...] Furthermore, Israelis and Palestinians *must* avoid unilateral acts and declarations [...]

and also because they can be 'reproof' words, can be used to rebuke one's opponents and critics:

(3)   MR LOCKHART: [...] if that's all he has to offer to this debate, he ought to stay out of it.

0.3.2   *Hiding information*

The modality system allows speakers/authors to be as precise as they want to be. The transitivity system often forces people to be *more* precise than they might want to be (see Section 0.2.3). But language also offers a number of techniques for being vaguer or for giving *less* information than one might.

0.3.2.1   *The absent quantifier*

The first of these is the *removal of the quantifier* from a noun phrase, beloved of journalists (and just perpetrated by the present writer). Examples are not hard to find:

> Angry voters in the married barrister's Essex constituency urged him to quit [...] And ministers were counting on the local party to order him out.
>
> (*The Sun*: in Reah 1998: 71)

How many voters, how many ministers – all, most, a few, two? The writer either could not or did not want to be more precise, and as long as at least two members of the categories in question want the poor barrister 'out', he or she cannot technically be accused of lying. This can be a highly misleading and pernicious argumentative ploy. In particular, it can lead to prejudicial over-generalization of minority (or even majority) groups, for example, *blacks are violent, men are rapists* and so on, because the hearer/reader can be left to understand the missing quantifier in such cases as 'all', on the analogy of *mountains are high* or *cats are feline*.

To study this phenomenon, one might prepare concordances featuring the significant protagonists in the texts one is studying. To cite an example regarding the briefings corpus, the item *Yugoslavs* appears six times in the briefings corpus, all but one of these in journalists' turns, and the one time the word is uttered by the podium it is in echo of a question:

(4)   Q: You don't really expect the Yugoslavs and Milosevic to agree to the Rambouillet accords at this stage of the game, after the bombing, do you?
      MR LOCKHART: The Yugoslavs and President Milosevic needs to accept the essence of those accords

In contrast, the podium often speaks of *Americans*, for example, 'things that Americans recognize', 'the long-term benefits Americans have come to expect'. He is, presumably for diplomatic reasons, very careful not to over-generalize and speak of (all) *Yugoslavs*, but is often quite ready to assume the voice of (all) *Americans*.

0.3.2.2 *Nominalization*

The second information-impoverishment technique is nominalization, the representation of a process as a noun. This is a classic example of what Halliday (1995: 321) calls a 'grammatical metaphor', that is, the presentation of what in nature would be one kind of phenomenon in language as quite another. It is characteristic of all adult language and indeed is so pervasive that, like many other forms of metaphor, is barely considered by speakers as being metaphorical at all, for example, 'Bad weather has delayed many trains this morning. *Delays* are particularly severe on the east coast'. It functions as an information-packaging or *encapsulation* device (Thompson 1997: 170), especially when referring cohesively to events already mentioned, and as Halliday himself notes is particularly frequent in some genres, such as scientific discourse (Halliday and Martin 1993).

The characteristic of nominalization which interests us here, however, is that it removes the indications of time and modality that are generally present in a verb clause. It can also remove participants in a process:

> These ideas have been subject to widespread *criticism*
> The *coming* of writing.
>
> (Thompson 1997: 167)

Who has criticized these ideas? Where did writing come to? Sometimes these can be recovered from context or by using one's knowledge of the world. Alternatively, they can be reintroduced in some other part of the utterance. But if they are not they can be lost from view or hidden from view. As Fowler remarks:

> Nominalization [...] offers extensive ideological opportunities [...] To understand this, reflect on how much information goes unexpressed in a derived nominal, compared with a full clause: compare, for example, 'allegations' with the fully spelt-out proposition 'X has alleged against Y that Y did A' [...] Deleted in the nominal form are the participants (who did what to whom?), any indication of time – because there is no verb to be tensed – and any indication of modality – the writer's views as to the truth or the desirability of the proposition.
>
> (Fowler 1991: 80)

Fairclough (1989: 124) also discusses nominalization as one of the features of grammar that is particularly powerful in building a picture of the world (which has, in his terms, 'high experiential value').

Nominalization in given texts can be studied, like other metaphorical forms, by examining the frequency lists that derive from them, especially the relative frequency lists (keyword lists, see Section 0.4.1), which tell us which words are more frequent in the types of text we are examining. A comparison of White House briefings with a corpus of news interviews and another corpus of written news texts revealed a number of interesting aspects of nominalization use. They included, for example, *operations* and *strikes* which, like other modern euphemistic military vocabulary, can be used to render war victimless. We find *air operations, field operations* and *NATO strikes*. Only infrequently do we have the full complement of protagonists, including the goal, appearing in the phrase, as in *NATO air strikes against Yugoslavia*.

Another example is illustrated by items like *cooperation, agreement*, which are not always accompanied by indications of who the parties agreeing/cooperating are or what they are agreeing to do or cooperating in:

(5)   Q: [...] It sounds like there's a lot of convergence here, that military *cooperation* can be enhanced without getting into this definitional rankle.

Note also the nominalized term *convergence*. The press are in fact very aware of the indeterminacy of these items. They frequently ask the podium to define what is meant by *agreement* (the long hyphen indicates an inaudible passage):

(6)   Q: Joe, can I ask one more question on this *agreement* definition? Can *agreement* be implicit so that if, say, Serbian forces are basically destroyed – opposition that there's an implicit *agreement* that U.S. ground troops are allowed?
        MR LOCKHART: Again, I don't know how the *agreement* manifests itself, but I'm not sure that there can be an implicit understanding.

Agreement, convergence, understanding and *cooperation* have been reified, have practically reached a status of independence from human beings doing the agreeing, etc. *Agreement, cooperation*, etc. are seen as 'good things' in themselves. We should probably be wary of reading too much that is sinister in this use of language – the nominalization of such items is fairly typical of political talk. Having said this, it does seem that *agreement* in the context of the Kosovo crisis tends to really mean Yugoslavia giving in. This is more explicitly expressed with the nominalization *compliance*, also present in the keyword lists.

0.3.2.3   *Adjectivization*

The third linguistic means of hiding information is *adjectivization*, that is, the employment of nouns as modifiers of other nouns. This is also a type of grammatical metaphor but one that has received much less attention than nominalization. And like the latter, adjectivization is such a standard feature of the language that we are rarely aware of the possibilities for choice and of the ambiguities it can allow. Consider a phrase like *the American President*, which means both 'the President of the Americans' and 'the President who is an American'. The ambiguity is not important in most contexts. But in, say, *Muslim leader*, the descriptive term can also mean something more than just belonging to a nation or ethnic group, but being a *real, proper, authoritative* Muslim.

We might also reflect on sentences such as:

(i) AIDS is a gay problem.
(ii) BSE is a British problem.

Do these mean:

(a) AIDS/BSE is a problem *of* (besetting) gay/British people;
(b) AIDS/BSE is a problem (caused) *by* gay/British people;

or

(c) AIDS/BSE is a problem *for* gay/British people *to solve?*

The adjectivization of *gay* and *British* hides the relationship between the group and the *problem* which, instead, is apparent when a preposition is present. Again, this can offer substantial ideological opportunities. A speaker who was both homophobic and hypocritical could use sentence (i) to mean (b) that AIDS is *caused by* gay people – but, if challenged, could instead claim they only meant (a), it *afflicts* them.

In the briefings we find the following:

(7) Q: Joe, one of the reasons that you didn't want this conflict to spread is because, if there were mass amounts of refugees, it would destabilize the region. And now that there are [...] do you feel that you can handle *the refugee problem* indefinitely, and prevent it from becoming a destabilizing force?

What is meant here by *the refugee problem*: besetting the refugees or caused by them? And, if the latter, a problem for whom? Probably aware of the particular semantics of the term *problem*, the podium prefers to use *issue* and *question*.

Since they are noun-like in appearance, adjectivized items are not immediately obvious in frequency lists. In the briefings frequency lists, however, a number of words appeared as possible candidates, for example, *ground* (collocates with *forces* and *troops*), *security* (*advisor, arrangements, force, guarantee* and several more – but whose *security?*), *defense* (*concerns, spending*), *air* (*campaign, defenses, power, strikes*) and *peace* (*agreement, deal, process, settlement, talks*). All the above appeared in at least 50 per cent of cases in modifier position.

If one is interested in researching these items for their own sake, one or two heuristics can be used to spot likely areas. Nationality or group nouns, especially if found in singular form, for example, *American, Irish, Catholic* generally modify other nouns. It is worth concordancing items like *problem, issue, question, concern, situation* and so on to see how they are modified. A very good place to find them is, of course, in newspaper headlines (see Morley 1998 for a detailed discussion of extended noun phrases in this genre and especially of how to interpret the relations between their components).

0.3.3   *Semantic prosody*

A third way in which corpus technology can help expose speakers' and writers' attitudes is in uncovering choices of *semantic prosody* they might have made. Some words regularly collocate with items of a favourable or unfavourable connotation and are said to have a 'good' or 'bad' semantic prosody. The item *prosody* is borrowed from Firth (1957), who uses it to refer to phonological colouring that spreads beyond segmental boundaries. Here, meaning is spread beyond word boundaries since it belongs to both the word and its collocate. An example I have used elsewhere (Partington 1998: 67) is *rife*. The denotational meaning of this word is simply 'of common or frequent occurrence, prevalent' (Webster's Encyclopedic Dictionary 1989). But, as the following concordance (*Newspaper corpus*) reveals, it collocates almost exclusively with unfavourable items, such as *crime, diseases, corruption* and *violence*:

1   They are seedy, run-down areas where crime is **rife** and the misery of unescapable poverty stalks
2   when rickets and other deficiency diseases were **rife**. He stayed with Glaxo all his working life,
3   to be managing director. Uncertainty is already **rife**. Several months ago, when rumours circulated
4   in an economy void of privatisation laws and **rife** with corruption. Delegates also voted to defend
5   chumminess is more popular, so mistakes are **rife**. The change has been gradual since the Second
6   ding societies ripe for takeover: Speculation is **rife** in the building society industry. Patrick Hosking
7   management group last month. Speculation is **rife** that it will soon sell the reconstituted Lehman
8   n to democracy: Vote-buying and violence are **rife** as Thais prepare for polling day, writes Teresa

The phenomenon becomes especially interesting when people diverge from the expected profiles, when they upset these normal collocational patterns. Louw (1993) argues that this can be done consciously, in search of ironic effect. A phrase like 'conservatism is *rife* in middle England' would almost certainly be so heard.

But Louw also argues that writers can also diverge from a prosody by accident, in which case the reader may detect a difference between what the speaker or writer is apparently saying and what he/she really believes. I found several examples in these briefings, for instance:

(8)   MR LOCKHART: I think General Clark has answered that question, which is he could *deal with success* quite quickly.

The concordance of *deal with* in these briefings shows it very often collocates with unpleasant items: *aggression, situations of conflict, the scourge of terrorism* amongst others. If we take Louw's argument that a speaker's unconscious upsetting of normal prosody may reveal something of their real attitudes, that of the phrase *deal with success* may be telling us that the podium (or General Clark) is in his heart fearful about the prospects of success. In addition, the kinds of *people* whom the podium and his clients have to *deal with* are usually enemies or, at the very least, problem groups of some type. They include *Milosevic, the Belgrade authorities, China*. We might then be surprised by Mr McCurry's reply to the question of who the podium works for:

(9)   So you work for both sides of this equation. I like to tell people, my office is perfectly situated as a geographic metaphor here in the White House – 50 feet in one direction is the Oval Office, and 50 feet away is here where we are *dealing with you*.

He claims to be working as much for the press as the President but the phrase *dealing with you* suggests that he really sees the press as a problem not a client.

Another example of misfiring prosody is:

(10)   MR LOCKHART: President Milosevic has proved to be *quite adamant in his campaign of atrocities* in Yugoslavia and in his willingness to pay a price.

The concordance of this item from the *BNC* shows that whoever is *adamant* has strongly held beliefs and convictions. In general, it is fairly honourable in its connotations, for example:

1   Lawyers are *adamant* about the need to remain independent of the state.
2   Joanna's grandfather was also *adamant* she was telling the truth.

To be *quite adamant* in a *campaign of atrocities* is odd on a number of levels. The podium has other words at his disposal: *stubborn* or *pig-headed* to express Mr Milosevic's determination; *unscrupulous* or *Machiavellian* to express his supposed villainy. Following Louw's reasoning once again, does the podium's use of *adamant* reveal a suspicion that Mr Milosevic may, by his own lights, have a case?

Without help, it is very difficult to study prosodic effects. Native and non-native speaker analysts may instinctively *suspect* items are being used in unusual ways, but without being able to concordance a corpus to look at the usual patterning, it becomes impossible to prove anything. Both groups can profit equally from corpus technology.

0.4   The importance of comparing corpora

It is impossible to over-emphasize the philosophical point that all work with corpora is properly comparative. Even when a single corpus is employed, it is used to test the data it contains against another body of data. This may consist of the researcher's intuitions, or the data found in reference works such as dictionaries and grammars, or it may be statements made by previous authors in the field. In the case of language students, the other body of data might be what they have learnt from some authority, such as their textbook or teacher.

Such use of corpora is, therefore, clearly subversive, but it is also in line with empirical methodology. The testing of intuition and/or received knowledge against a body of data is the very spirit of scientific experimentation. Moreover, observations from a single source (even an authentic text) are of limited value and are essentially anecdotal: 'by and large, we are not methodologically justified in interpreting the significance of a particular linguistic event unless we can compare it with other similar events' (Partington 1998: 146). Testing observations and findings against corpus data can provide 'background information' against which particular events can be judged, as we shall see several times in the course of this book.

A word of warning is, however, in order. The corpus should never be treated as the final word. All corpora have limitations, imperfections, *lacunae*. No corpus is fully representative of the language as a whole, or even a subset thereof.[8] In addition, the process of comparison, as we will see, is fraught with dangers. There has been a tendency in some branches of corpus linguistics to raise 'the corpus' to the status of the new authority. But all findings resulting from corpus study should, wherever feasible, be tested anew, very possibly using other corpora.

A good deal of language research, therefore, avails itself of more than one corpus. For translation studies (as well as translation practice), it is clearly useful to have at one's disposal similar or comparable or parallel corpora in the languages of interest (Teubert 1996; Aston 1999). Similarly, it is often profitable to compare sub-sections of the same language, for example, different registers (Biber 1988), the language of different historical periods (diachronic studies) or of different geographical areas (e.g. the English used in United States, United Kingdom,[9] Australia, India and so on) or different text-types, as here.

0.4.1   The means of comparison: frequency, keyword lists and concordancing

As implied in the previous section, simple frequency of occurrence of an item in a corpus is not especially informative: the fact that *you*, for example, occurs more often than *therefore* tells us very little. However, should *you* occur significantly more frequently in one corpus than another (say once every 100 words as opposed to every 300), this may well imply something (probably that the first comprises spoken, the other written texts). One might suspect that if, of two written corpora, one contains *therefore* significantly more often than the other, it probably consists of texts of a more formal register, although nothing can be inferred with certainty from a single item.

WordSmith Tools, a suite of programs for language analysis designed by Mike Scott at Liverpool University, provides a *Wordlist* facility that can be used to provide lists of the most frequent lexis in two corpora, one of which is taken as the *foreground* corpus, that is, the one whose language is the object of study, the other the *background* or *reference* corpus. The *Keyword* facility then compares these and produces lists (one alphabetical and one ordered by significance) of all words that are significantly *more* frequent in the first corpus than the second and also of those that are significantly *less* frequent.

Such frequency lists are clearly of their nature blunt instruments but, where appropriate, the clues they provide can be followed up by concordancing the relevant items to get a closer picture of the role they play in briefings texts. In addition, both *MicroConcord* and the *WordSmith Concordance* tool provide a facility that lists the most frequent collocates of a word. This is most useful when examining concordances of very frequent items.

0.4.2 Choosing corpora for comparison and controlling the variables

There are, however, a number of practical and methodological pitfalls frequently encountered when attempting to compare corpora.

The main difficulty (and danger) is in controlling the number of variables in play. In choosing a corpus to compare with one's main foreground corpus it is vital, first of all, to compare like with like and, second, to be aware and in control of the differences that inevitably exist between them, in relation to the aim of the comparison. To cite a simple example, if the researcher wishes to uncover differences between varieties differing on the basis of geography, between British and American Englishes, for instance, it would introduce a confusing uncontrolled variable if one of the corpora were of the spoken language and one of the written. If the aim of the exercise is to study differences between the written and spoken forms of the language, a factor of disturbance would be introduced if one of the corpora were of legal texts, the other of doctor–patient interviews, that is, if there were important differences in content. In a *reductio ad absurdum* case, if we compared a corpus of spoken, highly informal, British working class conversations with one of written, highly formal, Canadian government papers, it would be impossible to assign the observed differences in linguistic data to any single cause.

Unfortunately, it is not easy to isolate hermetically the variable to be studied. The general corpora available for commercial or academic use often contain very many different registers but it is not always possible to use them wholesale for comparison. Thus, it is often necessary to compile one's own corpora or tailor those that exist to one's particular purposes, as here.

Even so, the results may still not be perfect. In order to compare the language of the White House briefings corpus (henceforth *WHB*) with another very similar text-type, the news interview, I compiled a separate corpus, and gave it the name

INTS. This contains interviews of political figures conducted on British television by Jonathan Dimbleby (ITV: *The Dimbleby Interview*), John Humphrys (BBC: *On the Record*) and David Frost (BBC: The *Breakfast with Frost* interview) in 1999–2000. It is deliberately the same size as *WHB*, containing around 250,000 words. This genre was chosen in order to attempt to isolate features particular to briefings. For example, since both corpora consist mainly of questions, any differences discovered might tell us something about the particular types of questioning they involve. However, *INTS* is a collection of texts from *British* environments since I was unable to collect sufficient suitable material from US sources. This inevitably introduces a second maverick variable into the comparison. However, attempts were made to control this second variable by checking results against the data in the *Frown* and *Flob* corpora. These are general corpora, a million words each, the first of current American English and the second of current British English, which were designed to be comparable, that is, they contain exactly the same variety of text-types. Thus, if a word or phrase was found to be more frequent in *WHB* than *INTS* (or vice versa), the same word or phrase was looked up in *Frown* and *Flob*, to see if the difference in frequency was the product of a systematic difference between the two language varieties.

A couple of comparative examples should illustrate this point. It was no surprise to find words like *sometime, defense, gotten* included among the significantly more frequent words in *WHB*, since they are 'American words' or spellings, little used in the United Kingdom (although the last does appear twice in *Flob* in the expression *ill-gotten gains*). However, the keyword lists gave the term *problem* as significantly more common in *INTS* (171 occurrences to 58). But is *problem* simply more frequently used in British English? According to the comparison between *Frown* and *Flob*, the answer is no: *problem* was actually *more* common in the American texts (296 to 217). On the other hand, *solution* was four times more common in *WHB* than in *INTS* (44 to 11), whilst their occurrences in *Frown* and *Flob* were roughly equal (65 to 69). Thus, the use of these items is probably saying something about these sets of texts, not about American or British English. *Problems* greatly outweigh *solutions* in the news interviews, whereas there is just about one *solution* for every *problem* in the briefings. The podium, in fact, prefers to use the words *issue* or *concern* – both of which are in the keyword list. The podium is clearly keen to portray an optimistic vision of events, whereas many of the news interviewees, perhaps hostile to the government of the day, are happy to talk at length of any *problems* it may be encountering.

The picture is more complex when whole sets of items are found to be more frequent in one of the corpora. *INTS* is significantly richer than *WHB* in a large number of adverbs, many of which are intensifiers: *perfectly*,[10] *extremely, absolutely, indeed, very, really* and *quite*.[11] From this cue, a second look at the keyword data, along with subsequent concordancing of likely items, also showed that a fair number of other items frequently used to intensify were much more common in the news interviews: *whole* (found e.g. in 'a whole new system'), *huge* ('huge work', 'a huge task'), *all* ('all across the country'), *everybody* ('everybody knows that ... '), *nobody* ('there is nobody more determined ... '), *always* ('I always argue that ... '), *never* ('he never said any such thing ... '), along with *much, more, big* and *better*. Of all these, only *perfectly, indeed* and *quite* were also found to be more frequent in *Flob* than *Frown*. A high degree of intensification, of hyperbole, would seem to be a feature of these interviews in relation to the briefings. This is somewhat surprising given, first of all, the folk reputation of American speakers as being more expansive than the British and, second, the temptation for the podium to exaggerate his clients' virtues. However, as we shall see (Section 7.5.2), there are brakes on his boastfulness, and overstatement is likely to be mocked by his audience (Section 11.5). There are no such immediate restraints on news interviewees. Moreover, it may also be the case that intensification is a common feature of the kind of language used in *formulating an argument*, in making a case *for* or *against* something or someone, which is by far the principal activity of the political interviewee. A popular tool of political argument is *comparison* and *contrast* and the speakers often wish to stress that their side's approach is *extraordinarily* good and that of their opponents *extremely* poor, for example:

(11) JIM CALLAGHAN: [...] the government's done *very well indeed*, I think it's been *extraordinarily* good, had good circumstances and done well.

(12) ANN WIDDECOMBE: Well of course what Tony Blair has done is to be *extremely* cynical about this.

The podium has many other duties to perform besides constructing such arguments – issuing statements, discussing presidential and other business, engaging in banter with the members of the press and so on, and, therefore, features of argumentative prose, including intensification, are relatively less common.

There can often, then, be considerable difficulties in finding the 'perfect' comparable corpus and in controlling the number and degree of differences. Moreover, for our purposes, it would scarcely be advisable to measure one corpus against another that was too *similar*. For example, comparing *WHB* to another corpus of briefings, perhaps from a different source or a different period of time would probably reveal very little about the essential nature of briefings, about their linguistic peculiarities. The keyword lists would only throw up lexis highlighting different topics of discussion and different personalities of the day, everything else, being the same, would be invisible.

0.4.3 Other pitfalls in comparing corpora

The word and frequency lists used in this study are unlemmatized, that is, the machine does not distinguish between different words written the same way, or between different forms of the 'same' word (say noun and verb) if they are written the same way.

This can spell danger to the unwary. The word *strikes* appears in *WHB* far more often than in *INTS* (40 to 4). Does this suggest an inversion of trend – the dawn of a new era of industrial harmony in the United Kingdom, and the exacerbation of labour strife in the United States? This theory is quickly dispelled by a look at the collocations of the word in *WHB*: *air*, *NATO*, *bombing*. The item *steps* is relatively frequent in *WHB* (60 to 12), but as a noun or verb? The concordance shows it to be almost always a noun and a 'government business' word (Section 0.5) found in expressions such as *take steps to ...*, *positive steps forward*, *the latest steps in this process*.

A final problem, particular to spoken corpora, is that posed by transcription. One needs to be aware of some of the choices made by the transcribers. For example, expressive items such as *oh*, *ah*, *well* might be found in a keyword list, perhaps alongside eye-dialect spellings such as *aint*, *gonna* and the like. One might decide that this was evidence of a greater informality of style. Items such as *I've*, *you've*, *she's* might be among the keywords. Does this prove that the texts of the foreground corpus are person-oriented? It could simply be that the transcribers of the reference corpus have decided to 'improve' the language by ignoring interjections and using only standard spellings. Thus, *oh* and *ah* will have disappeared, *aint* and *gonna* become *are not* and *going to*, whilst *I've*, etc., will be recorded as two separate items. It should be sufficient to read parts of the corpus, or concordance it for contractions or colloquial spellings, to uncover the major transcription decisions.

Given these difficulties, then, it is advisable to compare one's foreground corpus with more than one other set of texts. In Section 0.5, three other corpora are used for comparison with *WHB*. The first is *INTS*. The second is *USPR* (for *US press*), a collection of about 380,000 words of written journalism from the United States. It comprises sections A and B, that is, the sections containing news texts, of both the *Brown* and *Frown* corpora. The third is *WSC*, the Wellington (New Zealand) spoken corpus, a one-million word collection of spoken texts of a variety of genres from the early 1990s.

0.5　Keywords in the briefings

Many of the items in all the relative frequency keyword lists (and in any such list) refer to people and places, the scenes and the players in the particular events: *President*, *Mike*, *Joe*, *Milosevic*, *NATO*, *Congress*, *Monica*, *Albanians*, *Bosnia*, *Kosovo*, *China* and a multitude of others. Just as predictably, many more relate to the major ongoing topics of debate, the current affairs of the period. These include the Kosovo crisis: *war*, *bombing*, *targets*; the Clinton–Lewinsky crisis: *impeachment*, *attorneys*, *testimony*; and alleged war crimes: *crimes*, *atrocities*, *repression* and so on.

In addition, there are numerous items pertaining to what we might call the various *spheres of business* being conducted in the briefings. First and foremost is the business of briefings themselves, whose typical lexis includes: *reports*, *statement(s)*, *readout*, *meeting*, *update* along with quite an array of deictic expressions. These indicate the time and place events occur in, as well as the people involved.[12] Many of these items are very high on the keyword lists, that is, their relative frequency is very great. They include: *here, this, those, there, today, yesterday, tomorrow, Monday.*[13] The word *now* is more frequent in *WHB* than in *USPR* or *WSC*, but is actually significantly *less* frequent than in *INTS*. It is clear from this that deictics are widely used in face-to-face interaction and, therefore, in both interviews and briefings. Temporal deictics are particularly common in *WHB* because there is a particular sub-category of briefings business, which we can name 'calendar business', 'calendar talk', that is, questions and replies about planned future events, travel arrangements, when the next meeting is and so on.

Other spheres of business well represented by keywords include government administration: *budget, supplemental, session, bipartisan,* etc., diplomatic affairs: *alliance, autonomy, region, provisions, delegation* and so on, and presidential business (overlapping calendar talk): *trip, schedule, Arkansas.*

As well as deictics, a number of other lexical sets are well represented in briefings. Many verb auxiliaries are relatively very frequent, including *will, has, does, did, have, are, going.* This is largely due to the sheer quantity of questions being asked in the briefings, and even if interviews also consist of questioning, they are of a different type, longer but fewer in number. On the other hand, perhaps surprisingly, the items *what, who, when, where, why* are all more frequent in *INTS*. This, however, is because the use of these items in questions is swamped, in both corpora (and in almost all genres of text) by their use as relatives ('in spite of *what* happened yesterday … ', 'those *who* are responsible', etc.). Their greater frequency in *INTS* is an indication of the greater syntactic complexity of the interview texts compared to briefings (an indication supported by other evidence, for example, greater average sentence length, 31.21 words to 15.97).

A number of other items attest to the essential question–response structure of briefings including *aware* (typically used by questioner's in *are you aware … ?, is the President aware … ?* and by the podium's *I'm not aware of … .*), *think* (*I think, do you think … ?*), and *believe* (*I believe*) as opinion giving and seeking expressions, and *correct* (*is it correct … ?, that's correct*) and *accurate* (*is that accurate … ?*) as truth checking questions and responses. The word *again* is also relatively common in briefings. It is used by the podium as a response introduction ('Again, I'm not going to get into that … ') to imply that the question has already been dealt with. In addition, it has the function of clearing the channel of communication: *Say again* meaning 'please repeat'. The word *saying* – typically used in reformulation of the interlocutor's move (e.g. *so what you're saying is …)* – is highly significantly frequent in both *WHB* and *INTS* (Section 9.2). Many of the items mentioned above are discussed in the following chapters, and indeed it was their appearance in these lists that led me to investigate them further.

The presence of most of the above words or sets of words is to some extent predictable. However, other items are more difficult to explain; in particular a number of determiners are significantly more frequent in *WHB* than in all three of the other corpora, including *USPR*, a written corpus. These include the items *any, some* and *an.*

The word *the* is twice as common in *WHB* as in *WSC* (making up about 6 per cent of all items compared to 3 per cent), still significantly more frequent than in *USPR*, equally as common as in *LNTS*. The word *several* is as common in *WHB* as in the written *USPR* and many times more frequent than in the spoken *LNTS* or *WSC*.

The reason why so many determiners are so frequent in these briefings is not immediately self-evident. The syntactic simplicity of many of the exchanges could well result in a high relative density of determiners. Moreover, the closed world and shared knowledge of the participants lead to the frequent use of the definite article *the*. Collocational evidence indicates that the item *several* is certainly so common because it is often used by the podium in the expressions *in the past several days/weeks/months*. Nevertheless, at the time of writing I am not satisfied that I have yet fully accounted for determiner frequency in these texts.

A good number of prepositions or adverbial particles are also relatively frequent in *WHB*: *on, forward, to, toward(s)* stand out in particular, and *as, of, in, with, within, through, beyond, back, about* are all found in at least one frequency list. Concordance evidence helps explain why. For example, *about* appears in press requests such as *Can you tell us about … what about …* and in podium replies such as *the President talked about, I don't know anything about … . On* is also used as shorthand to refer to topics of questioning: *on the issue of, can I follow up on that?, the President's view on … .* The frequency of both these items show us how much briefings talk is explicitly *about* or *on* 'issues'. The item *back* is often involved in the control of discourse topic: *if we can go back to …, can I come back to you on that?*, and as a kind of podium admonishment: *go back and look at the facts*. The item *to* is relatively the most common of all, being part of some very frequent 'briefings expressions' including 'talk' words: *say to/speak to/talk to*, discourse managing items: *(just) to follow up/to get back to*, future action or intention phrases: *try to, going to [we're going to, I'm not going to (get involved in …)], plan/are planning/plans to …, do you want to …?, I don't want to …, we/they have/ought/need(s) to …*, and several others. When the subject in this last group of expressions *(have/ought/need(s) to …)* is *we*, it is characteristic of high-flown rhetoric. Instead, when the subject is third person, we are in hectoring style, for example, 'he knows what he *has to* do'.

We can conclude this part, then, by noting the strong evidence we have unearthed to suggest that the relative proportions of certain prepositions and particles in texts can be strongly indicative of the genre they belong to.

0.6　Politics, language and the news media

As mentioned at the beginning of this chapter, this work is also a case study of the relationship between politics and the press using linguistic tools. As Schäffner (1997: 1) points out, language is vital to the process of transforming political will into social action, 'in fact, any political action is prepared, accompanied, controlled and influenced by language'. Fairclough (1989: 23) goes still further. Politics is not just conducted *through* language, but much of politics *is* language: 'politics partly consists in the disputes which occur in language and over language'. Schäffner (1997: 1) stresses the need for a closer cooperation between political scientists and linguists. The first are 'mainly concerned with the consequences of political decisions and actions [...] and they may be interested in the political realities which are constructed through discourse'. But since, as Fairclough argues, political actions include language, they *must* show an interest in how political discourse functions from a linguistic point of view, if only to discover its particularities, how it differs from other forms of the language, other forms of rhetorical persuasion. Linguists, in turn, are interested in 'the linguistic structures used to get politically relevant messages across to the addressees in order to fulfil a specific function', that is, in uncovering the relationship between language forms and what speakers do with them. But this approach cannot afford to ignore 'the broader societal and political framework in which such discourse is embedded' (Schäffner 1997: 1). Otherwise, it will be impossible to predict or evaluate what speakers want to do. The present work, though principally linguistic, is offered in the spirit of cooperation between the two fields.

There are two ways to link the linguistic to the political, continues Schäffner. One is to start from 'the linguistic micro-level and ask which strategic functions specific structures (e.g. word choice, a specific syntactic structure) serve to fulfil' (Schäffner 1997: 2). The other is to begin with 'the communicative situation and the function of a text and ask which linguistic structures have been chosen to fulfil this function' (Schäffner 1997: 3). Although both approaches will serve, the methodology and especially the tools used in this work will favour the first, that is, beginning the analysis from the linguistic data. Moreover, it is not always possible or even desirable to establish *a priori* the function of a text. In any case, the two levels, the political situations and the discourse organization are linked 'by way of an intermediate level: that of strategic functions' (Schäffner 1997: 3). Language is functional; people use it to achieve ends. In briefings, these ends are both personal and political. A close study of how participants interact linguistically will give us a picture of the strategies adopted to attain both kinds.

These briefings are of course not only political texts but also news texts, though of a very peculiar kind. That 'news is a representation of the world in language' (Fowler 1991: 4) and that journalism is essentially a process of manufacturing news has long been argued by many analysts of the media (Glasgow University Media Group 1976, 1980; Tuchman 1978; Fowler 1991). Fowler calls this 'the standard position' and talks of the 'social construction' of news. At the most basic level, the media are part of the cycle of power: what they report, what they decide to make newsworthy, becomes influential and their decisions affect the unfolding of events themselves.

Our texts, however, illustrate how the process of news manufacturing by the media goes deeper still. Briefings, as other political interviews, are news-making activities where no newsworthy events occur outside the words themselves. The news is in the language – the topics, the controversies, the arguments among sources real and invented. Moreover, the majority of the 'facts' that are the topic of briefings debate are, in Tuchman's (1978: 89) terms, 'nonverifiable': 'facts that could be verified in theory but not in practice – and certainly not in time for deadlines'. If a fire breaks out the reporter can go and see it for himself. But to know what happens in Congressional committees, in the President's office, during a NATO summit, the press must depend upon sources, on the *words* of other people. Thus, facts and words are seldom divisible in news: 'newsworkers explicitly recognize the mutual embeddedness of fact and source' (Tuchman 1978: 90). Unfortunately, the sources for much of the information on the doings of powerful institutions are the institutions themselves. This is why the questions try to be so testing. Like a cross-examination in court, they can be the only means of finding out 'what really happened'. The journalists, in recompense, are the ones with the power to compose and present the 'final' story, the version of the truth to be published, and in this sense 'in the course of accomplishing this copresentation (of fact and source), newsworkers create and control controversies as news' (Tuchman 1978: 90).

In simple terms, then, the journalists in these briefings are not only reporters of events as they are when, say, covering a fire or a murder, responsible for the way the event is presented but generally unconnected to the original incident. They are also chief players in the drama itself. This is an all-important difference between copy based on news interviews, including briefings, and other news texts. In the former, the journalists themselves are actors in the stories being presented, they 'get the opportunity to make the news and not just report it' (Jones 1996: 21). In one sense, of course, that of the observer's paradox (Labov 1972: 209, on the lines of Bohr's principle of complementarity),[14] the observer can never be separated from the phenomenon observed. Here, the issue is especially complex. The press is both one side in the dispute and also reporter of the dispute; they are, as it were, counsel for the prosecution and jury all in one. In particular, they have the chance to shape the news stories themselves by shaping the kind of language used in the encounter. The questions they choose to ask will determine to a large extent the course of events. And very frequently, as we shall see, they also try to remodel the responses, the wording of the podium's replies, to suit their purposes (Section 9.2 on *reformulation*). Finally, their interpretation of an event that they have had a hand in manipulating will become the written or spoken record of that event.

The increasing wariness in the press' attitude towards governmental authority over the last few decades has brought to the fore problems inherent in this dual role of participant and observer. Douglas Hurd, foreign minister during the government of Mrs Thatcher, for example, 'took issue with journalists [...] over the way he thought they were becoming actors as well as spectators in foreign affairs' (Jones 1996: 26). On a slightly different but related matter, many students of communication have noted the rise of the phenomenon of 'superstar interviewers' (Jucker 1986) whose reporting is as much a media event as the statements of those they report. Partly to counter this plural power of the press, there is increasing use by government in the United States of direct appeals to the public, the so-called presidential broadcasts on television (known as 'going public' – Maltese 1992: 3–4). It is in this context that Mr McCurry also made the decision to permit live broadcast of White House briefings, presumably so that the world could see for itself what happens and not rely totally on the press-manufactured account.

1 Briefings as a type of discourse

1.1 The pragmatics of briefings as institutional talk

As mentioned in the Introduction, this book attempts to relate corpus linguistics to other fields of linguistics. It is meant as a contribution to the pragmatic study of press briefings as one type of *institutional talk*. This is basically defined as talk between professionals and lay people, but the definition can be stretched, as here, to include talk between two groups of professionals with an audience of lay persons (the TV and Internet audience). The main object of study in this field is 'the ways in which institutional contexts are manifested in, and in turn shape, the particular actions of […] participants' (Drew and Heritage 1992: 24).

1.1.1 Institutional talk and conversation

Institutional talk has been studied mainly by exponents of Conversation Analysis (CA), one of whose principal interests is to discover how it differs from ordinary day-to-day conversation.

Conversation is generally seen within CA as the prototype of all forms of talk. It is, as Levinson puts it:

> the prototypical kind of language usage […] the matrix of language acquisition […] the central or most basic kind of language usage.
>
> (Levinson 1983: 284–5)

According to Scannell (1991: 12), it has a 'bed-rock' status in relation to other forms of speech, which are, therefore, derivative. Institutional forms consequently tend to be studied 'in terms of the manner in which they depart from the norms and conventions of ordinary talk'. Harris discusses Habermas' (1984) distinction between *communicative* discourse, essentially forms of conversation, which 'is oriented to reaching an understanding' (Harris 1995: 121) and *strategic* discourse, which 'is oriented to success' and 'is basically instrumental in mode, power-laden and often located in institutional sites' (Harris 1995: 121).

Institutional talk, then, is instrumental, is both talk *at* work and talk *for* work, in the sense that it aims to accomplish the work of the relevant institution whilst, in contrast, one of the defining characteristics of conversation is that it is not principally necessitated by a practical task (Cook 1989: 51). A word of caution, however. This is not to say that conversation is not goal-oriented, that participants do not have aims and strategies to achieve those aims. As Harris (1995: 122) remarks, 'most linguistic contexts contain elements of the "strategic", even those which might be considered the prototype of discourse oriented to reaching an understanding'. The difference is that in institutional talk the *overall aims* are principally defined by the nature of the work being done and the institutions being served. Conversational participants may well not have any overall aims in this sense at all. Institutional interaction:

> involves an orientation by at least one of the participants to some core goal, task or identity (or set of them) conventionally associated with the institution in question. In short, institutional talk is normally informed by *goal orientations* of a relatively restricted conventional form.
>
> (Drew and Heritage 1992: 22)

What the particular working goals of the two sides are in these briefings is an empirical matter that we investigate throughout the book. Drew and Heritage are here talking about relatively long-term goals and not the kind of goals that exist at the micro, speech act level (discussed later), although the latter are to an extent determined by the former.

Institutional settings also predictably impose particular limitations on the kind of language behaviour which can be produced. The interaction:

> may often involve *special and particular constraints* on what one or both of the participants will treat as allowable contributions to the business in hand.
>
> (Drew and Heritage 1992: 22)

However, a distinction is necessary between highly formal settings and informal ones such as these briefings. The behaviour expected of a professional in the first kind (e.g. a barrister/attorney in court) is highly constrained and any deviations will either be very minor or heavily censured (by the judge). In less formal settings, on the other hand, there can be interpersonal communication between participants on more than one social level, a 'business' level, but also more unofficial, conversational levels. This will be reflected in the kinds of language used. In these briefings, the participants often know each other very well, and one of the most interesting aspects of the genre is the way the talk moves from one kind into another, from one social *register* to another.

Institutional settings also create another set of constraints on participants, closely associated with those on language. They also determine the possible *roles* that can be adopted. These roles have various rights and obligations conventionally, sometimes legally, associated with them. The non-formal setting of the briefings allows both sides the possibility of moving between roles, of speaking in many different social voices. The podium can, for instance, speak for the

White House at one moment, but for himself the next. But each of these roles or *footings* comes with its set of opportunities, of strengths and weaknesses. The way in which these opportunities – and those offered by shifting between one footing and another – are exploited by speakers is the topic of Chapters 3–5.

The roles of institutional participants also tend to be asymmetrical, that is, different participants have access to different discursive resources, they do different things with their talk and very often intervene in different moments. Often, this reflects a difference in status, and even power, between participants. We might think of a barrister and a witness or an interrogator and suspect. As Linell and Luckmann (1991) point out, asymmetries are normal in conversation too – between speaker and hearer at any given moment, between the initiator and respondent, there may be differing levels of knowledge of the topic, differing levels of conversational skills – but these are not systematic and most of them are short term.

In sum, then, conversation and institutional genres can be said to differ principally in terms of:

- participants' goals;
- participants' roles;
- participants' rights and obligations;
- permitted types of interaction;
- permitted contributions to the business in hand;
- long-term symmetry/asymmetry of opportunity between participants.

It is the task of the analyst to study how the *language*, which is produced in the course of the talk, can throw light on each of these aspects. Corpus/concordance technology can be a powerful aid in this process.

1.1.2   *Speech act theory*

In its view of talk as a vehicle for social action, CA has drawn heavily from the *speech act theory* as devised by Austin (1962) and refined by Searle (1969). This theory treats the utterance as a series of actions or *acts* each (a) deriving from an intention on the part of the speaker (the *illocutionary force* or *intent*) and (b) having an effect on the hearer(s) (the *perlocutionary force* or *effect*). The two are not always co-extensive, the effect does not always match the intent. Moreover, the intended *force* of a linguistic action may be different from its apparent *form* (or *locution*). We might consider this example from the briefings:

(1)   Q: You must have given him a deadline.

is formally a statement of fact. More precisely, the speaker has formulated a state of affairs which 'must' be the case. However, the speaker intends the utterance as a question – 'have you given him a deadline and if so what is it?' The locution and the illocutionary intent are non-aligned; in other words, the action is *indirect*. The podium's reply moreover does not provide the requested information:

(2)   MR LOCKHART: … between a path of peace and a path of violence.

Thus, the illocutionary intent and the perlocutionary force are also out of line. In such cases, the illocution is said to have *misfired*. In fact, the questioner is not satisfied and repeats the question:

(3)   Q: You must have given him a deadline.

To which, this time, the podium replies:

(4)   MR LOCKHART: No, we must not have, Helen.

He denies that the state of affairs presented by the questioner is the case. This time the perlocution is to some extent aligned with the illocution in that an answer of sorts is supplied – 'we have not given him a deadline'.

Notice, however, that this outline has not exhausted all the activity in the above exchanges. An utterance like *you must have given him a deadline* attempts to constrain the respondent's reply in a way that, say, *did you give him a deadline?* does not. The *spin* put on the former makes it much harder for the podium to give a negative response and, in fact, his first attempt to reply is an affirmative – if rather creative – reinterpretation of what the deadline might consist of. But Helen insists and repeats the question in exactly the same words. Such bald repetition is no accident. It suggests rather testily that the podium is being uncooperative. The latter is thus forced into an equally bald negation of the question's preferred affirmative direction. At the same time, he attempts to save some *face* (Chapter 7) by suggesting that the question's direction was misguided – *we must not have*, that giving a deadline was not such an obvious and reasonable thing to do.

As this example illustrates, speech acts are profitably studied in combination with an analysis of the detailed tactics adopted by speakers in authentic utterances to get the best out of the local situation. In strategic talk these tactics tend to be particularly varied, especially when the goals of the participating parties are in contrast. As Harris points out:

> A number of […] researchers in pragmatics (e.g. Leech 1983: 231; Levinson 1983: 38; Wilson 1991) have also maintained that universal pragmatic hypotheses should be tested against a corpus of empirical data and have highlighted the advantages of applying pragmatic theory systematically to real language behaviour, particularly in strategic contexts.
>
> (Harris 1995: 120)

In this book, although I cannot claim to be 'applying pragmatic theory systematically', an attempt is made to connect a number of ideas from pragmatics to just such a large corpus of authentic data in strategic contexts.

1.2 The structure of briefings discourse

1.2.1 The turn: context and expectations

The main structural unit of spoken discourse as studied in CA is the *turn at talk*. It is in and with the turn that the actions of participants are performed. Given the linear nature of speech, turns at talk are organized into sequences. One of the major insights of CA is that the way these sequences are organized can have considerable consequences on how and what meanings are conveyed [Greatbatch (1988) discusses turn-taking in news interviews].

Thus, to understand any single turn in institutional talk, the analyst must take into account its context. This context is of two principal kinds: the immediate co-text (or *context of production*, or *micro-context*), and the wider institutional, generic context (or *context of communication*, or *macro-context*). Both set up expectations in the minds of the participants, which determine how they will interpret utterances. The analyst too needs to be aware of these expectations.

1.2.2 The macro-context or context of communication

People who know how to behave in an institutional setting – who have a mental *frame* (Minsky 1975) or *script* (Schank and Abelson 1977) of the event – are able to do so largely through having experienced previous examples, previous tokens of the genre. These prior experiences give them expectations of what will happen, of what their own and other people's behaviour should be. Any single event is interpreted in the light of these expectations. In the type of talk where one party is a professional but the other is not, it is the former who generally takes the lead precisely because they possess greater experience of what is required behaviour in the circumstances.

These generic expectations thus shape any single event. But they are also shaped *by* them. As Halliday (1992) points out, every instance has an effect, however infinitesimal, upon the system. In this context, each new briefing has an effect on the relationship between the participants, can improve it or impair it, and can teach new members the rules of the game. In a particularly tense and competitive genre like this one, in fact, the rules of the game are under constant negotiation and each briefing can alter the relationship – and thus future expectations – to a considerable degree.

1.2.3 The macro-context of White House briefings

Following some of the parameters laid down by Hymes (1964, 1971), we can at this early stage give the following description of the macro- or communicative context of the discourse under analysis here.

Setting (place): The briefings normally take place in the office of the White House Press Secretary, inside the White House itself. However, when the President moves away from Washington on business, the Press Secretary may go with him, followed by a number of reporters who thus become a travelling band. Other locations where briefings have been held include Zagreb, Kampala, Tokyo, the International Trade Center, the Waldorf Astoria Hotel in New York.

Setting (*time*): The vast majority (39) of the briefings in the corpus took place between June 1997 and April 1999, although a few (nine) predate this period (the earliest is from August 1995).

The channel is mainly spontaneous speech but the podium will occasionally read from a prepared statement or *readout*. The podium has regular planning meetings with his aides to second-guess potential questions and work out responses. This means his talk is not always fully spontaneous. But very few genres of speech are, apart from simple conversation.

The code varies from informal to formal (even highly rhetorical) registers of modern-day US English.

The topics range widely. The White House library search engine requires a user to enter one or more search words and collects those briefings that contain these. The word chosen was *Yugoslavia*, largely because at the time of compilation (February–April 1999), the Kosovo crisis was the most prominent news item. Thus, it is a prominent topic in the corpus. However, all in all, I was surprised by how *little* time was spent on it. Many other topics were also covered. These included the Clinton–Ms Lewinsky affair and the threat of presidential impeachment, the President's relationship with Congress, financial and budgetary matters, the White House's reaction to various Congressional proposals, and sundry criticisms of the administration's record.

The participants: There were two main podiums in the period of time covered by the corpus. Mr Mike McCurry was the chief White House Press Secretary from January 1995 until October 1998, when he retired and was replaced by Mr Joe Lockhart. One or two others, either members of the Office of the Press Secretary or government officials occasionally stand in or help out, including Mr Barry Toiv, Ambassador Dobbins and Colonel Crowley.

The podium is usually appointed from within the ranks of the governing party and will have had experience of spokespersonship for other official bodies. Mr McCurry began his career as spokesperson for the Senate Committee on Labor and Human Resources and had been spokesperson, communications expert and political strategist during various election campaigns and for a number of Democratic institutions including the Democratic National Committee. He also worked for a time for a public relations company.

Mr Lockhart had also worked as press secretary in various campaigns and was assistant to the President immediately before his appointment as chief Press Secretary. He also had a background in journalism, having worked for ABC Network News, CNN and SKY Television News (UK).

The journalists are both print and broadcast. They represent many of the most prestigious US news outlets. The senior member (or 'Dean' as she was called by her fellow reporters) at the time was Helen Thomas who was employed by UPI, one of the main US news agencies. Those media outlets with easy access to Washington are clearly favoured by this briefings process, whilst those who lack such access have to rely on the wire (press agency) correspondents. This is a major bone of contention with the non-Washington based press and may be one reason these briefings are so heavily criticized in some media quarters.

One hugely important feature of context deserves separate mention. The podium is in charge of the microphone which resides, in effect, on his podium. His voice is by far the most dominant in the on-line broadcasts, a fact that is not to be undervalued in this study. The journalists ask their questions from the 'floor', from the seating space in front of the podium. The latter can to some extent choose the questioner, but the number of journalists is generally quite small (around 20) and any attempt to ignore someone would not escape notice. He can, of course, always decline to answer the question once it is posed.

1.2.4 The micro-context or co-text: topic coherence and cohesion among moves

We have already seen in examples (1)–(4) how, in interactive discourse, in order to understand what an utterance does, we need to look at its neighbours, especially the preceding co-text. 'The sense of an utterance *as an action*', say Drew and Heritage (1992: 18), 'is an interactive product of what was projected by a previous turn or turns at talk and what the speaker actually does'. In other words, to understand the illocution of the current utterance we must take into account the 'perlocutionary dimension', that is, the recent history of the interaction.

The vast bulk of the discourse of these briefings consists of questions and responses (I use this word in preference to *answer* which implies a response which satisfies the questioner: Harris 1991 and Section 12.1). Or rather, it consists of a series of questioner turns or moves,[1] which may or may not contain a question of some sort, followed by podium response moves that react in some way to the previous questioner move.

The so-called Question–Answer (Q–A) adjacency pair is one of the most studied forms of turn-taking in CA. Moreover, it is by far the dominant kind in institutional talk, to a degree that we might say it is the basic bed-rock form for this kind of discourse. Participants in institutional talk communicate via means of questions and responses, which most often belong, as Drew and Heritage (1992: 39) point out, 'to the institutional and lay participants respectively'. Thus, the Q–A pair has been studied in courtroom dialogue (Atkinson and Drew 1979), doctor–patient relations (Fisher and Todd 1987) including, among many other types of discourse, psychiatry (Bergmann 1992), the classroom (Mehan 1985).

In effect, in all the above genres, the questioner is the professional, the respondent the lay participant. This makes the news interview, including briefings, a highly unusual type of institutional talk in that both sides are equally professional. This, of course, has major repercussions in the power relations between the two sides (Chapter 7).

Other writers, however, claim that, in some forms of institutional discourse, the basic exchange is not question–response, rather question–response followed by evaluation of response on the part of the questioner (generally the professional), that is, Q–R–E [see especially Sinclair and Coulthard (1975) on classroom interaction]. There is evidence that this kind of exchange does occur in the briefings:

(5)   Q: Do you feel any pressure because of this pending crisis to change your strategy away from an air campaign to perhaps using troops to bring in relief?

   MR LOCKHART: I would question the foundation of the question that somehow leaves with NATO the responsibility for what's going on. NATO did not ethnically cleanse a million people out of the country. NATO did not close the border and force them back in, for whatever reason only Milosevic can explain. And I think if we allowed this to go on with impunity these and more unspeakable horrors would occur.

   Q: Well, how is that an answer?

What is particular about this kind of discourse, however, is that any kind of journalistic evaluation of the podium's response itself functions as a form of question, even if no explicit interrogative is forthcoming. Since questioner moves are supposed by all to comprise questions, and since any questioner move that falls short of complete agreement with the podium is taken pragmatically to constitute a problem for the podium to respond to, any evaluation is seen as requiring a further podium response [Hoey (1983: 81–96) discusses how negative evaluation in texts generally constitutes a problem requiring solution]. In other words, an evaluation is seen as a kind of question in itself. In the following, the podium has been asked to explain how President Clinton's lying to the press differs from President Nixon's over the Watergate affair. The podium gives a list of supposed differences, but the questioner retorts 'we're nevertheless still talking about lies':

(6)   Q: But he was still talking about lying to the American people, if I read his statement correctly.

This evaluation of the podium's reply needs addressing as if it were a question and the podium pulls out one of his *we've already dealt with this question* type responses:

(7)   MR LOCKHART: We went through yesterday the enormous difference between Watergate and the issues that have been affecting this President.

Thus, the structure of this kind of exchange is question–response–(evaluation + question), or Q–R–E/Q. Note also in (7), by the way, the presentation of the

President as 'done-to' (or Affected) rather than 'doer' (Actor), as well as the use of the neutral term *issues*, preferred to *problems* or *scandals*.

One of the basic concerns in all discourse analysis – and one of the main reasons utterances are best studied in context – is the question of how speakers maintain and exploit *topic coherence*. In all Q–A based genres, the question of topic coherence is of fundamental interest in evaluating the perlocutionary relation, exchange by exchange, between questioner move and respondent move. In political interviews, moreover, a study of topic coherence could hardly be more important: it will help us explain why a response seems to answer the question or why conversely it is seen (first of all by the questioner, but also by the analyst) as evasive. This will be a major theme in this book and Chapter 12 is a summary of observations on the matter. The study of coherence between a response move and the immediately following questioner move is also necessary to investigate how the questioner appraises the response and whether they decide to develop or shift the topic. However, the perlocutionary dimension goes beyond a scrutiny of the immediately preceding move. In a multiquestioner context, such as these briefings, it is interesting to study how much, if any, coherence there is among a series of questions. Moreover, any strategic manoeuvres on the part of the respondent, the podium, will only be apparent by examining the coherence among a series of responses.

Some insight into coherence can be achieved by examining the clues offered in the *cohesive devices* employed by speakers, that is, the linguistic signals they use to indicate connections among portions of the discourse they are producing. These devices can, of course, be concordanced. Here, we will look at both the form and function of questioner and response moves as they occur in these briefings and the kind of coherence that exists among them. The methodology adopted was to look at both the questions and responses in isolation in the Q and R subcorpora, and then to look at how they combine in the full texts that these subcorpora derive from.

1.2.5   *Questioner moves: form and function*

Dealing first of all with the list of question moves in the Q-file, one or two structural features stood out. When journalists wish to install a new subject as the current topic of debate, they do so in a limited number of ways. The most common is to state the background to the topic first and then ask the question:

(8)   Q: Joe, Clinton's going to meet with Presidents Mahuad and Fujimori later on. Can you explain to us what this meeting is about?

Often, the question itself appears as a simple appendage:

(9)   Q: The White House supposedly refuses to intervene to try to resolve the tobacco dispute. Is that true?

Another, though much rarer mechanism, is the reverse: the question first then the background:

(10) Q: Joe, does the White House stand behind the statements that Sid Blumenthal made after he came out of the grand jury several months ago, where he characterized his testimony? Now it appears that he was discussing things that didn't happen or didn't happen the way he wanted.

This projects the background as an *account*, that is, a justification for asking this particular question. Finally, they can employ a tripartite structure: announce the topic very briefly, ask the question and finish off with the account:

(11) Q: On the ozone rule that's put out by EPA, how close are we on that? I understand that there are some compromise deals being cut already.

This last example contains a typical example of the way topics are very frequently signalled with the utmost economy in these briefings. The word *on*, followed by the briefest indication of topic, often a place, is common: *On East Timor..., On China...* , *Joe, on gun control...* , *On Jesse Jackson.* These topic introductions are a kind of preface to the question, and although question prefaces are very common in these briefings they tend to be short. There is, in general, a pressure to keep questions as concise as possible. First of all because others are waiting with their questions ready and second because the potential topics of debate – current affairs – are already in the foreground of debate and long introductions to them are unnecessary.

On the whole, however, questioners are loath to be seen as installing a new topic out of the blue. They much prefer to preface their questions with an indication that they are pursuing an old one. The most common way of doing this is to claim that the podium or one of his clients raised the topic first (*yesterday the President said, you said earlier*, etc.) and the question is just a request for further elucidation. If the topic has already been broached this frees the journalist from having to justify their intervention. For the same reason questioners frequently state explicitly that they are returning to an old question, using *back to* either on its own – *back to Kosovo* – or preceded by *coming/going/getting*: *Mike, getting back to that Nixon question.* More frequent still is a preface indicating that the question about to be asked is a *follow-up*, and, therefore, not a fresh question. In the following we have what certainly looks like a new topic introduced as a *follow-up* justified by a whole battery of *you saids*:

(12) Q: Let me *follow that up*, Joe. *You talked* yesterday about Senator Byrd had a valid point when he talked about, you know, the White House shouldn't tamper with the jury. But *you said* that talking to a member of the Senate, making your case to a member of the Senate, would not constitute tampering with the jury. But *you said* there were some things that might constitute jury tampering. What are those things?

It is in any case not easy to decide what exactly comprises a *fresh* topic. Even if it has not been mentioned during the current briefing, it could still be 'in the air'. As Jucker (1986: 127) points out, 'obviously no question of an interview can introduce an entirely new topic'. For example, do the following questions – one on land mines and the other on chemical weapons – contain two separate topics or is the second the same topic with a shift of emphasis (they have in common the idea of banning both)?

(13)   Q: Mike, do you have any comment on Senator Leahy's land mines legislation? [...] Is the White House ready to join him in this effort to ban land mines?

[Podium's response followed by two more brief questions and responses.]

Q: But how does that square with our stand on the Chemical Weapons Treaty where the administration, of course, pushed to have that ratified [...]

The point is that, when either establishing or shifting topic, speakers try to reduce their imposition on the audience by establishing explicitly some kind of cohesive link with what has gone before, even if they have to stretch quite a way back:

(14)   Q: Mike, I wanted to revisit a question of a few weeks ago I brought up about the Mike Espy case [...]

Contrast this with the questions that occur when the topic is well established. They are unprefaced, shorter and openly, immediately interrogative:

(15)   Q: Will we sign on with Ottawa?
(16)   Q: Why can't you do both?
(17)   Q: Would such a limit be constitutional?

Question justification is, in fact, an important key to reading this type of discourse. Most of the question prefaces discussed so far have this as one of their functions. Questioners clearly feel the need to justify their intervention, partly for making demands upon the podium, but rather more for imposing on their fellow journalists' precious time (Section 3.3).

Another noticeable feature of structure is the frequent occurrence at the very beginning of questioner moves of the cohesive discourse particles *but, and, well* and *so*. Each of these has a very different function (Jucker 1986: 117–25), but they have in common the implication of coherence of some sort with the preceding response. When *but* introduces a question in interviews there is usually some implied contrast:

(18)   MR McCURRY: You can pursue both, but you won't get a global regime in Canada because there are countries not participating in the Ottawa process that would be necessary to have a truly global solution to this problem.

Q: *But* how does that square with our stand on the Chemical Weapons Treaty where the administration, of course, pushed to have that ratified, even though a number of countries known to be promoting chemical weapons have no intention of signing?

However, the contrast is generally, as here, fairly cooperative. The frequency of this use of *but* undoubtedly 'stresses the quantitative importance of disagreement' (Jucker 1986: 124), but disagreement is a way of developing topic and of encouraging the podium to expand a line of argument. *And*, instead, functions as an expression of continuity but without the contrast implied by *but*. Paradoxically, however, it can be pragmatically *less* cooperative, since it makes the interviewee work harder to develop their argument:

(19)   MR LOCKHART: The President's intentions were clear – at least I believe they were clear.
       Q: *And* the intention is to cooperate, simply put?
       MR LOCKHART: The intention is to work with them, to cooperate. *But* if you're going to ask me to define that specifically before the Committee sits down to talk about what they're going to do, I can't do that for you.

Notice that the podium in his second move, in order to do more than simply repeat the questioner's proposition, feels the need to supply his own *but*, his own topic-advancing particle.

Jucker reports on a number of studies of *well*, including R. Lakoff (1973a), Levinson (1983: 334) and Schiffrin (1985). The general conclusion is that it prefaces responses that are insufficient in some way, or that contradict or modify the move made in the first part of the exchange. Their occurrence in the *question* move has been studied much less. And, yet, it is not uncommon in the briefings as the start of a questioner move.

First of all, and fundamental to all its uses, it expresses a pause in the speaker's thoughts. This allows it to function as a boundary marker between (sub-)topics (Jucker 1986: 118–20). But it can also express a pause for reflection because – it intimates – there is a problem in the interaction at this point. The problem can be of two types. It can be backward looking or *anaphoric*, that is, the speaker has a problem with the previous speaker's turn, that is, the podium's previous response:

(20)   Q: Well, how is that an answer?
(21)   MR LOCKHART: [...] I think our position is well-known on all of those issues.
       Q: Well, what is it?

Often the anaphoric *well* is accompanied by a reformulation of the problematic previous turn:

(22)   Q: Well, clarify that. Are you saying the NATO spokesperson was speculating?

Or it can be forward looking, *cataphoric*, in which case it suggests that what the speaker himself or herself is about to say might be seen as problematic by the interlocutor, by the podium:

(23)   MR LOCKHART: [...] and the Republicans may be divided but the country
           is not.
       Q: Well, Joe, aren't the Democrats also divided on that?

The questioner's *well* indicates their appreciation that the podium, being a Democrat, might have preferred not to hear this question.

It can even express combinations of the above, a topic boundary *and* dissatisfaction with the previous reply, a sort of 'I'm not totally happy with that, but let's move on ... ':

(24)   MR LOCKHART: We've certainly made it as one of the objectives we're
           pursuing that the refugees can return to Kosovo.
       Q: Well, back to the refugees in Arkansas issue,

and, just occasionally, the pause for thought attested by *well* does not indicate a problem at all, just that the following words will convey the speaker's deeply considered opinion (or what he or she wishes to convey as such):

(25)   MR McCURRY: [...] And that's the role of the Press Secretary, to be
           equi-distant between two combatants in this adversarial relationship.
       Q: Well, you've done a good job, Mike.
       MR McCURRY: Thanks, sweets. (Laughter.)

The last of the particles to look at is *so*. This functions as the introduction to a whole new type of turn, the *reformulation* of the previous speaker's contribution. It is very often found with other indicators that the current speaker is 'summarizing' the thoughts of the previous one, for example, *So, basically, you're saying there is ... , So adjournment, just to be precise ... , So, simply put ... .* It might be thought that this kind of move is used simply to *check* the drift of the topic rather than to shift it, but this was not found to be the case – it performs both functions simultaneously. It is usually very sceptical, a kind of recapitulation in the most negative light possible of the podium's thought in order to put those thoughts to the test. Reformulation is discussed in detail in Chapter 9.

Earlier, the point was made that not all questioner moves contained questions. Many of them are in non-interrogative *form*, but still perform an interrogative *function*, for example, 'But you don't disagree with that'. Others seem less interrogative still. Some questioner moves outline a situation:

(26)   Q: One of the things that the Attorneys General are clearly concerned
           about is that they do a deal on punitive damages and then the White
           House pulls the rug out from under them and says, oops, that was a bad

idea for you to do that. So they're clearly looking for some guidance from you to say, does this work, does this not work.

What, of course, makes such outlines as these into questions is simply their position in the discourse. They occupy the question slot in the Q–A or the Q–R–E/Q exchange; they occur where a question is expected and are, therefore, interpreted as such.

Occasionally though, tables can be turned. The respondent can turn questioner and force the journalists to respond, perhaps as a joke:

(27) Q: Since your revelation about this –
      MR LOCKHART: What's a revelation?
      Q: It's in the Bible. (Laughter.)

But sometimes for genuine clarification:

(28) Q: [...] There have been two columns written – one of them in The
         New York Post – that deal with the President's firing of the White
         House doctor and a number of other drugs and the President questions.
         And my question –
      MR LOCKHART: Excuse me, what White House doctor?
      Q: The first one, when he came here – I believe it's Bell or – he was fired
         because he wouldn't inject something that they didn't tell him what it
         was. (Laughter.)

Or an exchange of discordant opinions can usurp the Q–A form in moments of tension:

(29) Q: [...] where was the President's moral butt when innocent victims were
         being slaughtered by the Viet Cong, and where 591 other young men
         from Arkansas lost their lives?
      MR LOCKHART: Next question.
      Q: Next question – you're ashamed of this, Joe? Is that what you're saying?
      MR LOCKHART: Lester, I don't have time for this today. Next question.
      Q: You don't have time for it, okay.
      MR LOCKHART: And you can put that in your report. That doesn't
         bother me.
      Q: I will. Oh, I'm delighted to.

Such departures from normal roles, however, are always short-lived. As in almost all political interviews, participants follow the Q–A or Q–R–E/Q formula obediently.

1.2.6 *Response moves: form and function*

Response moves tend to be longer and structurally more heterogeneous than the questioner moves. However, the following features are noticeable. In the response subcorpus (R-file), only two replies begin with the word *yes* and only five with *no*, compared to 28 which open with *well*. We noticed above how *well* signals pause for reflection, which makes it absolutely typical of responses. It can give the respondent a moment to organize their thoughts and at the same time it can even serve to compliment the questioner, to imply their question merits proper consideration, even if all you are doing is stressing common ground:

(30)   Q: Is it something to veto a bill about?
       MR LOCKHART: Well, we certainly have a veto threat on it.

When, however, the previous move is seen as particularly troublesome or patience testing, the response is quite likely to begin with *look* or *listen*:

(31)   MR LOCKHART: Look, that's an unfortunate characterization.

The R-file also contains a whole series of self-referential openings involving *I*, which have three functions. They can express opinion: *I think ... , my understanding is ... , I'd say ... , I'm saying ...*; agreement or disagreement *I (don't) think/believe so*; or they are used to avoid giving an answer: *I don't know, I'm not aware of/familiar with ...* . There are also a good number which use *we* when the podium is claiming to speak for one of his clients (Chapter 4).

Another very striking feature of the podium's prose is his frequent use of parallel structures:

(32)   MR LOCKHART: The President has talked about investing in education. He's talked about improving education. He's talked about protecting the environment [...]
(33)   MR McCURRY: It looks like it's politics; it doesn't look like it's doing the constitutional business of the American people.

This device is both highly rhetorical in effect and creates a strong internal cohesion to the move. It is discussed in detail in Chapter 11.

It is often important for the podium to demonstrate explicitly the cohesiveness of his response with the previous questioner move. There is considerable *lexical* cohesion created by the podium; he frequently picks up and repeats in some way items from the previous move:

(34)   Q: Do you have a clear position on *criminal liability*? Any limits in that sense?
       MR McCURRY: I'm not aware that *criminal liability* has been an issue.
(35)   Q: Is *the census* a non-negotiable item?
       MR LOCKHART: *The census* is certainly something that we feel strongly about [...]

This reiteration is not strictly necessary – he could have used the pronoun *it* – but it serves two functions. First of all, in the less than perfect acoustic conditions of a press conference, it does no harm to repeat the topic in one's response, and it also creates a useful impression that the response is addressing the question properly, whether or not this actually is the case.

It can, however, have a quite different effect:

(36)   Q: Does that mean, though, that you're saying that complying with subpoenas, to fully comply is really a *relative* term?
MR McCURRY: No, it's not *relative*, and that's an artificial construct.

(37)   Q: I understand that there are some *compromise deals* being cut already and that Erskine Bowles has participated in the –
MR McCURRY: I'm not aware of any *'compromise' deals*.

Here, the repetition is a kind of sarcastic echo and expresses a shortness, a testiness with the question on the part of the podium. This should be contrasted with other possibilities available to him. It is more normal *not* to repeat a questioner's exact words, to perhaps choose a stylistic alternative:

(38)   Q: Do the Democrats have a unified position yet?
MR McCURRY: They're coalescing around some things.

The semantic link is created between *unified* and *coalescing*, but any hint of sarcasm is avoided.

Finally, the podium might pick up a term as the prelude to a joke:

(39)   Q: Joe, this is the *honeymoon weekend* for the Clintons. When was Mrs Clinton's trip –
MR LOCKHART: I thought this was my *honeymoon week*? No?
Q: It was. (Laughter.)
MR LOCKHART: This was my *honeymoon*?
Q: You're having it. (Laughter.)

Continuing the topic of reiteration, we mentioned above how frequently questioners reformulate a podium's response in a negative light. This generally means that the podium must then offer a counter-reformulation, a more positive version of events, to defend himself and his clients:

(40)   Q: Does that mean, though, that you're saying that complying with subpoenas, to fully comply is really a relative term?
MR McCURRY: No, it's not relative, and that's an artificial construct. In any courtroom in this country, questions of privilege are dealt with all the time.

Such reformulations are often signalled linguistically in some way – *What I'm (we're) saying is …*, *look, listen*, etc. Podium reformulation is discussed in detail in Section 9.2.3.

The podium can also create cohesion with the previous move by actually commenting on the question:

(41)   Q: [...] What is the President's best estimate of how this is going to play out, this final barn dance between the two sides?
        MR LOCKHART: That's an apt illusion. (Laughter.)
(42)   Q: Joe, I want to go back at something. I think *it's a fair question* and maybe deserves a thoughtful answer, which perhaps we haven't received so far. (Laughter.)
        MR LOCKHART: Do I get to decide whether *it's a fair question*?

In sum, reiteration of part of a previous move which, as we have seen, can take a number of forms, is a salient feature of podium talk.

Lexical links can of course extend over more than two turns, as in the following (edited) example (Senator Roth has presented a taxation reform bill, the Republican House has devised a different one):

(43)   Q: Tax. *Senate tax plan* – reaction.
        MR McCURRY: [...] too much in *Senator Roth*'s marked skews towards the highest income.
        Q: So you like *Roth* but [...]
        MR McCURRY: [...] some things that are better in *his version*.

This is, of course, a totally normal way for cohesion to be created co-operatively by speakers.

Cohesion between moves is also created using *grammatical* devices, in fact this is probably the most normal way of doing so: personal pronouns take the place of proper nouns, demonstratives are used to refer to parts of the previous text and 'generalizing' items, like *anything* in the following example, appear in the response to substitute a more precise term in the question:

(44)   Q: But, Joe, isn't the way to move it along to cooperate fully and free up aides to testify?
        MR LOCKHART: I have done nothing here today to preclude *anything*.

A feature that seems to be typical of cohesion in this discourse type is the use of *that* by both parties. It seems to be used with the meaning of either 'what you just said':

(45)   Q: Look, *that's* an unfortunate characterization.

or it refers to something *in* what has just been said (here, the presidential initiative):

(46)   Q: [...] If it was important enough for the President to step into the baseball strike, why not important enough to step in and resolve this –
        Q: Because *that* was a big mistake. (Laughter.)

The ability of *that* to refer to parts of the previous discourse can lead on occasion to a rather promiscuous use:

(47) MR McCURRY: Well, I haven't said – the parties themselves have said *that*, I don't need to say *that*. They say *that* themselves.

Q: But you don't disagree with *that*.

MR McCURRY: I think *that*'s almost obvious.

Q: *That*'s pretty obvious, okay. Then *that* gets to the next question:

1.2.7 Conclusion on cohesion and coherence

We should note, finally, that exchanges like these are only fully comprehensible to the participants. Despite the cohesive devices and abundance of repetition noticed earlier, the analyst is liable to find the discourse much less coherent than those involved. Background information is taken for granted, topics are often broached without an introduction, public and private figures are mentioned without a presentation. This, of course, is typical of in-group discourse, of talk among people who know each other well and have a great deal of common, shared knowledge. Although these briefings are broadcast, this study of their cohesion seems to show that few concessions are made to the wider lay audience.

2 Footing

Who says what to whom

2.1 Footing or participant roles

The concept of *footing* in the sense relevant to this book was described by Erving Goffman in his paper *Forms of Talk* in 1981. It has since had a considerable impact in a number of social sciences, and its importance in linguistics is outlined by Levinson (1988).

Goffman was concerned with issues of precisely how people participate in social encounters. Talk can only be analysed if the analyst is able to take into account the participant status, that is, the level, degree and nature of participation of those present. Traditional dyadic classifications of participants as simply *speaker* and *hearer* were shown to be clearly inadequate. The roles described by communication theory models:

$$\text{sender} \rightarrow \text{transmitter} \rightarrow (\text{via channel}) \rightarrow \text{receiver} \rightarrow \text{destination}$$

were also unable to capture the complex participant roles encountered in natural speech events. Goffman therefore devised a three-party distinction for production roles, as follows [in brackets are the page numbers in Goffman (1981); this scheme follows Levinson (1988)]:

Production roles:
Animator: 'the sounding box' (p. 226)
Author: 'the agent who scripts the lines' (p. 226)
Principal: 'the party to whose position the words attest' (p. 226)

and a multiparty distinction for reception roles:

Reception roles:
A: *ratified*
Addressed recipient: 'the one to whom the speaker addresses his visual attention and to whom, incidentally, he expects to turn over his speaking role' (p. 132)
Unaddressed recipient: the rest of the 'official hearers', who may or may not be listening (p. 133)

B: *unratified*

Overhearers: 'inadvertent', 'non-official' listeners (p. 132) or *bystanders*
Eavesdroppers: 'engineered', 'non-official' followers of talk (p. 132)

Though recognizing it as a 'notable advance' on earlier schemes, Levinson criticizes Goffman's system on a number of counts. First, he argues, it does not maintain a sufficient distinction between analysis at the level of *speech event* and *utterance event* (of which more later). Furthermore, it does not comprise a sufficient number of categories, does not provide for enough distinctions. In addition, having been designed to account for face-to-face conversation, it cannot cope adequately with other forms of talk, including what he calls 'podium talk', of which press briefings would be an important example.

2.2   The rank structure of White House briefings

On the first of these counts, the structure of the analytical model, Levinson, as mentioned earlier, emphasizes the need to maintain a distinction between *speech event* and *utterance event*.

For our purposes – and perhaps for all institutional talk – we need at least three tiers. The highest level, for which we will preserve Levinson's term *speech event*, is the *discourse genre token*, that is, the kind of event of which the current item of talk is an example. Genre tokens or speech events tend to have plain English denominations: a conversation, a political speech, etc.; in the present case, we are studying occurrences or tokens of press briefings.

The second level, we will call *speech routines*. These are the subparts which make up the speech event. Any single routine is defined as that part of the event during which the overall activity of the participants remains constant. The routine is also the level at which any relevant conventions about turn-taking allocation, who is allowed to take the floor and when etc., will be applicable. Of necessity these definitions are rather vague. Taking as an example a radio phone-in programme (see Hutchby 1991, 1996), this might consist of perhaps four routines: the *introduction*, in which the host outlines the topic for discussion and presents the studio panel of experts; the *calls* in which callers normally address their remarks to the host (otherwise they explicitly nominate one of the panel), the *response/discussion* of the caller's point by the panel; a *closing* routine at the end of the programme in which each of the experts gives a summing up of their arguments. Obviously the calls routine is recursive, that is, there will be more than one call and follow-up discussion, but this part of the genre token can be counted as the same routine, because the activity remains, with minor variations, the same.[1]

White House briefings are quite simple in structure and can generally be divided into the following speech routines: *introduction*, in which the podium either reads out or summarizes a prepared statement on the latest White House business (or that part he/she wishes to be known); a *question and response* routine which makes up by far the longest part of the whole event; an optional *closing* routine in which the briefing is wound down, the week's future events are outlined and leave is taken. The occurrence of this last routine, however, is far from being the norm since briefings often end very suddenly for a number of contingent reasons.

The third tier is the *utterance event*, defined as 'that stretch of a turn at talk over which there is a constant set of participant roles mapped into the same set of individuals – that is, that unit within which the function from the set of participant roles to the set of individuals is held constant' (Levinson 1988: 168). Since it is thus defined by its function, Ensink (1997: 9) identifies the utterance event with the *speech act*. This is not necessarily co-existent with a single turn at talk, since participant roles, relations and acts can alter during the course of a turn. For example, it is quite possible for part of the podium's move to be addressed to a single, nominated addressee, whereas another part is addressed to the whole audience of journalists.

2.3   Levinson's participant roles and binary distinctive features

As regards the second of Levinson's criticisms of Goffman's work, the deficiency of categories for making role distinctions, it is clear that for the purposes of analysing press briefings, we need to add an important distinction at the level of *unaddressed recipient*:

> unaddressed recipient:
> *Target*: official hearers for whose sake the discourse is actually being produced
> *Non-target*: the rest of the 'official hearers' who may or may not be listening

This would differentiate – in, for instance, the classic situation where A says to B, in the presence of John: 'Tell John I'm not speaking to him' – between the unaddressed target (John) and all the other non-target participants in the talk event. Levinson (1988: 166) illustrates the distinction in the following dialogue (which I have edited slightly):

(1)   (from Sacks *et al.* 1974: 29)
       SHARON: You didn't come to talk to Karen?
       MARK: No, Karen- Karen and I're having a fight, after she went out with Keith and not with me.
       RUTHIE: Hah hah hah hah
       KAREN: Well, Mark, you never asked me out.

This distinction is more than ever vital in *broadcast* podium talk and other media communication, for example, advertising. Politicians' speeches and radio or TV commercials are very often tailored for a particular section – the *target audience* – of all those listening and watching. The highly complex concept of *audience* will be explored in Section 2.5.3.

Levinson (1988: 171), proposes instead to break down participant roles into 'polythetic defining characteristics', that is, into their binary distinctive features (both terms are borrowed from the field of phonology). He analyses the elements of production into:

> ± participation (i.e. present and involved);
> ± transmission (the actual delivery of the message);
> ± motive (having the motive or desire to communicate the message);
> ± form (devising the format of the message);

where the symbol ± (plus or minus) means activated or not activated. The real life examples he gives include:

> *Barrister*: + participation (he/she is present and involved during the utterance event), + transmission (he/she does the actual speaking), − motive (he/she does not have the motive or desire behind the communication – presumably Levinson intends that this is a property of the client), + formulator (since he/she decides exactly what to say, writes their own speeches etc.);
> *Reader of statement*: + participation, + transmission, − motive, − form;
> *(Distant) source of military command*: − participation, − transmission, + motive, + form.

The elements of reception, on the other hand, are:

> ± participation (as above);
> ± address (who the message is physically given to, being singled out by a feature of address, vocatives, gaze, gesture etc.);
> ± recipientship; (who a message is *for*);
> ± channel-linkage (ability to physically receive a message).

Real-life examples here include:

> *Indirect target (like John above)*: + participation, − address, + recipient, + channel-link;
> *Committee chairman*: + participation, + address, − recipient, + channel-link;
> *Overhearer*: − participation, − address, − recipient, + channel-link.

This scheme clearly allows a much greater delicacy of distinction than Goffman's original one. We can now, for example, differentiate between *target unaddressed recipients* and *non-target unaddressed recipients* through the recipientship feature:

> *target unaddressed recipient*: + participation, − address, + recipient, + channel-link;
> *non-target unaddressed recipients*: + participation, − address, − recipient, + channel-link.

To this analysis, Levinson adds the consideration that it is necessary to maintain a distinction between the participant roles and the incumbency of those roles. An example (also a limit case) would be *talking to oneself* where the roles of speaker (producer) and hearer (receiver) are occupied by the same individual. In terms of the current study, any individual participant in a briefing generally occupies at any one time more than one production or reception role. Precisely *which* roles is an empirical question to be studied event by event, and the possibility of changing and remixing footing roles is, as we shall see, a frequently exploited strategy. Moreover, 'any role may be occupied by any number of incumbents simultaneously' (Levinson 1988: 181), and in the case of the press when the podium is speaking, this is the usual case. Conversely, one individual can stand duty for a joint incumbency (as when the chairman of the jury pronounces the verdict). Similarly, the extent to which the members of the press present at a briefing are representative of other press people, of their newspapers, of their readership is a complex and intriguing question.

There may, however, be some limitations to this essentially binary system of analysis. The first we have already seen in the description of the *barrister* above, which included the feature '− *motive*', presumably since the motivator of the court case was deemed to be the client. Although it is undoubtedly true that the barrister in court speaks on behalf, and for the benefit of, the client, they normally also desire to win the case, they also have 'the motive or desire to communicate some particular message' in their own interest − for remuneration, to enhance their reputation, and so on. Both client and barrister ought to be marked '+ *motive*' in a binary system, even if the motivation is on a different level. But such a system fails to capture distinctions in types, and also in degrees, of motivation. This is clearly relevant to the present study, where the White House podium is in some ways analogous to a barrister in being a paid representative of a certain interest. Thus, for example, even when giving a statement for which the administration has the principal motivation, the podium may also have involvement as a Democrat, as the President's friend, and so on.

Recitation is also resistant to binary analysis. Who is the motivator (Goffman's *principal*) and who the composer or formulator (Goffman's *author*, the party responsible for the *form* of words) when an actor is speaking Hamlet's lines? Shakespeare, the play's director and the actor collaborate in both the *illocution* (i.e. the expression of meaning) and the *form* of the language itself (Shakespeare their written base, the actor − under instruction − their shape in sound). Much of spoken communication is collaborative in this sense but a binary scheme has problems with concepts such as *part-motivator* and *composer to a certain degree*.[2] Even if Shakespeare, the director and the actor are all designated '+ *motive*' and '+ *form*', it is nevertheless highly reductive for any system to consider all three as the same.

Again, there are strong analogies between recitation and political briefings. In the latter, both 'sides' − podium and press − recite their designated roles, and, as we shall see, are acutely aware of the role-playing aspects of the situation.

There also seem to be complications regarding the concept of *participation*, defined, as Levinson himself admits, rather vaguely as having 'something to do with what Goffman (1981: 174) calls a "ratified role" in the proceedings'. It seems possible, however, for an individual to be treated as both participant and non-participant at the same time, as in the following example:

(2)   MR BERGER: I'm not going to make another statement. I do feel a little bit like we are the Allen and Rossi of this show. You may remember that Allen and Rossi was the act that followed the Beatles on the Ed Sullivan Show in the early 1960s – small piece of trivia.
    Q: You're dating yourself.
    MR BERGER: If you're too young, ask Wolf. (Laughter.)

Wolf, in traditional terms the *butt* of the joke, occupies two roles here. On one level he is, momentarily, for the occasion of the joke, excluded from the group, treated by Mr Berger as non-ratified, as at best an *overhearer*, since the addressee of *you* is everyone but Wolf.[3] Therefore, in the binary analysis he would be marked as ' − *participant*'. On another level, of course, he is the *indirect target* [like Karen in (1)] of the utterance and it would not be such a good joke if he were not present and part of the proceedings. His role on this level would therefore be marked '+ *participant*'. In Levinson's analysis, Wolf would be seen as participant at the speech event level, but momentarily non-participant target in the utterance event. However, on all such occasions of singling-out an individual from the group there is a deliberate ambiguity as to whether they are ratified participants at that moment or simply the object of attention.

   What is important here is that participation is not simply a physical affair, that is, a question of presence in the speech event and/or attention in the utterance event, but is how parties are *projected*, are treated by the speaker. This has important repercussions for the concept of audience (see Section 2.5.3).

2.4   Participant roles in the White House briefings: production roles

2.4.1   *Podium and press*

In contrast to everyday conversation, where a dyadic model with minor variations is often adequate, participant roles in institutional talk can be very complex. Any individual tends to have more than one role and, conversely many roles tend to be distributed over more than one individual. Levinson gives special mention to settings where individuals speak in the institutional role of spokespersons:

> they may at times speak for themselves as well as for others (acting in the *author* role but as representatives of other like-minded *principals*), while at other times they may act as mere *relayers* (for some *indirect source*) or *spokesman* (for some *principal*) in our restricted participant role sense.
>
> (Levinson 1988: 203)

The distinction between *relayer* and *spokesman* in Levinson's scheme lies in the fact that, while neither are *motivator/principal*, the latter is responsible for the *form* of the message (thus *relayer* is: + participation, + transmission, − motive, − form; *spokesman* is: + participation, + transmission, − motive, + form).

The job of the analyst is to try to decide which of these voices is speaking at any one time (in Levinson's terms in any one utterance event). There may often be blends of voices, as when someone speaks both for themselves and also others. And on behalf of precisely *which* others? In the case of the podium, for example, are the others the President alone, the administration, the Democratic party, the American people, the nation of the United States of America? In the next two chapters, we will attempt to address some of these questions with the aid of concordances. For the time being, then, we can analyse the figure of the podium into the following roles:

> *principal* (or *motivator*) either as:
> (a) *Private individual*: speaking for self alone, or
> (b) *Member/representative of group*: claiming to speak for self plus some like-minded group,
> in both cases, solely responsible for message and form;
>
> *Spokesperson*: speaking for a distant principal or motivator, but in his/her own words. Responsible for the form but not the message;
>
> *Relayer*: speaking for a distant principal or motivator, using a prepared form of words. Responsible for neither message nor form.[4]

The roles enacted by the members of the press are generally similar but with important differences in detail. They too can interact as private individuals, they can claim membership of a group, for example, the press, their own newspaper, the American electorate and so on. Someone may elect themselves as spokesperson for a position, and may *relay* a position by quoting from a document. However, this is clearly somewhat different from the briefer's role, since the newsperson has made a deliberate choice of what to represent or to quote. He or she will always, therefore, be motivator, at least in part, of the message.

2.4.2   *Absent motivators*

The podium represents, by definition, one or more absent motivators or principals. Here again, however, we must be aware of a possible blending of roles: a statement from an absent source may be accompanied by expressions of agreement from the relayer, making the latter partly spokesperson and even partly principal. Moreover, there may be strategic fudging as to who precisely is the motivator, the party responsible for a message.

From the point of view of the principal, as Levinson notes, there are advantages in using official spokespersons (including briefers):

> The potential vagueness of the participant role associated with the institutional role is of course an exploitable resource – the utterances of official spokesmen can be repudiated if expedient.

(Levinson 1988: 203)

But the expediency of using an intermediary goes well beyond this. Briefers can develop a very different interpersonal relationship with the press than that possible for an official principal. In particular, they can shift between formal and informal roles far more easily. When convenient, they can claim ignorance of both official and private matters, they can claim lack of competence (e.g. Mr McCurry: 'I'm not a lawyer. I wouldn't know how to speculate an answer to that question'). Likewise, they can claim lack of authorization to respond ('the lawyers' won't let them). These are beneficial as much to the absent principal as the podium himself.

2.5   Participant roles in the White House briefings: reception roles

2.5.1   *The podium*

The podium is, for the majority of the briefings, in the position of an interviewee, but an interviewee of a particular kind. In political news interviews, the interviewee is normally, in Levinson's scheme, an *interlocutor*, that is, he or she is both addressee and recipient of the questions. This is a consequence of their being directly responsible for the response message. The role of the podium in these briefings is far more complex. At times he is asked personal questions and is therefore simple *interlocutor* (e.g. 'Mike, are you going to write a book?'). But in his institutional role, he is responding on behalf of an absent principal, and is an *intermediary*, that is, he is addressee but not recipient. And yet, as we shall see, the two roles of *interlocutor* and *intermediary* are very difficult to keep apart. The briefer is generally identified with his various principals, and the very nature of the institution of the press briefing seems to require a fusion of the two roles. He *stands for* the President or the government for the occasion of the briefing and is held responsible – not just for maintaining lines of communication as, say, a committee chairperson (as *intermediary*) – but for response content, accuracy and for any evasiveness. In fact, the podium's responses are to a large extent the point of the exercise as far as the press is concerned, since a controversial response, a slip or a contradiction of himself or another government source are in themselves newsworthy events.

2.5.2   *The press*

The press footings need to be divided into two sets, the press as a group and journalists as individuals.

As a group, while listening to a podium statement, the press is occupying a role of joint-*interlocutor*, along with the papers, networks, etc. they represent. While listening to a debate between the podium and one of their number, the rest of the press slip technically into the role of Levinson's *audience* (neither addressed nor recipient), though they may well also be part-*beneficiaries* (see Section 2.5.3) of the debate. Finally, as the addressees of the joke targeting Wolf in (2), and on other such occasions, they are classifiable as *intermediary* (i.e. addressed but no longer recipient), but are again part-*beneficiary*.

As individuals, in a debate with the podium they can be *interlocutor* if the subject of talk is personal or joint-*interlocutor* (with the organisation they represent) if it is business. See the discussion of example (2) for their possible roles when targeted.

2.5.3   Present and absent audiences: who are these briefings for?

These briefings are televised. How does this affect their nature? First, there are none of the 'stage-setting' routines which mark the normal news interview as an encounter 'prearranged for the benefit of the viewing audience' (Clayman 1991: 54). Moreover, the presence of cameras is referred to explicitly only twice. On the first occasion, being on television is referred to simply as a constraint on the podium's physical movements as he threatens to look in 'the bins' (the recent documents archives) to prove his point over a questioner:

(3)   Q: Were you going to ever announce this, or was there some reason – (laughter.)
MR LEAVY: It's in the bins, back there.
MR LOCKHART: What do you think, guys? I think I've got them now. Should I let it go, or – (laughter) – come on, Terry, let's go find it. (Laughter).
Q: Wait a minute. You're on television. You can't do that.

On the second occasion, Mr Lockhart has just responded affirmatively to a question asking whether the President was due to visit Texas. He is interrupted by Mr Toiv, a White House representative:

(4)   MR TOIV: Joe, we're not ready to announce Texas.
MR LOCKHART: Okay – (laughter) –
[…]
MR TOIV: We don't have any specifics.
MR LOCKHART: Gotcha. (Laughter.) Okay. Everything I just said about Texas – strike. That was off the record. (Laughter.) Got it back there? Off the record. Okay, now, that's all I have.
Q: Tell your C-SPAN viewers as well.

MR LOCKHART: Yes. (Laughter.) To my C-SPAN viewers: those of you who
don't like me, please stop writing. (Laughter.) I am very thin-skinned, and
it really gets to me. (Laughter.) Guarantees about 300 next week.
(Laughter.)

In the last turn, the TV viewers are addressed directly ('To my C-SPAN viewers')
for the one and only time in the corpus texts. Even here it is a joking address, the
viewers being *addressees* of the utterance; the real *recipients* are the press, which is
made clear by the theatrical aside – 'Guarantees about 300 next week' – directed
to the 'real audience', the one in the room.

The effect of a TV audience can be various and complex[5] and the concept and
role of *audience* needs to be properly defined. The term is used by Levinson (1988:
170) to indicate 'those participants who are not *producers* (= sources or speakers)
and not *recipients* (= addressees or targets)' and thus, is a definition at the utter-
ance-event level. The general, lay sense of audience, however, is a definition at the
level of speech event or genre token, for example, the audience of a play, or a TV
programme remains the same for the duration of the event (even if the incumbents of the role can change – people may leave, new viewers may switch on).
However, since a TV audience maintains the same role throughout all the utterance events of a programme (with the exceptions of moments when they are
addressed directly, as in example (4), and so become *interlocutor*, or when members
can contact the studio in phone-in programmes, thus becoming producers as well
as receivers), the definitions at utterance- and speech-event levels can normally be
conflated.

There remain, nevertheless, crucial differences between the role described by
Levinson as *audience* – and occupied by Ruthie in (1) – and that of a TV audience.
In the first case, the audience is physically present. If necessary, its reactions can
be monitored by other participants. The channel-link is two-way: it can receive
but also emit signals. It can provide immediate feedback. The TV audience generally can only receive, and can only be monitored subsequent to the event and
very loosely.

But a more important distinction still is that the TV audience is generally the
beneficiary of the discourse, is the reason *why* the discourse is enacted in the first
place, in a way that Ruthie in (1) is not. The concept *beneficiary* is not the same as
Levinson's recipientship, which he admits 'is hard to define – informally it is about
who a message is *for*'. But 'who a message is *for*' covers a multitude of potential
destinations. Consider Mercutio's dying words in *Romeo and Juliet* [actually quoted
by one of the journalists, see Chapter 11, example (51)] 'a plague o'both your
houses'. Who is the utterance *for*? It is *addressed to* Romeo, but the *recipients* (of the
curse) are the entire Montague and Capulet families. However, the real *beneficiaries*
are the people in the audience who have bought their theatre tickets. It may be
argued that *beneficiary* is a role which properly only belongs at the speech-event
level of analysis. However, it is possible for the role to be projected onto different
groups from one utterance to the next – as in a pantomime, some jokes

(the political or risqué ones) are strictly for the parents. In normal conversation, the beneficiaries are generally the participants themselves. This is one of the defining characteristics of the genre. But not necessarily all the participants are equally *beneficiary* all of the time. For example, in the situation illustrated in (1) Ruthie could be made temporarily sole *beneficiary* if Karen were to tell a joke for her amusement alone.

Normally, the *beneficiary* of a TV transmission is the distant (home) audience. If there is also a studio audience, the situation is more complex, with one distant audience and one present audience, the latter more or less in the position of Ruthie. Who is the principal *beneficiary* on such occasions? When, as in the case of these briefings, members of the present audience often change footing to become discourse producer and individual interlocutor, the situation is more complicated still. In the White House briefings studied here, the primary *beneficiaries* are the journalists and their newspaper principals. The distant audience, although obviously ratified, is treated as almost incidental. In fact, the briefings were not originally intended for TV broadcast, they were born to cater for and continue to be designed for the physically present audience. But this may well *not* be the case for all press conferences. There is evidence that the briefings held by NATO during the period of the Kosovo crisis, organized in a superficially similar way, with a professional podium 'fielding' journalists questions, had the American home audience as primary *beneficiary*. Although the official languages of NATO include French, questions were only taken in English. Questions asked by British or American journalists – likely to be known to the podium, who was British but also worked in the United States – received longer responses than those put by other nationalities (Michelangelo Conoscenti, personal communication). The purpose of the exercise was at least as much to keep the US audience on board as to keep the newspapers informed.

Levinson's scheme also includes a category, among the reception roles, designated as *ultimate destination*. Although a reception category, it is also designated as *non-participant* (non-ratified) and not channel-linked. Thus it clearly cannot include our TV audience. But there are often important *ultimate destinations* for the podium's message. Since the briefings are televised live, are also available on the Internet and the transcripts are obtainable from the White House library, they can be studied by political organizations all over the world. These include the podium's own political masters but also some that will be potentially unfriendly. I have the impression that some of the podium's statements, especially on delicate foreign policy matters are delivered with these bodies in mind. During the Kosovo crisis, the podium's insistence on NATO's solidarity had not just the newspaper audience in mind, but also the Yugoslav leadership. He is generally very careful to be polite when referring to foreign states [Chapter 7, example (22)] and he also goes to great lengths to avoid antagonizing any party engaged in diplomatic talks with the US or its partners [Chapter 12, example (29)] or even the adversary in war [Chapter 7, example (63)]. Finally, in contrast, when engaging in bouts of pro-Democrat bravado or when vaunting the administration's achievements, the *ultimate destination* – his Republican opponents – are made to wince.

2.6 Conclusion: indirectness

It is probably the case that the normal, default, conversational situation is dyadic: the speaker incorporates all production roles and the hearer all the reception roles. Any departure from this circumstance allows participants to act *indirectly*.

In speech act pragmatics, an utterance is said to be indirect when its 'linguistic form does not directly reflect its communicative purpose' (Crystal 1997: 194), that is, when it performs one *act* under the guise of another. Speakers can, for example, use a question to give an order (*Can't you be more quiet in there?*), or a hypothetical statement to issue a threat (*If you know what's good for you, you'll pay up by Friday*). In terms of footing, speakers can also perform one *role* under the guise of another. This is the case when the speaker who has the current turn implies they are representing someone else. It is also the case when one party is addressed but another is the target or recipient (Levinson's examples of indirectness). In other words, we must maintain a distinction between the formal role that a speaker adopts or claims, or into which they place an interlocutor, and the underlying function of that role, between, if we like, its locutionary form and its illocutionary intent.

These distinctions are, of course, vitally important in the study of briefings. The podium is speaking indirectly – representing his clients rather than himself – most of the time. The questioners too claim to speak with many voices. The following chapters are dedicated to a detailed study of the roles, the footings adopted and projected by the two sides. But just as speech act indirectness exists for very practical purposes – for example, to ask someone to do something without imposing, to be vague so you can deny you meant something if challenged – role-performance indirectness offers speakers the possibility to exploit shifts between footings for *strategic* purposes. As we shall see, both sides exploit the strategic potential of role indirectness to the full. These practices should not, however, necessarily be seen as particularly disingenuous or deceitful. It is part of an adult human being's communicative competence (Hymes 1971) to know how to employ footing for purposes of politeness (the topic of Chapter 7), that is, to make one's points most effectively and avoid creating unnecessary tension or offence.

3　Voices of the press

3.1　Introduction

In the next two chapters, we look at how participants in the briefings realize changes in their footing and the effect this has on interlocutors. As Goffman (1981: 128) himself says: 'a change in footing implies a change in the alignment we take up to ourselves and the others present as expressed in the way we manage the production or reception of an utterance'. In other words, in the course of the speech event, a participant can often change from 'I am speaking as representative of *x*' to 'I am speaking as representative of *y*', and also 'I am treating you as representative(s) of *x*' to 'I am treating you as representative(s) of *y*', where *x* and *y* can be anything from single individuals to groups, to nations, to humanity. Of particular interest here will be to study how shifts of footing are employed deliberately or semi-deliberately as manoeuvres to protect or further speakers' rhetorical interests.

3.1.1　Footing and pronouns

One useful technique in the analysis of the different voices, the different footings adopted by speakers is to study their use of personal pronouns (Hardt-Mautner 1995; Wortham 1996). Ensink (1997) looks at how these are employed in a speech given to the Israeli Parliament, the Knesset, by Queen Beatrice of the Netherlands. Politicians, as Schäffner (1997) points out, do not deliver such addresses as individuals, rather as representatives of institutions (which tends to render the use of *we/us/our* very frequent). But politicians have personal beliefs, personalities and consciences (and so *I/me* may well occur). Ensink shows how the referents of *we* in the speech shift between: 'we, my husband and I'; 'we, those gathered in this room'; 'we, the Dutch people'; 'we, the Dutch and Jewish people together', amongst other possibilities. *You/your* is applied by the Queen to the Knesset (which as it happens is also coreferential with 'those in the room except myself'), the people of Israel and the Jewish people. 'At times', he observes, 'it is remarkable how easily, and almost imperceptibly, the formulations oscillate between the various (possible) referents' (Schäffner 1997: 15).

The particular interpersonal situation of briefings discourse renders the study of footing especially complex. The podium speaks partly as an institutional figure, as a politician representing institutions, and so his contributions bear some resemblance to the discourse studied by Ensink and Schäffner, including the frequent use of *we*. But he also has a much closer, more informal rapport with his audience, which makes parts of his discourse similar to conversation among intimates, where *I* is more common.

The journalists too have cause to use both *we* – when one of them claims to speak for them all, or when they take on the role of representative of a body, perhaps their readers or the American public – and *I* when they wish to show they are speaking for themselves. This dual requirement, of both the podium and the press, is perhaps borne out in the approximate statistical parity in the uses of *I* and *we* in the corpus of briefings. The occurrences of these items in the briefings held by the two main White House secretaries, Mike McCurry and Joe Lockhart break down as follows:

	McCurry	*Lockhart*	*Total*
We	1185	2328	3513
I	1113	2907	4020

The slightly more frequent employment of *I* in Mr Lockhart's sessions perhaps reflects his greater tendency to indulge in interpersonal banter with members of the press audience.

Chafe (1982) found that *I* was more frequent in unscripted than in scripted speeches and the reverse was true for *we*. There is, however, far more unscripted interchange than scripted in these briefings and the high occurrence of *we* relative to Chafe's findings is presumably due to the representative nature of most of what the podium does.

Concordancing of the relevant items was felt to be an important step in studying pronoun use in these texts. Since concordances of these items in the whole corpus would be unmanageably long, and since it was necessary to distinguish between the way they are used by the podium from how they are employed by the press, I used only the Q-file (containing journalist's moves) and the R-file (containing podium responses) (see Section 0.3.1).

3.2 Pronoun use by the press: first person plural

Taking the Q-file first, there were a total of 20 occurrences of *we* in the journalists' questions:

There are several examples of the 'inclusive' use of *we* to refer to *us* and *you*, that is, journalists and podium, for example:

(1) Q: Joe, speaking of money – *we* were just talking about money –

The footing here on the part of the speaker seems to be that of participant in a debate. There is also an exclusive use, that is, *us* but not *you*:

(2)   Q: Joe, I want to go back at something. I think it's a fair question and maybe deserves a thoughtful answer, which perhaps *we* haven't received so far. (Laughter.)

In this case, the speaker's footing is that of representative, mouthpiece even, of the assembled journalists in the room.[1] However, it is often impossible to tell who precisely the journalist is claiming to represent:

(3)   Over the last nine months during the Starr investigation, *we* saw the White House go to the Supreme Court three times to prevent the testimony of staff members and that sort of thing. Is that the general tenor of what *we*'re going to see with the Judiciary Committee? Or are *we* now going to see a different sort of White House with a different strategy that is much more cooperative than that?

Is the *we* doing the *seeing* here the assembled journalists, the press as a whole or the general public? The indefiniteness of *we* in such cases allows journalists to maintain a useful confusion as to whether their questions represent the press's or the public's interest.

Another common use of *we* is quotational to represent the words or thinking of another party:

(4)   What if the parties came to the White House and said, this is as far as – here's the trade-offs *we*'ve made on these two issues, and if *we* don't get any clear guidance from the White House that this would be acceptable to you, then the talks will collapse?

The body who is quoted most frequently is the administration itself, in one of its various guises (the White House, the President, the podium, etc.):

(5)   So, basically, you're saying there is no contradiction to be saying *we* will comply with this subpoena and asserting executive privilege to fight some of those –

We often represents the administration without any introductory reporting expression (such as *you're saying* in (5) above):

(6)   On the ozone rule that's put out by EPA, how close are *we* on that? I understand that there are some compromise deals being cut already [...]

This is, of course, an example where *we* really means *you*, and this is fairly common practice in these texts. This use in politics is discussed at some length by

Wilson (1990: 47).[2] It is usually explained in terms of politeness/power theory as communicating solidarity with the addressee. But what is interesting is that speakers who employ it generally occupy – or are trying to express – a position of superior power over the addressee. It is interesting to note that the press seem to feel they are in a position of supremacy with regard to the podium (for power relations, see Sections 7.1.3 and 8.7).

To illustrate the frequent difficulty of pinning down the exact referent of *we* in these briefings, we might consider the series of exchanges on the Ottawa process which envisages the complete but unilateral banning of land-mines. The question is posed:

(7)   Q: Will *we* sign on with Ottawa?

Here *we* would again seem to mean *you* and indicates solidarity. However, since the topic is about *countries* signing up, *we* could well include a reference to the United States, and so the footing of the journalist would be as representative of their country. Mr McCurry's response outlines the administration's reluctance to pursue unilateral action and its preference for more general talks on disarmament. Nevertheless, he is happy to continue using *we*:

(8)   MR McCURRY: *We*'ve said *we* see that as a complementary process, and *we* will continue to monitor that, but *we* think that an effective global regime has to be written in a venue like the Conference on Disarmament in Geneva.

suggesting as it does that speaker and hearer are on the same side. The next question, however:

(9)   Q: Why can't *you* do both?

changes to the use of *you*. There is clearly less solidarity here, more distance between questioner and addressee. The responsibility for any decision is placed squarely at the administration's door. The next question however, switches back to *we, our*:

(10)   Q: But how does that square with *our* stand on the Chemical Weapons Treaty where the administration, of course, pushed to have that ratified...?

and yet the administration is also mentioned explicitly as the agent behind the treaty ratification.

What seems to be happening in this extended example is that speakers shift their footing both unconsciously and strategically. Some questioners judge it more fruitful to use an empathetic *we* on certain occasions whilst others, on other occasions, feel they are likely to get a better answer by using a more distant and potentially more antagonistic *you*. Alongside this choice system however lies another, the semi-or un-conscious expression of affiliation or lack of it felt by the speaker with parties in question, in this particular case, their mother country. If we remember that *we* can also have a quotational function, its analysis on some occasions can be particularly complex.

3.3 First person singular

There were 38 occurrences of *I* in the Q-files. The majority are found in discourse management items, a large number of which have special roles in managing the particular discourse of briefings. Many are turn initial with the function either of claiming a turn, for example, *can I just clarify one point, I have a question*, or of requesting an extra turn (a *follow up*) in an environment where it is usual to pass the word around: *can I follow up on that, if I could follow up on that*. Notice these often also contain an indication of the *type* of intervention the journalist desires to make: *I have a question, Can I just clarify one point?*. These are similar to other moves, not necessarily introductory, which are used to *justify* taking a turn, for example: 'I wanted to revisit the question of a few weeks ago ...', 'I want to go back at something, I think it's a fair question ...'. One case is somewhat exceptional. The journalist tags 'That's all I was asking' onto his question as a most explicit self-justification. He feels the need to do this because his previous intervention was challenged by the podium. The full exchange is:

(11)   Q: Did they talk last night?
         MR LOCKHART: Sam, I have no idea. Is that important?
         Q: I mean, it was a day for the President, I thought maybe he and his wife talked on the phone. That's all I was asking.

More generally, why should journalists deem it necessary to offer a justification for asking a question in a conference, when that is the very purpose of the exercise? Similarly, it is quite common for them to ask permission perhaps with requesting hedges, for example, *if I can, if I may*. To answer this question, a concordance of *if I* was prepared from all the corpus files which was then divided according to whether the speaker was podium or press.

The majority of occurrences of *if I* in the press moves are permission requests. More particularly, in most cases, permission is being sought to ask a follow-up (e.g. *If I could just press the point* and *If I could just wrap that up*), occasionally to repeat or reformulate a question (*you don't mind if I pose it again, just to be precise, if I may* and *let me rephrase that, if I may*), or to finish a question (*let me finish, if I may*). On each of these occasions what is happening is that the journalist requests a further, supplementary move either to clarify matters, reformulate a question, finish unfinished business or simply get another question in. Since the etiquette of the briefings is one question per journalist at a time, these permission requests are probably addressed primarily to the other members of the press, who are being required to wait longer for their turns. Requests of this nature are absent from the podium's discourse. The following extended example shows how the process works:

(12) Q: Joe, can you clarify again, do the Russians now accept the notion that this must be a NATO-led force?

MR LOCKHART: Well, I'm going to let the Russians speak for themselves. I think we've been clear. I think there's a lot of work going on, particularly in Germany with Foreign Minister Ivanov...

Q: But on that principle, *if I may*, on that principle, what have the Russians told you? That they accept it, or no?

Permission is also sometimes sought when a speaker wishes to book a further move in advance, for example, 'Two things, if I may, Joe', or as in the following:

(13) Q: Joe, *if I can just clear up one point* you just made, and then *follow up*. You said that the Rambouillet agreements would have preserved Kosovo as part of Serbia –

MR LOCKHART: Yes.

[Three more exchanges occur before another questioner takes the floor.]

The other occurrences of *if I* in the above concordance are all in what we might call *accuracy hedges*, including *if I remember/understand (understood) correctly, correct me if I'm wrong*. Speakers use these to display tentativeness which can have one of three strategic ends. The first is to disarm potential attacks on the factualness of what they are saying. Second, it is used for politeness purposes, to appear to impose less upon the listener. Finally, it enables the speaker to avoid appearing overly didactic or expert and adopt the part of 'fellow mortal'.

For comparative purposes, the concordance of *if I* from the podium's response moves was also examined. Many occurrences were of the same kind of accuracy hedges discussed above. They include: *if I got this right, if I'm not mistaken, if I remember, if I understand correctly*. It is convenient on occasion for the podium to project a footing of equality with the audience, rather than that of a distant, possibly haughty expert. This is a good example of the working of the principle of the *efficiency* versus *solidarity* trade-off, by which, in the right circumstances, the semblance of a certain bumblingness can be more effective than that of expert proficiency.

There were only very rare cases of permission requests. In each case an *if I may (just) add* request is made by a second podium speaker, who wishes to supplement or revise information given by the main podium, and this latter is the addressee of the request as much as the audience of journalists. The absence of permission requests on the part of the podium should not come as a surprise. In normal conversational practice, being asked a question generally presupposes a desire for a response and no preliminary request for taking a turn is required: in fact, a response which began *if I might answer* would probably be seen as marked behaviour, implying 'if only you would let me get a word in edgeways'.

3.4   Second person

There were 87 occurrences of *you* in the Q-files. In 25 of these, the keyword was linked to a verb of reporting, either *say, tell, talk* or *comment*. Many of these relate to the podium's footing as information-giving body. A particularly clear example of the press requesting news in this sense is the following:

(14)   Q: Mike, talking about bipartisan, *can you tell us* about how Jack Kemp came to be among the invited guests today?

This role can be referred to explicitly when a questioner wishes to inquire further or challenge information they have received, for example 'you said from that podium that ... ' or:

(15)   Q: Joe, some of us *were given guidance* yesterday *by you* and others at the White House that the President would say in his remarks yesterday that he was going to cooperate with the investigation. He didn't say that. And I'm wondering, the word 'cooperate' was not used.

There is more than one type of possible footing involved in information supply, however. In the following, the podium is asked if they have a *readout* (prepared statement) on some topic:

(16)   Q: Do you have *a readout* on the President's meeting with Bishop Belo?
(17)   Q: One other question – do you have *a readout* on the meeting with the Macedonian President?

There are a number of similar questions in the rest of the corpus, for example:

(18)   Q: Will you all give *a readout?*
        COLONEL CROWLEY: I think we'll have – in some fashion, either *a piece of paper* or some – we'll be around after.

When a prepared statement is requested, the podium is being treated as a simple conduit for the information. His footing, in Levinson's terms, is that of simple *relayer* with no responsibility for the content or the form.

In contrast, the podium is also frequently seen as an informed commentator on the situation:

(19)   Q: Mike, the Senate voted today on State Department authorization bill and I wonder *if you could comment* on two aspects?
(20)   Q: Mike, *do you have any comment* on Senator Leahy's land mines legislation?

Comments made by a White House press secretary can, of course, be news-worthy in themselves. On such occasions, the podium is no longer simply a *relayer*, but to what degree he is *spokesperson*, liable for the form of words of the message but not its content, and how much he is *responsible* for both (in other words, to what extent his opinions are his own) has to be judged case by case.

On this topic, many of the occurrences of *you* clearly do not refer to the podium as a single individual, but as member of some body or group. Cases of the two extremes – when the podium is projected as either totally personal or totally representative – are relatively easy to interpret. In the final move of the following, the podium is patently addressed as a private individual in a totally personal predicament:

(21)   MR LOCKHART: Again, let me look at the first question, and I'll come back to you.
         Q: When will you come back?
         MR LOCKHART: Maybe next week, maybe never. (Laughter.) Next, please. (Laughter.)
         Q: *You* wanted this job, right? (Laughter.)

But at other times, he is clearly the other extreme, little more than a conduit, and the real addressee is the administration behind the scenes:

(22)   Q: […] as I understand it, the bill now goes to conference. Do *you* still have an opportunity then, do *you* feel, of improving the bill or might *you* have to swallow those restrictions?

There would obviously be little that Mr McCarthy could do personally to affect the bill either way. But what should be noted in this example is how the question still includes what would generally be seen as an appeal to the podium's opinion with the interpolation 'do you feel'. Thus the journalist is asking for *the administration*'s 'personal' opinion, if such a thing is possible. In fact, anthropomorphization of the administration, through its identification with the podium, appears perfectly normal to the press, who can attribute likes and dislikes to it:

(23)   Q: So you like Roth but you only like it in comparison to the House version?

Emotive language is also quite commonly associated with *you* when it means 'you the administration'. Among the occurrences of *you* we find: 'Because if you're saying you're *nervous* about blessing something in advance …', 'The provisions that you say *concern* you …'. The podium does little to discourage the process, presumably because humanizing the administration has its advantages.

However, the podium is not always clearly projected as either individual *principal* or institutional conduit, and since *you* in a question can be either singular or plural, the podium can often choose whether to respond with *I* or *we*. In the following we have an easy switch from one to the other: responses seem to frequently contain intermediate or mixed states of *I* and *we*:

(24)   Q: Well, Joe, are you saying that there are people in the United States who
        do not believe what you are saying about the level of atrocities going on
        inside the former Yugoslavia?
        MR LOCKHART: *I* hope not, because *I* think what *we* say is subject to great
        scrutiny, and *we* defend as best *we* can the statements *we* make based on
        the reports that *we* have.

3.4.1 'Do you feel … ?': prefaces which call for the interviewee's opinion

Following up the hint provided by *do you feel* in example (22), concordances of *you*
in the company of verbs of opinion-giving – *feel*, *think* and *expect* – were made in
the hope of studying the intermediate states the podium's footing seems to occupy
between entirely private and entirely representative body. Jucker (1986), in his
work on news interviews, calls expressions such as *Do you feel …* , *Do you think*, and
so on, 'prefaces relating to the interviewee's opinion'. The utility for the questioner
is that 'the preface reduces the possibility of hedging for the interviewee'; they
cannot reasonably dodge the question by claiming ignorance: 'the interviewee
might not actually *know* the details […] but she cannot fail to have at least some
opinion on the issue' (Jucker 1986: 104). These were among the examples found
in the briefings:

(25)   Q: Because he's been hit so bad *do you expect* some more fake diplomatic
        overtures soon?
        MR LOCKHART: I'm not going to get into the prediction game.
(26)   Q: *Do you expect* that Palestinian Authority President Arafat, now, and the
        PNC, will not declare an independent Palestinian state?
        MR LOCKHART: Well, I will leave it for Mr Arafat and the people there to
        express their own views. We have reiterated here our view that we don't
        believe that unilateral declarations should be made.
(27)   Q: […] It turns out, he wasn't really asked those questions. Does that
        trouble the White House? *Do you feel* he has a duty to be straightforward
        with –
(28)   Q: – the White House is willing – and all the good public policy objectives
        that *you think* might come out of it, the White House is willing to
        walk away and not step in at this juncture if it meant not having
        a deal?

To the first of these, the podium responds using *I*. He takes on his own shoulders
the responsibility for giving no answer. In the second, he shifts from the *I* of *I'll let
them speak from themselves* to the *we* of reiterating our official statement. In prefacing
their questions with opinion-seeking formulas such as *do you feel / think / expect*, the

press is generally hoping for a personal opinion, a particular slant over and above the official line. As these two examples show, they are rarely successful. The podium does not dodge the issue by claiming ignorance, but he has other tactics for evasion at hand.

In examples (27) and (28), there is an easy shift in the question from *White House* to *you* and back again; they seem to be interchangeable. The *he* in example (27) is the President, and both the *White House* and *you* are clearly treated as very separate entities to the President, in fact, they are asked to sit in judgement on him. This was a feature of the Clinton–Ms Lewinsky crisis: the press treated the President more and more as a separate entity from the rest of the administration and looked via their questions for any signs of a rift between the two.

3.4.2 *Confusion over* you

There are occasions when attention is directed explicitly at the podium's footing, where the status of *you* is misinterpreted or under negotiation. This happens most frequently when there is some confusion between *you*, the podium and *you* the President's proxy:

(29) Q: You have not provided us a real opportunity.
     MR McCURRY: I dispute that. We come out here every single day. We offer up all kinds of stories –
     Q: I'm not talking about you, I'm talking about the President.

This second example is a little more complex:

(30) Q: Do you believe that settlement in the Jones case would change the President's exposure to questions like perjury, anything that's involved in the original case?
     MR McCURRY: I'm not a lawyer. I wouldn't know how to speculate an answer to that question.
     Q: No, I wasn't asking you personally. I was asking you if the White House believes –
     MR McCURRY: I don't know that the White House has any corporate view on that question.

The question begins with an opinion-seeking preface *Do you believe...?* Mr McCurry interprets the *you* as directed at himself and, contrary to Jucker's expectations, sidesteps the question by claiming ignorance on the grounds of not being a lawyer. The questioner retorts, however, that the question was not aimed at the podium *personally*, but at the White House. Mr McCurry then evades once more on its *corporate* behalf. Even so this evasion is still presented as personal opinion prefaced by *I don't know that....* Very occasionally the questioner specifies the exact referent of *you* to obviate the danger of unconscious or wilful evasion:

(31) Q: Bob Dole is calling for Slobodan Milosevic to be tried in The Hague for war crimes. Do you think that's feasible? Does the White House think that's feasible?

This final case illustrates a somewhat different tactic by the questioner:

(32) Q: Well, let me ask you this. Governor Wilder said that most Richmonders are not interested in obliterating history, and he protested the removal of General Lee's mural from a new city exhibit, and then he saluted the Confederate battle flag in a gesture of unity. Does the President believe Governor Wilder was right or wrong, Joe?
      MR LOCKHART: The President is not aware of the circumstances by which any of this happened –
      Q: Well, I've just made you aware. Does he think that Governor Wilder was wrong, Joe?

This time the question preface is *Does the President believe...?* Technically, the podium is being asked to respond for the President's opinions and in fact does so, but claims that the President is unaware of what happened. Since the questioner has recounted what happened, the podium himself cannot claim ignorance and the journalist insists that they have *just made you aware*. The *you* here can logically only refer to the addressee present. But the rest of the question is nonetheless about the absentee President's beliefs. The complete identification of the podium with the President would appear absurd, but the hidden underlying motivation is probably that the journalist does not accept that the President is unaware of the incident and that therefore the podium's evasion through ignorance is disingenuous. The podium's final shot in this exchange turns the accusation back on the journalist, suggesting that the question itself was less than candid:

(33) MR LOCKHART: It should come as no surprise to you that I take some of what you say with a grain of salt.

In this case, the standing of *you* was under negotiation, the questioner refusing for a moment to accept any distinctions among the possible referents of *you* in order to forestall any potential footing shift.

In summary, the flexibility of *you* makes it difficult for an analyst to state with much confidence precisely which of the many bodies the podium represents is called into account to answer the particular question, except, as mentioned above, in limit cases, or when it is the object of explicit attention. This generally means that the podium has a certain freedom in choosing the footing to adopt in their reply and can turn this to their tactical advantage.

3.5 Conclusion: concordancing for participant roles and strategies

In this chapter, we have seen how concordancing pronouns in spoken discourse can shed light on how participants project themselves and others. We have seen how footing choices can allow speakers to take less or more responsibility for what they say and also to shift allegiance, as it were, between one group and another. At the same time, they can also attempt to constrain the footing choices of their interlocutor. The next chapter contains an investigation of the highly complex picture of politician and interviewee footing, as represented by the podium.

4   Voices of the podium

4.1   Use of pronouns by politicians

Wilson (1990) discusses the use of personal pronouns by political figures. He talks of two conflicting pressures they experience. The first, which is keenly felt in what he terms 'personality-led' politics (typically found, he says, in the United States but the term would also seem to be ever more applicable to the United Kingdom as well), is to use the singular *I* in the stressing of personal achievement, especially in competitive democratic systems. At the same time, the wise politician will avoid authoritarian or coercive rhetoric and will shun the risks inherent in assuming too much personal responsibility for actions and policies, both of which policies advise the use of *we*. First person pronouns can thus be used tactically:

> One of the major aims of a politician is to gain the people's allegiance, to have them believe that the decisions that are being made are the right ones. At the same time […] it is also useful to have the audience believe, in some circumstances, that any actions are perhaps not only, or not fully, the responsibility of one individual. First person pronomial forms can assist the politician in achieving these almost contradictory aims
>
> (Wilson 1990: 76)

Wilson divides the use of *we* into two main types: to group the speaker and the listener(s) (inclusive *we*) and to group the speaker and some other(s) excluding the listener(s) (exclusive *we*). The first is used to express solidarity and avoid the semblance of coercion, the second can be exploited to share responsibility. He then reports the work of Urban (1986) on the employment by representative political figures of the second of these uses, on the so-called 'expanding circle' of *we*, from *I + one other* through infinite stages to *I + the universe*. The examples of political spokespeople he gives – highly relevant here – include the following referents of *we*:

> *The President and I we*
> *The Department of Defense we*
> *The Reagan administration we*
> *The US government we*
> *The United States we*
> *The United States and Soviet Union we*
>
> (Wilson 1990: 53)

From an analysis of the briefings texts, we may well be able to add other footings of *we* to this list.

Wilson also makes the following germane observation. Although the term 'inclusive' describes the use of *we* to embrace speaker plus listener(s), according to Urban (1986) it very frequently implies the exclusion of some other group, that is, it implies a division of the sphere of discourse into *us* and *them*, which can be an important ingredient in what he calls the 'rhetoric of fear'. We might add here that this is equally true of exclusive *we*, where often enough, three parties are implied: the *we* group, comprising speaker and a set of others (e.g. the Democrats), a *them* group comprising the antagonist(s) of the *we* people (say, the Republicans) and third, the listeners.

4.2   First person plural

There are 176 occurrences of *we* in the R-files, the subcorpus of podium responses. There was the odd trace of inclusive *we*, for example: 'This is the year we've had a trillion dollar tax cut from Republicans on the Hill, down to an $80 billion tax cut ... ', where *we* is all the world, including you and me, which has seen and judged Republican bluster. There is also an instance of the use of *we*, which really means 'you' (mentioned in Section 3.2), for example: 'The President's statement, I think, was clear. We can spend all the rest of the afternoon going around on the difference between work with them or cooperate with them'. It is obviously 'you the press' who quibble over words like this but the podium is too (tactically) polite to put it this way.

However, the most frequent referent of *we* is, predictably, the exclusive one indicating 'we, the administration of the United States'. However, the administration has various roles depending on the sphere of action: national, international, party-political and so on. Moreover, the particular *us* in question is frequently defined in terms of an opposition to a particular *them*.

First of all, *we* can be the US administration, representing the nation on the world stage. One occurrence, where the talk is about Serbia, merits some attention (my italics):

(1)   MR LOCKHART: Well, I think President Yeltsin, the Russians and the entire international community agree that it's of urgent importance that President Milosevic come into compliance with U.N. Security Resolution 1199. If you – at the Contact Group yesterday, there was unanimous belief that the Serbs are not in compliance. *We believe* that they need to come into compliance immediately, that it's verifiable and durable. And if they don't *we reserve the right to take further action*. We further reserve the right to take that action based on consultation with *our NATO allies*.

There is clearly the possibility of confusion over the exact referent of *we* in 'we believe': is it the United States alone, the Contact Group or 'the entire international community'? When the podium goes on to say 'we reserve the right to take further action', the indeterminacy is not resolved and the referent becomes a vital issue: will the United States be acting unilaterally and alone? He, therefore, feels obliged to specify that, although *we* means the United States, the responsibility for 'further action' will be shared with 'our NATO allies'.

This is not the only occasion on which the issue of whether the footing of *we* is the United States alone or the United States together with NATO is given careful attention:

(2) MR LOCKHART: […] I will let the Secretary General speak and make his own statement – but *we believe that* – *the NATO allies believe* this is not sufficient to end the campaign

It was an important part of the podium's job at the time to give the impression of NATO solidarity, not only for the journalists but as a political message to its adversaries. On one occasion it even leads the podium into making *gaffe*:

(3) MR LOCKHART: We will take the steps that we believe that *we need to take in our national interest and that NATO believes that we need to take in our national interest.*

This could be interpreted as proving that the United States is using NATO to further its own national interest – a gloss its enemies might make but which the podium surely did not intend.

Elsewhere on international issues, the podium expresses explicitly that the footing of *we* is the United States:

(4) Q: The Vatican issued a statement saying that the whole world would notice this and would – the international community would take note of this, implying that it's another indication that Castro is opening up. Do you agree with that?

MR LOCKHART: Speaking for the United States government, *we* noticed and *we* welcome. (Laughter.)

The laughter is due to Mr Lockhart's conciseness and his playful echoing of the questioner's language 'would notice'. Similarly:

(5) Q: Amnesty International has asked the *United States* to clarify its position on the Pinochet case. So what is *your* position?

[…]

MR LOCKHART: Again, as we said, *we* have not expressed a view on the litigation that's going on both internally in the United Kingdom and between the United Kingdom and the government of Spain.

The podium accepts without demur the equivalence established by the questioner between the United States' position and 'your position'.

However, *we* can be employed with a degree of vagueness for tactical reasons. In the following discussion of the Ruanda massacres, *we* loses any specificity:

(6) ASSISTANT SECRETARY SHATTUCK: Certainly, *we* should have – and I think there's no question that everyone now looks back and says, *we* should have seen more closely what was occurring and called it at that point.

The *we* in the first occurrence of 'we should have' might be interpreted as an admission of special culpability on behalf of the administration and so the speaker replans the utterance so that it comes to refer to 'everyone'.

The Press, however, are not happy and try to pin down responsibility:

(7) Q: But isn't it precisely the United States that also bears responsibility? *We* in the United Nations opposed efforts at that time to get a peace-keeping force together or do something more forceful.

The *we* here is the 'nationalistic' use mentioned in Chapter 4, but it rather implies 'you'. The response to this:

(8) ASSISTANT SECRETARY SHATTUCK: Again, the focus of this trip and the efforts that are underway is to learn from the past, to address the cycle of impunity, to stop genocide from occurring

uses only moodless verbs – *to learn, to address, to stop* – which have no subject, no actor and so no one is fingered for blame. The pronoun *we* is conspicuous in its absence.

This *we* for sharing-out responsibility is not confined to foreign affairs. On the issue of TV and movie violence (in the wake of the Littleton school killings):

(9) MR LOCKHART: Because I think it just reflects the fact that from everything we know, from every study you can see, there is – children are impacted by what they see, and the games they play. And *we* need to continue to look at whether *we*'re doing enough on that front.

The *we* used here is ambiguous. It could be *we*, the administration, or *we* all decent-minded folk who need to examine our consciences. In the first sentence, in fact, it alternates with *you*.

On the home front, the *we* of the administration is often represented in contraposition to a Republican-dominated Congress. It is worth repeating the point that footing is often largely defined in terms of what a speaker projects themselves as being in opposition to, the *them* which plays opposite to the *us*. In this vision of the world, the administration is serious, responsible and patriotic; the opposition, that is, Congress (often referred to as 'the Hill') and the Republican party are self-seeking, partisan and divisive. *We* are steadfast:

(10)   MR LOCKHART: I think clearly we have demonstrated that, despite what some in the Republican Party want to focus on, we have the ability to focus on the people's business. We will continue to do that.

They, meanwhile, are petty and unfocused:

(11)   MR LOCKHART: [...] They have to make choices. They have to make choices about what the Republican Party's about. And right now [...] it's about investigation, it's about scandal.

We are also your average guys caught up among the Washington political sharks:[1]

(12)   MR LOCKHART: Let me refer you back to my answer that there are politics at play here, but we're not smart enough to figure out what they are.

Although this latter projection can backfire:

(13)   Q: I noticed the President this morning in his speech pointed out that he hasn't been around Washington too long, he's still learning about Washington [...] Is the President now projecting himself as an outsider in Washington?
       MR McCURRY: Well, he has not – does not come from the culture of Washington, has not been a regular insider here, has not been stuck up on Capitol Hill for most of his career –
       Q: Georgetown University, working on Capitol Hill –
       Q: Governors Association –

Here, it is the President who is casting himself as an outsider to Washington, which is greeted by sarcasm, if not incredulity, by the press, who list episodes from his Washington career.[2]

Despite complaining in this way of Republican politicizing, the podium is by no means reluctant to use their position to engage in a spot of party-political tub-thumping themselves:

(14)   MR McCURRY: Gingrich didn't vote for George Bush's program, and Armey didn't vote for it, and DeLay didn't vote it, and Kasich didn't vote for it. They opposed it. They said it would ruin the economy. And they said

the exact same thing about Bill Clinton's program in 1993. John Kasich went so far to say if it worked he'd turn himself into a Democrat. And we've got the DNC sending him a membership application now. (Laughter.)

Section 7.5.2 looks at podium boastfulness and its dangers.

The last use of *we* to be mentioned here is that referring to the actual White House staff or employees of the Office of the Press Secretary. Very often it is tied up in phrases such as *we'll have more news/ more to say on that later, we'll give you a readout/ an update tomorrow* and so on. The staff are portrayed as a player in these briefings, usually as a harassed but blameless intermediary between two factions:

(15)   MR LOCKHART: [...] That's a recurring theme here: White House staff, difficult circumstances.

Finally, *we* is often found in situations where the podium slips into what I call 'rhetorical mode' [Sections 11.3.3 and 12.2.5, and example (27)].

4.3   First person singular

4.3.1   Discourse managing I

There are 132 occurrences of the pronoun *I* in the subcorpus of responses. A good number of these are involved in expressions the speaker uses for discourse management. The simplest of these are fillers, expressions employed, at least in part, to gain time to think, and they include occurrences of *Well, I think* as in, for example, 'Well I think broadly speaking'. Notice they frequently begin with *well* which, according to Holtgraves (1997: 233), is used to 'displace' or delay some kind of disagreement or difference of opinion with the preceding speaker – moments when it is vital to gain thinking time in order to choose one's politeness strategy with care (see Sections 1.2.5 and 1.2.6).

Another discourse managing expression is *as I said*, for example, 'Well, as I said this morning'. This can also be a filler but can have more than one ancillary function. It can be used to say simply, 'I know this is a repetition for some of you',[3] or it can mean 'this is an important point worth repeating':

(16)   MR BELL: Well, the CFE Treaty required the destruction, physical elimination, *as I said*, of over 50,000 pieces of equipment.

Or it can be saying 'please, you've asked me this before, don't ask me again' (usually because he has no more information to give):

(17)   MR LOCKHART: [...] *As I said*, I can't tell you how things will ultimately be synchronized.

A third discourse manager in these texts is *I mean*, whose function is rather intriguing. It is generally used to introduce the reiteration or reformulation of a proposition:

(18)   MR LOCKHART: That it would be inappropriate – in fact, I'd draw your attention to a lot of what he said. *I mean*, you should go back and look at the whole speech.

This is a reiteration which also emphasizes what was said before, roughly 'I would even go so far as to say ... '. Or the reformulation can be to propose an alternative form of words, 'let me put it this way/another way':

(19)   MR LOCKHART: Well, I think we intend to go up and get a sense of where the committee is going before we decide – *I mean*, we're not going to go up and tell them how they should run their proceedings.

The phrase *I mean* is discussed briefly by Quirk *et al.* (1985) in a section entitled 'Reformulation', part of a chapter on 'Apposition'. However, the only function discussed is that of 'mistake editing', that is:

> the use of *I mean* in order to correct a phonological or semantic mistake (which is common enough in impromptu speech), e.g.
> *The thirst thing*, I mean *the first thing* to remember is that ...
> Then you add *the peaches* – I mean, *the apricots* ...
> (Quirk *et al.* 1985: 1313)

From the evidence of a concordance prepared from these briefings, however, the functions of *I mean* are several and complex. Perhaps related to 'mistake editing' is its (quite frequent) use to introduce replannings, that is, changes in direction of a speaker's utterance, for example:

(20)   Q: Is there, in fact – *I mean*, how would you describe this map proposal?
       Q: Joe, your answer is – *I mean*, forgive me, but implies a naivete that's not there about how NATO works.

In the second of these there is a change not only in the direction but the tone of the question, which is evidently softened for reasons of politeness.
    It is also used by the podium to mitigate, to soften the brusqueness of an abrupt response. It frequently follows immediately a single word response:

1   *No* – **I mean**, beyond some of the things we've talked about [...]
2   *No* – **I mean**, we've seen the same kind of anecdotal reporting [...]

3   *No*, **I mean**, I think it's unfortunate that Boeing has had to take this step.

4   *No*. **I mean**, three weeks from now, if we sign, if we can agree [...]

5   *No*. **I mean**, not unless we manage to geographically realign the continent.

6   *No*. **I mean**, I would quibble a little bit with the question.

7   *Oh, sure*. **I mean**, I think if you watched the President's speech earlier

8   *Sure*. **I mean**, the United States is still a full partner in the United Nations

9   *Yes*, **I mean**, there has been a lot of – there is a lot to say –

10 Do I believe it? *Yes*.**I mean**, I believe what I see on television some days.

We might coin the expression 'a continuer' to describe this function of enabling the speaker to expand upon their response.[4] The press, for their part, regularly use it to introduce a follow-up, to press home a question, or possibly to ask a further question pretending it is simply a reformulation of the old one (concordance of *I mean* with context word *q*):

(21)   Q: Joe, why is the President signing this Kosovo funding package despite all the pork in it and stuff he doesn't like

   MR LOCKHART: Well, I think we have a real emergency here [continues]

   Q: *I mean*, if he had vetoed this, do you really think the Republicans would have denied money to the troops in the field?

The final use of *I mean* to be discussed is explanatory. It is used by speakers to introduce the explanation, justification even for a preceding utterance:[5]

(22)   Q: But with winter coming there's now some 50,000 people homeless. When are we going to act? *I mean*, people risk freezing to death and worse.

Such a justification can be used to pre-empt, to gainsay potential objections on the part of the interlocutor:

(23)   MR McCURRY: – and it's been Monica, Monica, Monica, Monica. And you know that, and I know that. *I mean*, you can't pretend otherwise.

This explanatory, self-justificatory meaning of the expression may well be the one underlying all its other uses. The employment of *I mean*, thus, generally implies full personal responsibility on the part of the speaker for what is said, both the form of words and the propositional content. Its recurring use by both the press and more interestingly (because less predictably) by the podium is evidence that, in terms of footing, they very frequently claim to be acting as the *principal* (Section 2.4.1) of their contributions to the discourse.

4.3.2   'Doing the job' – I for relaying information

Another group of occurrences of *I* is related to the podium's job as relayer of information. The concept of relaying as one of the basic footings a speaker can adopt is discussed in Chapter 2. In terms of the briefings podium, he is a relayer when he acts as a simple conduit of information that passes from the White House sources to the press. There are a number of more-or-less stock expressions used to carry out the functions of this role. These include: *I'll come back to you, I've got the week ahead, I'll have to check for you.* One interesting technical expression that is found four times in this corpus is *I'll take the question* (alternatively *Let me take the question*), which is used to mean, 'I don't know the answer to that question, but I will take it to other informed sources and bring you their response':

(24)   MR McCURRY: *I'll take the question* and Amy Weiss will help you get an answer, because I don't know.

The podium thus adopts a role as two-way channel, relaying information not only from the administration to the press but also in the opposite direction.

4.3.3   Truth-hedging I

Nevertheless, even a conduit can be held accountable, if not for the content, then at least for the *accuracy* of the message they convey. Many of the *I* expressions in the concordance above, particularly *I think, I believe, I doubt, I'm not aware* are examples of hedges used to mitigate the responsibility for truth. They are very common in these texts and other kinds of dialogue. Holtgraves (1997: 232) contends they 'may represent the default mode for expressing an opinion'.

Hedges are items used in discourse to qualify or mitigate the force of what is being said (see a fuller definition in Section 7.6.2). The podium uses them to qualify the truth of the information he gives, that is, to declare '*to the best of my knowledge* what I'm saying is the case'. The clearest example is the following:

(25)   MR McCURRY: Well, I think we were out of the country when he was here last month, if I'm not mistaken.

which contains a double hedge *I think* and *if I'm not mistaken.* If it were subsequently to be discovered that *we* were not out of the country at the time, the podium has not told a lie, because he only said what he *thought* was the case. Similarly:

(26)   MR LOCKHART: We'll take a look at the tax cuts, but *I believe* that what they're talking about now is paid for, so we will look at them.

Should it later be revealed that they are *not* paid for, the podium cannot be held to account because he was simply expressing his *belief*. The following sentence concordance of the first ten occurrences of *I'm aware of* (out of a total of 28 in the R-file), one of the most widely-used truth hedges, shows how its overriding function is to provide the podium with an escape route in case later information should prove him wrong:

1   As I indicated earlier, there are no plans for meetings that **I'm aware of** at the moment.
2   MR McCURRY: There are no definite plans that **I'm aware of** at the moment for U.S. government officials to […]
3   MR TOIV: Not that **I'm aware of**, but I don't know who sits in those sessions.
4   MR McCURRY: Not that **I'm aware of**, but, again, let's develop more facts for you
5   MR McCURRY: There are no parallels that **I'm aware of**.
6   MR LOCKHART: Right now, what **I'm aware of** is the NATO military campaign continues.
7   MR LOCKHART: Not that **I'm aware of**.
8   MR LOCKHART: There's no assistance that **I'm aware of**.
9   MR TOIV: No change in those views. None that **I'm aware of**.
10   […] so it doesn't have any practical affect that **I'm aware of**.

Note that it always occurs in negative contexts here.[6] It is sometimes used to mitigate a previous more full-blooded *no* (line 9). On other occasions (lines 3–5), the tentativeness of the phrase itself is justified by an explanation, an account, of why he is not aware of some fact or other.

The frequency of these items in podium discourse clearly shows how sensitive they are, either consciously or unconsciously, to their accountability for the accuracy of their reports. In fact, if we compare the use of introductory expressions containing *we*, such as *we think, we believe, we remain convinced* to hedging expressions involving *I*, such as *I think, I believe* and so on, the items in the former group are used to express positive commitment to an idea, a policy, etc., whilst the latter overwhelmingly have an accuracy-hedging function. Compare the use of *I believe* and *we believe* in the following turn:

(27)   MR LOCKHART: Well, *I believe* that the Secretary of State had spoken to him this morning, so they've had – the Secretary of State spoke to a series of NATO foreign ministers.

We believe that the concept of a just peace where you have an autonomous Kosovo where the Kosovar Albanians have self-government, self-rule, the freedom to live free of fear, free of repression, is a concept that's not dead.

4.3.4   Speaking for the President

One striking use of the *I* hedge is in reporting the views and feelings of the President (concordance of *I* in the context of *President*):

(28)   MR McCURRY: [...] and the President *I think* believes on balance that some of those restrictions are useful and important

(29)   MR McCURRY: Oh, *I think* the President feels strongly, if not passionately, about the issue

(30)   MR LOCKHART: [...] If the local community believes there's an appropriate role for the President, *I think* the President would be anxious to play any positive role he can.

The podium plainly has the brief to speak for the President, to recount what he is thinking, what he is feeling, what he believes, what he wants. He can even wax quite personal and intimate. The following pre-prepared introduction to a briefing is a long list of the President's emotions that day:

(31)   MR McCURRY: I asked him a short while ago what were the high points of [...] the visit he just paid to the USS Independence, which he was *very moved by* and *excited by* and obviously *invigorated by*. He was *especially tickled* that at the very end of the long, inexhaustible rope line that he worked they had assembled all the sailors from Arkansas [...] and he *enjoyed that immensely*.

In these utterances, the podium's role is that of presidential mouthpiece. In terms of Goffman/Levinson footing, it is the closest he comes to the footing of *spokesperson*, that is, a figure responsible for the actual form of language but not the content, one who speaks for a distant principal or motivator, but in his own words. In the view of those involved in these briefings, this role is clearly seen as one of the podium's principal duties, and is in fact discussed openly. On one occasion, he is asked the question (*she* being Ms Lewinsky):

(32)   Q: Are you nervous about what she might have to say when she testifies before the Grand Jury?

He responds with the unrevealing:

(33)   MR TOIV: We have no view on it.

This, predictably, does not satisfy the journalists:

(34)   Q: You have no view on it? Surely, the President has a view if someone is accusing him of a crime?

Notice the identification, conflation even, of *you* with *the President*. The podium then moves to another topic, but the questioner is not to be denied:

(35)   Q: Barry, let me ask you this, when you say that you have no view of the possible testimony of Monica Lewinsky, does that mean that in the daily meetings that you attend at the higher levels in the White House, no view was expressed of her coming testimony? Or does it mean that you were told to express no view of her testimony? (Laughter.)

   MR TOIV: I don't think anybody here knows what anybody's testimony is going to be. So how can anybody have a view on it?

   Q: But I was asking about the view on it.

   Q: *But you have to come out here every day and express what the President's feeling.* I mean, we really are operating in the dark, a total black-out on how he's going to testify, what's the M.O. on it, everything – just absolutely given us no details.

The podium is criticized for not performing the role of presidential mouthpiece. Note how the podium's claim to have no information to give is not accepted as a defence. He can still, rebuts the journalist, express a view, an opinion. This is reminiscent of Jucker's observation, quoted earlier (Section 3.4.1), that interviewers regularly attempt to reduce the interviewee's room for hedging or evasion by asking for their opinion rather than their knowledge.

At other times, however, as mentioned previously (Section 3.4.2), when tactically convenient, the questioner can challenge this total identification with the President:

(36)   Q: You have not provided us a real opportunity.

   MR McCURRY: I dispute that. We come out here every single day. We offer up all kinds of stories –

   Q: I'm not talking about you, I'm talking about the President.

And they can exploit the different footing roles to disorient him as, in an example we have just seen:

(37)   Q: Barry, let me ask you this, when you say that you have no view of the possible testimony of Monica Lewinsky, does that mean that in the daily meetings that you attend at the higher levels in the White House, no view was expressed of her coming testimony? Or does it mean that you were told to express no view of her testimony? (Laughter.)

The *you* in 'you have no view' is clearly consistent with 'you as presidential mouth-piece'. But the next *you* is more personal, is the man with his own ideas and opinions who has to attend daily meetings at the White House. The final *you* in 'you were told' combines elements of the personal and the spokesperson, and above all is somewhat insulting. He is portrayed as passive both logically and grammatically, a man who merely and meekly obeys orders. The podium, in fact, reacts to the insinuation: 'I don't think *anybody* here knows what *anybody*'s testimony is going to be. So how can *anybody* have a view on it?' He removes all personal reference, all responsibility, by turning all parties into *anybody*. Better to be impersonal than a dogsbody.

The podium can also claim, when convenient, that legal circumstances restrict what he can say as presidential spokesperson. This was especially relevant during the Starr investigation into the President:

(38)   MR McCURRY: [...] You asked me questions about the President's actions. If I got those answers from him, he would have, in effect, forfeited his attorney–client privilege, and he would have been an open sitting duck for Ken Starr because he'd have subpoenaed me – and I wasn't interested in being subpoenaed. He certainly could have subpoenaed the President, saying that there is now no attorney–client privilege that exists because you have vitiated it by talking publicly or authorizing your press spokesman to speak publicly on these matters.

He was not able to answer questions in his role as spokesperson for the President because this, he claims, would have opened the door to the President's opponents, who would have dragged him – and the President – into court to answer more potentially damaging questions.

4.3.5   *The podium as political commentator*

In contrast to their role as *relayer* or *spokesperson*, a great deal of the time the podium is treated as though fully responsible for both the message and the form of words. Much attention is paid to the actual form of what is said by both sides, as in the following:

(39)   Q: Mike, did you say that if the benefits to the American people – namely, stopping children from smoking – are good enough, the White House would support a deal that would limit the punitive damages that the tobacco industry –

MR McCURRY: I was very careful not to say that and I won't say that because that's not where we are right now.

Words themselves are frequently the basis of a news story. This topic is dealt in more detail in Section 9.1.

The press often ask for the podium's comment as though it was his personal opinion which counted:

(40)   Q: Mike, why do you think the President isn't watching this closely [...] ?
(41)   Q: Joe, was it appropriate – along the same vein, is it appropriate for the President to be raising money for members of the Judiciary Committee in the Senate?

And the podium frequently responds to questions about administration policy using first person *singular*:

(42)   Q: But, Joe, isn't the way to move it along to cooperate fully and free up aides to testify?
       MR LOCKHART: I have done nothing here today to preclude anything.

We might even go so far as to say that the podium regularly personalizes their response:

(43)   Q: Well Joe, there were three signature issues: patients' bill of rights, tobacco, campaign finance reform. You're not saying that those can be resurrected by next week?
       MR LOCKHART: Well, I don't have much hope for campaign finance reform and tobacco because those have been killed.

On one occasion in the corpus, the podium even sides with the press against the Presidency. The question in the following example, is whether the Clintons have the moral right to protect the privacy of their daughter against the press. Journalists in the room are arguing that they have forfeited this right by in the past exploiting her themselves for positive publicity. Mr Lockhart finds himself in a tough spot because he can find no real counter-arguments:

(44)   Q: Joe, let me ask you this. In 1992, the First Family, while they were still campaigning, did a photo spread with People Magazine with Chelsea. So is the issue that when they decide to publicize her with People it's okay, but when People decides to, it's not?

At first he tries to stonewall:

(45)   MR LOCKHART: I think the issues here are fairly clear, and I don't see any more reason to elaborate on it.

But then he concedes that he has argued much the same but to deaf ears:

(46)   MR LOCKHART: He's not listening to what I tell him.

The press insist:

(47)   Q: […] what is this baloney? (Laughter.)
        Q: You said it better than he could say it. It's baloney.

And Mr Lockhart is forced to admit that their description of the President's arguments as 'baloney' is quite accurate:

(48)   MR LOCKHART: Sometimes it's hard to spin baloney into anything else.

This, predictably, causes something of a sensation among the journalists:

(49)   Q: What he just said is good.
        Q: What did he say?
        Q: He said it's hard to spin baloney into anything else. Thank you.
        (Laughter.)

They are so pleased because they have an excellent quote for their copy. Any hint of a rift, of a disagreement in the administration is always a good story (see Section 6.1).

There can be little doubt that the podium on this one occasion has abandoned his role as spokesperson and is speaking for himself. In footing terms, he has clearly become his own *principal*. This exchange was, of course, an aberration and things swiftly returned to normal.

Given that it is so dangerous, it is not immediately obvious why the podiums are so prone to personalizing their discourse in this way. By doing so they can be held accountable and culpable, and not just for the inaccuracy of their information but for the implications of what they say. Presumably, the rationale is as follows. First of all, the podium is expected to take some of the flak from the press, it is a part of their job to act as a whipping boy in place of the President or others in the administration (see Sections 4.3.6 and 7.5.3 on the podium's complaints, some humorous, others not, about the tribulations of his job). Second, there are benefits in making the interpersonal relationship between podium and press more intimate, more personal. The administration, when necessary, can present a more human face, in the hope of capturing a degree of sympathy and comprehension. The over-employment of *we* or third person agents (*the administration feels, the White House would like* and so on) would probably have an alienating effect on the audience.

Section 4.3.6, in fact, is a discussion of how the podium attempts to take the process of personalization still further, to personalize not only his comments on the news, as in the examples in this section, but also his whole interpersonal relationship with the audience.

4.3.6   *The podium as private individual*

A final use of *I* relates to occasions when the podium steps outside any of his official roles and presents himself as a private person. This is the case, for example,

when Mr McCurry announces the birth of a son to a fellow member of the White
House staff:

(50) MR McCURRY: I've got an announcement first of major import. No news.
      Good news. Good news. The arrival on this planet of Ryan Federico
      Pena, born today at 8:55 a.m. Little Ryan weighing seven pounds, six
      ounces, and Secretary Pena and his wife, Ellen Hart Pena, are doing
      well, and Secretary Pena is taking time off, taking advantage of the
      Family Medical and Leave Act.

His first words 'I've got an announcement of major import' serves to arouse
the audience's curiosity and also as the basis for the bathetic revelation that we are
speaking of a strictly private event. He is careful to give his announcement some
official gloss by talking of 'the Family Medical and Leave Act'. The press, unfortunately, was less than charmed by this happy news and got down to business
almost immediately, with the brusque question 'Tax. Senate tax plan –
reaction?'.

Where attempts to set up a more intimate interpersonal relationship appear to
be more successful are when the podium jokes about the trials and tribulations of
being a press secretary:

(51) Q: Joe, this is the honeymoon weekend for the Clintons. When was
      Mrs Clinton's trip –
      MR LOCKHART: I thought this was my honeymoon week? No?
      Q: It was. (Laughter.)
      MR LOCKHART: This was my honeymoon?
      Q: You're having it. (Laughter.)
      MR LOCKHART: Bye. (Laughter.) I told someone – someone asked me last
      week how long I thought the honeymoon would last, and I said it would
      end the first day somewhere between good and afternoon. (Laughter.)
      And I think I was right.

We might call this the use of *I* for joshing and telling personal stories. The
press seem to respond favourably to the podium's humorous portrayal of self
in a tough spot. We might hazard the explanation that the portrayal of themselves
as expert and gruelling grillers of official representatives appeals to the press'
collective ego and reassures them that they are doing their job properly,
especially given the frequent accusations of over-compliance from the non-
Washington press. And precisely because it works in smoothing the way to closer
interpersonal relationship, the podium is more than willing to play the comical
victim.

Chapters 6–8 investigate in more detail the fluctuating and volatile nature of
the interpersonal relationship between the podium and the press.

4.4   Conclusion: summary of the podium's footings

In Chapter 2, a number of roles for the podium were pre-hypothesized. After a closer look at the data, it is now feasible to take more accurate stock.

The podium acts as *relayer* when reading out a prepared statement (a readout) or making an announcement he has previously committed to memory. These phases of the speech event are usually quite brief, typically lasting seconds rather than minutes, and they either serve as an introductory basis to the question–response session or they are part of the response to a specific request for information.

He acts as *spokesperson* for a much greater proportion of the time. He uses his own words to respond to questions in the interests of: the White House administration, the White House staff, the President, the Democratic party, the United States of America, the NATO coalition, plus combinations of these. Or, rather, he *claims* to respond as their representative since, as we have seen, there is some doubt as to whether he can speak for these bodies, especially NATO as a whole, or the entire population of the country. What we can say with certainty is that it is possible for a *spokesperson* to further the interests of one *principal* (generally in the present case the administration or the President) while pretending to speak for another (e.g. the United States or party supporters). Shifts of footing, like all other forms of linguistic indirectness, are not always innocent.

This vagueness about precisely whose views are being represented is not confined to the podium. The journalists too, for their own purposes, can represent a third party's point of view in their question and leave that party indeterminate:

(52)   Q: Would you try to dispel the impression that Mexico was really very angry at the U.S. over this episode?
        AMBASSADOR DOBBINS: I'm trying to characterize a meeting between the two Presidents. I'm not trying to characterize a relationship between two countries. And when you talk about Mexico, are you talking about the press, are you talking about the Cabinet, are you talking about the Congress, Mexican Congress?

Who exactly do you mean by 'Mexico' the podium asks – its government, its President, its press? A disagreement seems more serious and newsworthy if it is between two whole nations rather than between two people, even if they are Presidents. We have already seen that the podium will identify *we* and the nation when it suits him, but here the Ambassador takes issue with a similar press conflation.

Another point to emerge from this study is that *spokespersonship* is not a single, unanalysable, unvarying role. At times the role of a spokesperson is very similar to the relayer. For example, when representing the administration's position on foreign affairs in times of conflict, the podium's language itself reflects his lack of any room for manoeuvre, becoming guarded and repetitive; more like a readout than conversation. At other times, when representing a body he feels a more personal association with, for example, the White House staff or the Democratic party, there can be strong elements of *principalship* in his language: it may be interspersed with modal indications of agreement, it may take flights of grandiloquence, it may, of course, be accompanied by coadjutant intonation, voice quality, gesture. Levinson's scheme, which does not contemplate mixed roles in the same utterance, would interpret such occasions as the speaker moving back and forth between spokespersonship and principalship from one utterance to another. However, it seems feasible that some features of the same utterance – the syntax say – might be typical of spokespersonship or even relayership, whilst others – for example intonation, gesture – might be typical of more personal involvement. Yet again, however, these *indications* of principal-like involvement can be used tactically to suggest the podium's personal alignment with the message to reinforce it. As mentioned elsewhere, there may be strategic smudging as to who precisely is the principal of a message.

Finally, the last major footing production role, that of *principal*, is one the podium professes to eschew. When Mr McCurry speaks his mind on his resignation leave-taking, the 'personality' of 'who stands here' is, he says, of no consequence to what goes on:

(53)   MR McCURRY: But the press secretary of the President – we come and go, but we didn't get elected to be anything [...] it's not about the personality of the people who are here. We have but one requirement, which is to report accurately and truthfully on the work the President has done [...] But personality and who stands here is not a part of it.

He claims to see the press secretary's role as essentially one of non-*principal*, of *relayer/spokesperson*. However, principalship *is* an important stance of the podium: he is an *exploiter* of this kind of footing and in two ways. First of all, as recounted earlier he can add tactical touches of principalship to messages from a distant source. Second, he can slip into the footing role of fully fledged principal to personalize his relationship with the audience. There is nothing necessarily sinister about either of these two procedures. It is normal human social practice for speakers to take advantage of the possibilities offered by footing and the potential of shifting and combining roles to one's own communicative advantage. In fact anyone who fails to do so is generally taken to be sociopathic, a social misfit. Perhaps the most interesting aspect of what we have seen in this data, however, is the sheer *number* of roles the podium can adopt and shuffle for both personal behavioural ends (to survive in a difficult job) and paid political ones (to protect and further the interests of his employees).

5   Footing shift for attribution

'According to the *New York Times*
this morning ...'

In this chapter, we examine one common technique employed by questioners to present for attention views which are potentially hostile or damaging to the podium and/or his clients. These tend to be attributed to third party sources. This technique is yet another form of *footing shift*, since when the questioner attributes an opinion to others they are changing their participant status in the communicative event.

5.1   Clayman and journalistic neutralism

In a study entitled 'Footing in the achievement of neutrality: the case of news-interview discourse', Clayman (1992) discusses the particular strategy of attribution as employed by interviewers in order to appear to maintain a neutral stance with respect to both the interviewee and their own questions. This entails crediting the presuppositions and opinion in the questions to others, especially other authorities (e.g. by quoting from the press, other agencies, including governmental ones, other politicians and so on).[1] The following is an example (with light editing) from a British phone-in radio programme:

(1)   CALLER: We're havin' a very very hard struggle at the present moment ...
      HOST: But what is your reply to the fact that – made by *some people including Nigel Lawson the Chancellor* – that some pensioners in fact are doing rather better than they've ever done before?
      CALLER: Yes, but it's the poorer ones that're feeling the pinch.

(Hutchby 1996: 35)

The host proposes a counter view to that of the caller, contradicts them in effect, and ascribes it to 'some people including Nigel Lawson'. As Clayman (1992: 170) points out, interviewers frequently afford 'special handling' to particular parts of their discourse, 'the more contentious or objectionable' portions. Extra care is taken at these points to distance themselves, to shift the footing, without which:

> the interviewer would seem to be taking a position on a controversial public issue; with it the interviewer remains personally disengaged from the

substance of what he or she is saying [...] Accordingly, they can fulfil the complex journalistic requirement, put forth in the standard interviewing textbooks (e.g. Lewis 1984: 117–28), of being interactionally 'adversarial' while remaining officially 'neutral'.

(Clayman 1992: 196)

In this way, the questioner is not held personally responsible for any hostile views expressed in their question (Heritage 1985).

To emphasize that the neutrality of the interviewer is an artifice, Clayman employs the term *neutralism* to describe it (Heritage and Greatbatch 1991). He points out that it is normal for interviewees to acknowledge and acquiesce to the neutral or neutralistic stance of their interlocutor. He claims that it is, in fact, constructed and maintained collaboratively. There is a default, or normal, assumption on the part of interviewees that 'the interviewers' own opinions are not at issue' and 'they regularly decline to implicate interviewers or hold them responsible for what was said' (Clayman 1992: 196). This, Clayman (1992: 196) maintains, helps to validate and stress 'the "journalistic" character of what is taking place'. This is entirely different from normal practice in conversation, where neutrality is not the usual presumption. Speakers generally act under a 'with me or against me' assumption (Pomerantz 1984). Impartial responses and lack of positive feedback (typical of news interviews) are normally taken as rejection or hostility (Heritage 1985: 115; Clayman 1992: 198). The footing shift used for the purposes of maintaining neutrality is a formal practice particular to this type of institutional talk, and therefore presumably its significance and use have to be learnt. We shall see later whether there are any moments of tension in these press briefings between the habits of conversation and the practices of institutional talk; in other words, whether the neutrality of a question or a questioner is ever placed in doubt.

Clayman goes on to point out that this neutral stance is not always totally innocent:

Although [interviewers] ordinarily refrain from affiliating with their more opinionated statements, this does not mean that they produce such statements with equal weight. They can influence the truth value or epistemic weight of what they report by the terms used to characterize the responsible party.

(Clayman 1992: 187)

There are a number of ways to colour the utterance:

Since there are a large variety of ways that any individual or collectivity may be formulated (see Sacks 1972), [interviewers] can select those formulations that either enhance or detract from the source's credibility.

(Clayman 1992: 187)

This 'variety of ways' includes, of course, exploiting intonation and quality of voice:

> when speakers are engaged in quoting others verbally, they can imply their own alignment towards what they are saying through the tone of voice they choose to adopt. In such cases the speaker's views are conveyed without being stated explicitly.
>
> (Clayman 1992: 198, following Sacks 1992)

Thus, attribution is used both to distance the speaker from the utterance and, strategically, to try to influence the interviewee's response. In fact:

> It is possible to conceive of the footing shift as a strategy that permits interviewers to smuggle their own beliefs into the discussion while claiming that they belong to someone else.
>
> (Clayman 1992: 194)

In other words, the interviewers could well be expressing their own views but are under no obligation to own up. This is an instance of the kind of indirectness described in Section 2.6.

However, this is by no means a non-risk strategy:

> interviewers cannot just say *anything* and get away with it, for they are necessarily constrained by the interviewees and how they choose to respond. This should provide a corrective to the viewpoint that news interviewers are inherently powerful and able to dominate their guests at will.
>
> (Clayman 1992: 194)

If the interviewee, in other words, feels that the interviewer is in bad faith, is not in effect neutral, they will cease to collaborate in the maintenance of the neutralistic atmosphere. Examples of such break-down are presented and discussed by Greatbatch (1998). In one of them, the British politician, Paddy Ashdown, leader at the time of the Liberal Democratic Party, takes offence at an interviewer's proposition that his party is 'immature' and 'undisciplined' (the punctuation in what follows is my own):

(2)   IR: So you have loose cannons on your deck [...] doesn't that suggest that your party is still immature, irresponsible, undisciplined, unserious?

     ASH: Well, prove that. [pause] You made the proposition, propose it to me.

Ashdown's challenge to the interviewer to 'prove that', indicates his belief that the interviewer is personally responsible for these opinions. The interviewer is rather taken aback:

(3)   IR: Well, I'm saying to you: that this eh is what appears that the allegations in ... [Ashdown interrupts] hang on, there are also allegations in uh by

Emma Nicholson of dirty tricks, there is … but this leads to the more serious charge, if I may put it like this, that you are maybe you are opportune – that you are opportunists.

After a moment's disconcerted confusion, the interviewer alludes to the 'allegations by Emma Nicholson of dirty tricks' (Emma Nicholson being a rival Conservative Member of Parliament), thus shifting the footing, that is, the responsibility for any accusations. Mr Ashdown then accuses the interviewer of 'recycling Conservative propaganda as fact', thus challenging the authoritativeness of the source (Clayman 1992: 187–9) and strongly implying that the interviewer has abandoned any neutral stance:

(4) ASH: You made a very serious charge. Perhaps you let … Perhaps you … Well, again, before you recycle Conservative propaganda as fact, justify it.
    IR: I am putting the charges Mr Ashdown […] it is not just Conservative propaganda nor is Labour propaganda it is widely believed that you tailor your political … you massage your message.

The interviewer understands the implication and claims that he is just 'putting the charges', and that what he has said is not just rival party propaganda, but 'widely believed' – that is, believed by many people, not necessarily including me – another footing shift. At this point, the interview gets back onto neutralistic rails: Mr Ashdown addresses and refutes the accusation of sail-trimming. He presumably thus accepts the interviewer's role as relayer rather than source, as he must do if the interview is to continue.

Harris (1991: 80–1) discusses a case where an interview broke down completely because the interviewer (the journalist Brian Walden) felt the interviewee (the British politician James Callaghan) was not answering his questions. The response of the public was strongly unfavourable to the interviewer, 'suggesting that there are fairly strict limits to the extent to which an interviewer can force a politician to provide what he (the interviewer) considers a satisfactory answer to a particular question' (Harris 1991: 81), and reinforcing Clayman's point above that an interviewer cannot simply act with impunity. From the extract Harris quotes, it is interesting to note that the interviewer, Mr Walden, refers to his own knowledge and beliefs, making explicit use of first person pronouns (e.g.: 'I know exactly what you think'). This may well have contributed to both the breakdown of the interview and the public's adverse reaction. He was felt to be the one 'breaking the rules' because he failed to attribute his beliefs to a third party and thereby failed to maintain neutrality by shifting his footing.

5.2 Attribution to newspapers

One frequent source of facts, stories and opinions is, of course, the newspapers. To investigate examples of attribution to the papers, sentence concordances were made of the words *Post* and *Times* since these words are common in newspaper titles (both Washington and New York have a *Post* and a *Times*). There were 14 occurrences of *Post* and 26 of *Times* as newspapers, the following are the most relevant:

5.2.1   *Post*

1   Q: Mike, two publications today, the **Post** and the Times, both used the word 'paranoia' to describe the way the President feels about the issues that are raised by current accusations and past accusations.

2   Q: Joe, but The Washington Times and The Washington **Post** rarely, if ever, agree editorially, but they both agree strongly that his statement, 'I'm not ashamed of impeachment', was itself shameless.

3   Q: In all seriousness, Mike, in a **Post** story this morning, there was an implication that George's companion may have attempted to badge their way out of this tight spot.

4   Q: There have been two columns written – one of them in The New York **Post** – that deal with the President's firing of the White House doctor and a number of other drugs and the President questions.

5   Q: – The Washington **Post** today – the Italian Prime Minister, in recent conversation with the President when he was here, asked what would happen if the bombing didn't work, and according to the story, the President didn't seem to have an answer.

5.2.2   *Times*

1   Q: Joe, is the story this morning – I think it was The New York **Times** – accurate that said that Clark told Pentagon officials that the air campaign might not be successful?

2   Q: Joe, CNN and the Washington **Times** and the Richmond **Times**-Dispatch, among other media, have covered the very sharp controversy raging in Richmond.

3   Q: Joe, does the White House have any reaction to the London **Times** and Berliner Zeitung reports that Germany's federal criminal agency, EuroPol, and Swedish police are all investigating numerous reports of major drug money going to the KLA?

4   Q: Joe, you've said the Yugoslav army is in worse shape. The New York **Times** article also says they're in worse shape, it just says they're not in much worse shape.

5   Q: Mike, I've got a parochial question with the Watertown Daily **Times** in New York.
MR McCURRY: A fine newspaper.
Q: Thank you.

6   Q: Joe, is The New York **Times** one of the papers that you read carefully?
MR LOCKHART: Some days, but they use a lot of big words, so it's sometimes hard to understand. (Laughter.)

7 Q: Joe, the New York **Times** reports the Pentagon declaring that that captured Yugoslav lieutenant is 'a prisoner of war'. But last week, I recall your telling us, it's not a war, it's a conflict.

8 Q: On this LA **Times** story about the Jackson–Vanik Amendment and Vietnam – is the President ready to take this step to improve relations with Vietnam?

9 Q: Joe, here was a report in the Los Angeles **Times** this morning that Secretary of State Albright was disappointed with the formulation that you and the President have enunciated,

10 Q: Joe, The New Zealand Star **Times** has just – (laughter) –
   Q: No way.
   Q: The New Zealand Star **Times** quoted General Schwarzkopf as saying in Auckland that the NATO bombing mistakes, as he termed them, in Yugoslavia, are, in his word, inexcusable.

There are a number of general formulae used when citing newspapers. One of these takes the general form: *do you (or the White House) have any comment on (reaction to) the story in the* Post/Times *about…?* for example, *Times* concordance, line 3. It is, however, sufficient to mention the paper's name (*Post*, line 5: – 'The *Washington Post* today…') and then launch into what it purports to say. There are various other brief introductions: 'On this *LA Times* story about…' (*Times*, line 8), 'in a *Post* story this morning…' (*Post*, line 3).

Sometimes, a paper is quoted using its own form of words (see Section 9.1). The attribution is thus emphasized, the paper is treated as both principal and formulator (author) of the message, and the questioner – in the role of simple relayer – can distance themselves all the more effectively. This happens when the report is particularly hostile or damaging, for example, when the President is attacked [which is the most threatening act the podium can face (Section 7.4.1)]:

(5) the Post and the Times, both used the word 'paranoia' to describe the way the President feels … (*Post*, line 1).

On occasion, newspapers are quoted as reporting other parties, frequently official sources:

(6) [The *Times* and the *Post*] both agree strongly that his [the President's] statement, 'I'm not ashamed of impeachment', was itself shameless; (*Post*, line 2);

(7) […] the New York Times reports the Pentagon declaring that that captured Yugoslav lieutenant is 'a prisoner of war'. But last week, I recall your telling us, it's not a war, it's a conflict (*Times*, line 7).

Once again, the illocutionary intent is to deflect the responsibility for highly critical comment or, in the last case, to suggest that it is not the questioner themselves who is trying to catch the podium out – which could be seen as somewhat puerile and a breach of neutralism – but a respectable organ of the press. Note in the following example the pains to which the questioner goes in order to stress that they are using someone else's precise form of words:

(8) Q: The New Zealand Star Times *quoted* General Schwarzkopf *as saying* in Auckland that the NATO bombing mistakes, *as he termed them*, in Yugoslavia, are, *in his words*, inexcusable and the bombings are a mistake. (my emphasis.)

On other occasions, third parties are quoted indirectly; the form of words is not reported by the questioner. Thus, the journalist adds the role of formulator to relayer, becoming, in Levinson's terms, the spokesperson.

In either event there is a complex chain of reporting involved. A primary source is indicated more or less by name [although we sometimes come across more nebulous sources, for example: ' … some close to the PUSH operation are saying … ' (see below)]. Often the critical slant is explicitly or implicitly attributed to this primary source, for example: ' … the NATO bombing mistakes, *as he termed them* … '. At other times, however, it is the newspaper report, or secondary source, which is said to apply the critical slant, for example: '*they both agree* that his state-ment … was itself shameless. The final link in the chain, the questioner them-selves, is able in both cases to apply the criticism but maintain a neutralistic stance.

5.3 The authoritativeness of the source

It should be noted that the parties who are quoted (whenever there is a specified source, that is – see Section 5.5) are almost always deemed authoritative sources, 'élite' people or institutions whose opinions are in themselves newsworthy (Galtung and Ruge 1973; Morley 1998: 145–53). It is obviously important to establish the authoritativeness of the source to constrain the podium to take the question seriously.[2] Notice too that the secondary source is often multiple: 'The *Washington Times* and the *Washington Post* […] both agree … ' (*Post*, line 2); 'the London *Times* and *Berliner Zeitung* reports' (*Times*, line 3); 'CNN and the *Washington Times* and the *Richmond Times-Dispatch*, among other media … ' (*Times*, line 2), as if the more newspapers carry a story, the more significant it becomes, and the more an answer is warranted. The authoritativeness, the quality, of the newspaper itself is also an issue. In *Times*, line 5, the representative of the *Watertown Daily Times* feels the need to hedge his question, almost to excuse himself:

(9) Q: Mike, I've got a parochial question with the Watertown Daily Times in New York.

The podium acknowledges this tentativeness and encourages the questioner:

(10) MR McCURRY: A fine newspaper.
     Q: Thank you.

Others are not so lucky. If the newspaper is less well known and foreign, its authoritativeness is liable to challenge, even ridicule:

(11) Q: Joe, The New Zealand Star Times has just – (laughter) –
      Q: No way.

Note that the derision actually comes from another member of the press. Disdain from the podium is reserved for questions which use or cite the so-called *tabloid* newspapers as their source:

(12) Q: A former White House steward named Mike McGrath was quoted today as having said that he was required to leave the President alone with –
      MR McCURRY: Wait, in the Star, right?
      Q: Wait, wait, wait.
      MR McCURRY: Was that in the Star?
      Q: That's in the Star, correct. Was there anything untoward about the way Mr McGrath left the White House? Is there any dissatisfaction.
      MR McCURRY: I don't know anything about the circumstances of his hiring, and I don't have any comment on stories in which people are paid to provide information.

The questioner does not initially mention the *Star* as their source, probably fearing the kind of response that eventually ensues, but has to admit it after Mr McCurry's insistence ('Wait, in the *Star*, right?'). The podium can generally avoid commenting on tabloid stories without greatly antagonizing his audience because of the professional distaste the latter tends to feel for their tabloid rivals.

On one occasion, however, the questioner takes sides with the tabloids (but note the initial hedge or disclaimer: 'I'm not here to defend the *Star* tabloid … '):

(13) Q: Joe, I'm not here to defend the Star tabloid, but it seems to me they broke the story of Gennifer Flowers and the Dick Morris sex scandal. Now, when both of those stories broke, defenders of the President said, oh, it's just the Star, it's just a tabloid, we're not going to dignify that with a response. And my question is, how can you use that same defense to just dismiss out of hand the story? I'm not asking whether the story is true, but wouldn't it be more instructive to just deny or acknowledge the facts that are in question here, rather than try to smear that tabloid?

The story in question is about an alleged illegitimate child of the President's.[3] The questioner characterizes the general White House response to tabloid stories as 'it's just a tabloid, we're not going to dignify that with a response' which is in fact fairly close to the attitude expressed in the podium's actual response:

(14) MR LOCKHART: I'm not trying to smear, I'm just telling you that unless you have some independent reporting that you want to bring to this room and ask me about, I'm just not going to comment.

To recapitulate, then, a question from the floor is both more difficult to avoid and also more difficult to answer if the primary source quoted is an official, governmental one, or one which might generally be expected to be friendly. It is a relatively simple matter for the podium to rebut the criticisms expressed by those expected to be critical of or antagonistic to the White House – political rivals, the Republican party, foreign enemies, the right-wing media, etc., because, since *they* are not neutral, the podium is under no requirement to be so either. Such criticism can be refuted directly on the grounds of preconceived bias:

(15)   Q: Joe, some Republicans have said the Chinese espionage scandal is at least partially responsible for President Clinton and congressional Democrats reversing course on the issue of missile defense. How do you respond to that [...]?

    MR LOCKHART: It's not. That is an example of the kind of partisan shot that I was talking about the other day.

It can even be treated as a cue for a session of party-political or patriotic tub-thumping:

(16)   Q: Back on Iraq for just one more second. What do you make of – at a time when Butler is going to the U.N. and these semi-official Iraqi newspapers coming out today and saying President Clinton is an ugly adolescent and saying he's pouring fuel on the fire [...]

    MR BERGER: I wish I had the clip. This is actually in the Iraqi news service, which does show that the American journalistic profession is superior to the Iraqi journalistic profession. (Laughter.)

which in this particular case simultaneously massages the press's ego, obviously a useful ploy for the podium.

Since it is far more difficult to counter criticisms whose apparent source should be 'on the same side' as the White House, the sources cited by the press are more frequently of this type. In the concordances of *Post* and *Times* above we find: a trio of Generals (Hawley, Clark and Schwarzkopf), the Pentagon, Secretary of State Albright and the Italian Prime Minister. These obviously can be neither accused of prejudice nor ridiculed, but have to be dealt with, if possible, on merit. The press try to uncover, even at times to provoke,[4] contradictions in the administration position, which would of themselves be newsworthy. These contradictions are often as much a matter of the words used as of fact (although the distinction is not an easy one):

(17)   Q: Joe, the New York Times reports the Pentagon declaring that that captured Yugoslav lieutenant is 'a prisoner of war'. But last week, I recall your telling us, it's not a war, it's a conflict. And my question is, is the Pentagon wrong, or is your it's-not-a-war-it's-a-conflict corrective now inoperable, as Ron Ziegler used to put it?

The podium counters by pointing out that he represents the White House and not the Pentagon, a separate arm of the administration:

(18) MR LOCKHART: My understanding of the situation is, the Pentagon is the best place to put these questions.

But the one time the podium cannot gainsay a contradiction is when his own statements are involved. Thus the following type of question is quite common:

(19) Q: Previously, you had identified the policy – or the structure of an international course as one that's NATO-led. Now they're saying with NATO as its core. Is there any difference between those two?

The example below, however, is more complicated and aggressive. The podium's actual words are quoted:

(20) Q: No, I'm quoting you. [...] 'I am very well familiar with the President's medical records since that was so extensively debated in the 1996 campaign. I have spoken to the President's physician. The President is not under any medical treatment for any psychiatric or mental condition.' Now, that being the case, isn't the sole alternative what Reuters News Agency quoted Angie Dickinson saying in Hollywood: Clinton has a very horny appetite [...]

A trap is set for the podium. The questioner quotes a previous podium statement that Clinton is not under medical treatment. Therefore, they argue, the only other possible explanation for his behaviour is his inherent 'horny appetite', deemed an unedifying conclusion. The opinion is attributed to the actress Angie Dickinson, not strictly an authoritative source, but a certain weightiness is added by a mention of the *relayer, Reuters News Agency*. The podium responds at first with a joke but the questioner insists, rather sarcastically, on an answer:

(21) MR McCURRY: Is that a medical diagnosis, or was that a – (laughter).
      Q: I wonder, would you agree, disagree, or give that an icy 'no comment'?

so the podium responds, equally sarcastically, by challenging the authority of the source:

(22) MR McCURRY: I'm not familiar enough with Angie Dickinson to know whether she's been in a position to render such an astute and explicit diagnosis, but I doubt that she has any informed ability to make that decision.

which is, as Clayman mentions and as we too have seen above, a common enough tactic of political interviewees (Clayman 1992: 187–9).

5.4   The main functions of attribution

Clayman lists the functions of attribution, as far as news interviewers are concerned. These are:

- initiating a topic;
- generating disagreement between interviewees;
- defending against criticism;
- presenting the other side.

The first of these is glossed: 'on many occasions, IRs (interviewers) make provocative statements to open the discussion, or to initiate a new topical line of talk' (Clayman 1992: 174). In these briefings there are a number of interviewers or questioners. Each new questioner to take the floor can open a discussion, a new line of talk (although follow-up questions do occur), and therefore provocative introductions, often accommodating footing shifts, may well be even more frequent than in news interviews. Some concordance evidence was found in support of this statement. In a comparison I made of the White House briefings corpus (*WHB*) and the similar-sized corpus of British political interviews (*INTS*), phrases such as *there are/were/have been reports ...*, *some reports are saying*, etc. which are generally used to introduce new topics, were found to be considerably more frequent in the former (26 to 11). Here are two examples:

(23)   Q: Joe, have you read these *reports* that Yugoslavian TV and movie theaters are showing reruns of the movie 'Wag the Dog'? (*WHB*)

(24)   JONATHAN DIMBLEBY: If *reports* today are correct, then the rate of violent crime, which was falling when Labour came to power is now on the way up again. (*INTS*)

We have already noted, however (Section 1.2.5), that journalists are generally reluctant to admit they are initiating fresh topics.

Since there is only one respondent, footing shift cannot be used for the second purpose in Clayman's list: to generate disagreement between interviewees. However, as we have seen, it is used to try to locate or produce differences of opinion between those bodies the podium is taken to represent.

As for the third function, the use of attribution to defend oneself against criticism, the press rarely employ it simply because they are seldom attacked openly by the podium, who prefers to blandish them whenever possible (Section 7.5.1). The podium, of course, may use attribution to defend himself (Section 5.6).

5.5   Presenting the other side

As regards the fourth of these functions, 'presenting the other side', journalists clearly see this as one of their main tasks. The following sentence concordance of *critics* and *criticism* casts considerable light on this practice:

1   Q: Joe, some **critics** are suggesting that by the time air power does what it's going to do, there won't be any Kosovars left in Kosovo.

2 Q: Joe, someone in the administration is saying – not in the administration, but some **critics** are saying that the administration is back-pedaling for not inviting the Reverend Jesse Jackson to the event yesterday.

3 Why shouldn't we believe **critics** who say this is a morass, they're not going to be able to get out, there is no exit strategy?

4 What I'm saying is, why should we give you credibility when you say it's not a permanent fix and not believe your **critics** who say it is.

5 Q: Joe, will the President elaborate on this tonight and how would you counter **criticism** by some in Israel who are going to claim this is interference in their elections?

6 Q: Joe, the President's gotten a lot of **criticism** for his handling of the Kosovo confrontation. I wonder if you think today's events amount to a vindication?

7 But could you at least answer that **criticism** – do you have a strategy for what happens after the first round of bombing?

8 Q: Joe, a couple of weeks ago, the biggest **criticism** of the President seemed to be that he didn't have an exit strategy. Now, you're hearing more and more that he doesn't have an entry strategy for ground troops.

9 Q: Do you have any response to **criticism** from the French and Finnish governments about the airlift out of Macedonia, that it's going to take too much pressure off of efforts to resettle the refugees?

The podium is asked on each occasion a question of the general type *how would you answer your critics who say … / the criticism that …*. Note that on only two occasions is a source of sorts provided for the criticism (line 5: 'criticism by some in Israel … '; line 9: 'criticism from the French and Finnish governments … '). It would seem that 'the other side' of the argument does not always need to be explicitly sourced since it can be considered 'in the air'. In actual fact the source for the counter-argument is often the press itself. This is clearest in example (8): 'a couple of weeks ago, the biggest criticism of the President seemed to be that he didn't have an exit strategy'. What the press meant by an *exit strategy* from the Kosovo crisis was ill defined. In fact the term seems to have rolled over from the previous action in Bosnia, where US troops had been deployed on the ground and where an exit strategy meant eventual plans for withdrawing them. The term was revived during the Kosovo crisis, but since no troops were deployed there it is hard to know what precisely it could mean. This did not stop the press from using it as a club with which to beat the White House and its representatives.

Phrases of the ilk *some X are saying/suggesting* are used in a similar fashion (concordance: *are saying*, context word: *some*):

1 Q: **Some** of our allies **are saying** that suddenly the U.S. seems more committed to being involved and finding a solution. Is that the case?

2 Q: Joe, someone in the administration is saying – not in the administration, but **some** critics **are saying** that the administration is back-pedaling for not inviting the Reverend Jesse Jackson to the event yesterday.

3   And **some** close to the PUSH operation **are saying** that it was a means of punishment because he pulled the three American POWs out.

4   Q: What I'm asking is can it be cast within the whole – **some** people **are saying** it must be passed within the whole context of a national settlement and others **are saying** it's separate.

5   Q: Okay, but **some are saying** the word – that the administration 'stole' this from Reverend Jackson.

6   Q: **Some are saying** that by attacking a residence, whether he was there or not, this was an assassination attempt.

7   Q: Joe, some Democrats are talking about, in a sense, taking a last shot at the President through censure, and **some are saying** that the censure motion should say the President lied under oath [...]

8   Q: Joe, there are **some** commentators, including General Brent Scowcroft, the former National Security Advisor, who **are saying** that the President should have made the speech that he made today two, or three, or longer, weeks ago.

There are varying degrees of vagueness of attribution here from simply 'some are saying', through 'some people', 'some critics', to 'some of our allies', to the most tangible 'some commentators, including General Brent Scowcroft'. In the case of both *critics/criticism* and *some x are saying*, the podium might be expected to comment on the lack of a concrete source for the criticism, which might be used as grounds for rebuttal. This happens on just one occasion:

(25)   Q: Some are saying that by attacking a residence, whether he was there or not, this was an assassination attempt.

      MR LOCKHART: Well, as Wolf said, probably the – some are saying that, the same some that Wolf referenced, and those some are still wrong. Try again.

The podium both underlines the vagueness of the word *some*, and suggests that, whoever they are, they must be partisan.[5] The accusation – that NATO attempted to assassinate Mr Milosevic by targetting his residence – is a serious and potentially deeply embarrassing one. Challenging a vague source is a tactic used sparingly by the podium. It is, after all, their job to answer questions and the atmosphere of collaborative neutralism is a convention to be preserved. But this occasion was felt to warrant it.

At this point, we can attempt a list of journalists' preferred options for quoting sources. The most favoured method is to cite a 'friendly' one, another administration voice, even the podium himself. Next favourites are press sources, best if authoritative and multiple. In third place, the kind of vague, unspecified sourcing we have seen in this section. In final place come 'unfriendly' sources, who are disfavoured precisely because the podium can easily reject them for presumed bias.

To conclude this part, of the four functions of the footing shift listed by Clayman, presenting the other side is undoubtedly the most relevant to these briefings.

5.6   Podium response strategies to attributed accusations

How does the podium answer the accusations carried within footing-shifts? The main strategies seem to be:

- deny the account;
- challenge or top the authority of the source;
- deny knowledge;
- challenge the neutrality of an attribution.

5.6.1   Denying the account

One strategy is flat denial of the attributed account as in example (25) and as in the following:

(26)   Q: [...] you and other administration officials have said that there were signs that the Yugoslav ruling coalition was split, that there were desertions and all that. Well, according to The New York Times this morning, that's not true; in fact, the army's stronger than ever – recruiting is going great and –

MR LOCKHART: Let me be very clear on this. The New York Times report is not accurate [...]

In these two examples there is a preface to the actual denial: 'Let me be very clear on this ...' in example (26), 'Well [...] some are saying that ...' in example (25). This is not always the case:

(27)   Q: The Senator from Virginia, John Warner, says the lack of a US exit strategy from Bosnia puts the US on the brink of disaster right now.

MR McCURRY: He is wrong that there is no exit strategy.

Here, there is no mitigating preface to 'He is wrong'. The difference lies in politeness choices. It is wise for the podium to be polite to the *New York Times* in example (26) and to the journalist in example (25), but Mr Warner, a mere Senator and a Republican to boot, can be dispatched without formality. When the source is a public hero, however, considerable politeness is required. The podium's disagreement with General Schwarzkopf over 'the NATO bombing mistakes' [see example (8)] is both preceded by a hedge which questions the authenticity of the relayer or secondary source – 'if he's quoted accurately' – and prefaced with 'respectfully':

(28)   MR LOCKHART: Well, *if he's quoted accurately*, I would *respectfully* disagree. I think we have gone to extraordinary lengths to avoid collateral civilian damage or casualties in this.

5.6.2   Challenging the authority of the source; topping the source

Another important strategy in meeting adversarial claims in footing shifts is to challenge the authority of the source. We have already seen this at work in example (12), where the source was a despised tabloid, and examples (20)–(22), where it was an actress. But this is far more problematic when the source is perceived to be an authoritative one. Clayman gives an example of the one-upmanship tactic, of an interviewee citing as their source the *present* President of the United States to counter the interviewer's citation of a *former* President. The podium in these briefings occasionally 'pulls rank', as it were, in similar fashion. The questioner refers to 'a report this morning':

(29)   Q: Joe, there was a report this morning that suggested that this Kosovo thing is 'Albright's war', and that the Secretary of State had miscalculated on the effect of NATO bombing. Is there any legitimacy to that, or is that just a Washington blame game?

Note that the eventual question allows no innocent response: it is an example of the 'have you stopped beating your wife?' type question (other instances are discussed in Sections 6.3 and 9.3.1).[6] Either the report is true, or there is dissension in government ranks (a Washington blame game). The podium responds by appealing to much higher authority:

(30)   MR LOCKHART: Oh, I think I'd just put it in a pile that's growing steadily of inaccurate reports. I think the President and his national security team have been united in moving forward this campaign. [...] And that is a view that has been shared throughout the President's foreign policy team. So I would just say that the story is not accurate.

It is, of course, convenient for the podium to imply that the first and perhaps most important source of authority is the President himself. In the above case, he also throws in the weight of 'his national security team' and 'foreign policy team'. Notice that he feels this is enough to allow him also to flatly deny the report, twice labeling it as 'inaccurate'.

5.6.3   Denying knowledge

Another useful – and extremely common – strategy is to claim no knowledge of a report. The examples below were all elaborated from the concordances of *I am not aware of* and *I am not familiar with*, both formulae used to disclaim knowledge (Section 12.2.2). Although it is part of his job to be informed, it is of course impossible for the podium to watch all the TV news and read all the day's papers, especially if foreign, like the UK's *Financial Times*:

(31)   Q: Joe, on China, there was a story in The Financial Times today that said
        that China is about to test launch a new submarine-launched ballistic
        missile [...]
        MR LOCKHART: I'm not familiar with the story; I didn't see that this morning.

But at times one has the impression that pretending ignorance is employed strategically as the best way out of a tight spot:

(32)   Q: Joe, here was a report in the Los Angeles Times this morning that
        Secretary of State Albright was disappointed with the formulation that
        you and the President have enunciated, that there would have to be
        either an explicit or implicit agreement from Belgrade before a force
        could go into Kosovo.
        MR LOCKHART: No.

Note that no actual question was put and so the podium's 'no' is ambiguous. The
question finally arrives:

(33)   Q: Did she express that to the President?

and is greeted by a thrice repeated 'I am not aware of ... ':

(34)   MR LOCKHART: Not that I'm aware of. I'm not aware of any disappoint-
        ment. I'm not aware of any disagreement on what that policy is.

He doth protest too much.
    Given this tendency to disclaim familiarity with reports, the wily journalist can
adopt strategies of their own:

(35)   Q: Joe, is The New York Times one of the papers that you read carefully?
        MR LOCKHART: Some days, but they use a lot of big words, so it's some-
        times hard to understand. (Laughter.)

By asking whether the podium generally reads the *New York Times* – it would of
course be a dereliction of his duty if he did not – the journalist prepares the
ground so that the podium cannot reasonably deny knowledge of the story. The
oddness of the journalist's preface alerts the podium that something might be
going on, so that his first reply, shrouded in a joke, is guarded, non-committal.
The questioner proceeds:

(36)   Q: I'm thinking of that report that indicated that there was a reduction
        in the map-making, in other words, there were two map-making

organizations that were pooled together and they ended up using maps that were outdated for this tragedy.

MR LOCKHART: I actually didn't read that story very carefully, so – but I would send you either to the Pentagon or to the Central Intelligence Agency.

In the event, the question – a serious and potentially damaging one regarding NATO bombing mistakes – still receives a disclaiming response. However, the podium replans his move, eventually referring the questioner to another interlocutor, possibly aware that he has partly fallen into the trap, possibly aware of the lack of credibility in disclaiming knowledge of an important story in a prestigious paper.

5.7   Conclusion: challenging the neutrality of an attribution

An examination of the final podium strategy for dealing with attributed accusations will also help answer the question posed earlier in this chapter. In Section 5.1, it was observed that the presumption, on both sides, of news-interviewer neutralism is very different from normal behaviour in conversation, where speakers expect their interlocutors to show some kind of affiliation and a neutral, detached position is read as disagreement or even hostility. In terms of footing shift, are there any occasions on which conversational practice rises to the surface in these texts, where there is conflict between normal social behaviour and the constraints of briefing talk? Do we find moments where the podium refuses to accept the neutrality, the 'innocence' of an attribution?

The most striking example is perhaps the following exchange between Mr Lockhart and the journalist Lester Kinsolving:

(37)   Q: Joe [...] I was wondering if you could answer a question faxed to us by a Marine Corps Force Recon veteran of Vietnam, where he was concerned about the President saying the bombing of the Serbs is the moral thing to do. And his question was, where was the President's moral butt when innocent victims were being slaughtered by the Viet Cong, and where 591 other young men from Arkansas lost their lives?
MR LOCKHART: Next question.

The podium is clearly irritated by the question which drags up the old chestnut of Mr Clinton's draft evasion during the USA–North Vietnam war. Lester explicitly ascribes the question itself to a member of the public: 'And his question was...'. Mr Lockhart, however, flatly refuses to deal with it. Mr Kinsolving, however, is not one to give in without a fight:

(39)   Q: Next question – you're ashamed of this, Joe? Is that what you're saying?
MR LOCKHART: Lester, I don't have time for this today. Next question.

Q: You don't have time for it, okay.

MR LOCKHART: And you can put that in your report. That doesn't bother me.

Q: I will. Oh, I'm delighted to.

My impression is that the podium's annoyance results from his (strategically convenient) conviction that *ad hominem* attacks upon the President are beyond the pale, are outside the journalistic conventions that underlie these briefings. Lester here is breaking the covenant, not least by using the kind of language he does – 'the President's moral butt'. In any case, at this point, the proceedings descend almost to the point of an open tiff, and a rather childish one as Lester mimics the podium's words ('You don't have time for it, okay'), whilst the latter adopts a 'see if I care' attitude (' … doesn't bother me').

This second example is a little more complex:

(40)   Q: The Israeli press is reporting today that Prime Minister Netanyahu has asked President Clinton to defer a decision on Pollard until after the impeachment trial. Is that why we haven't heard what the decision is, which had been expected last month?

MR LOCKHART: First off, there are several things wrong with the question. There was never expected to be a decision last month. Go back and look at the facts of this case.

At first, as is usual practice (see Sections 6.6 and 7.4.2), it is the question rather than the questioner which is censured ('there are several things wrong with the question'). But then the questioner is also reproached apparently for carelessness, but also possibly for bias ('Go back and look at the facts'). Mr Lockhart takes issue with an embedded statement (that the decision had been expected last month' is embedded in the final subordinate clause of the question) and it is perhaps this indirectness, this disingenuousness which irks him; similar ploys had been tried several times earlier in the course of this session (embedded accusations are discussed in Section 9.3).

Despite these examples, it is in fact quite rare for the podium to attack the neutrality of attributions. It is more common to find challenges to their accuracy, as in example (29): 'Well, if he's quoted accurately' and in example (31): 'Oh, I think I'd just put it in a pile that's growing steadily of inaccurate reports'. This is partly because, as we have seen, the press attempt, wherever possible, to quote authoritative sources, governmental ones if possible, and avoid those perceived as partisan. Second, as discussed in Section 5.5 above, the press is afforded ample license to present 'the other side', even in a fairly hostile manner. And finally, the podium is clearly trained to resist the temptation to get into tit-for-tat, to avoid full-blooded altercation where he might well let something slip that he would later regret.

Nevertheless, what these examples do show is that neutralism is not a steady state but a dynamic doctrine and a potential cause for dispute. Journalists will occasionally attempt to push the boundaries of the permissible, in terms of topics for discussion, of interrogation techniques, even of the language they can use. The podium, in common with other interviewees, will try to resist, appealing to propriety, to the rules, to a sense of when things are 'out-of-bounds'. 'Ground rules' can change if one side or the other attempts to shift the ground. The discussion of such argumentative techniques and claims to power is taken up again in Chapter 8. In the following chapter we look more deeply at the conflictual atmosphere of briefings and the rules of behaviour which enable business to still be done.

6 'Rules of engagement'

The interpersonal relationship
between the podium and the press

6.1 'An adversarial relationship'

At the end of his last briefing, the press ask Mr McCurry about his feelings on
retiring:

(1) Q: What are you going to miss the most about being the spokesperson?
     MR McCURRY: I'll miss the give-and-take here in the briefing room. I enjoy
       this – it's kind of fun.

The press want more details:

(2) Q: Do you have any words for the press? [...] Do you have any words
       for us?
     MR McCURRY: I am much too close to the combat that we've enjoyed
       here to make any profound comments [...] but, look, this is a
       contentious environment, and it is, by design, an adversarial relation-
       ship. But what I've tried to do is make it a professional relationship and
       one in which we can still have some measure of amicability in the
       proceedings.

Note the descriptions 'combat', 'contentious environment' and 'adversarial relationship'. It is the general perception of those working in politics and journalism,
as well as most commentators, that the relationship between politicians and the
press in both the United States and the United Kingdom is highly adversarial.
As Nicolas Jones, a British political writer and BBC journalist, explains:

> production teams are anxious to demonstrate that their editorial standards
> have not been compromised and that they did not shy away from posing
> tough and embarrassing questions.

> (Jones 1996: 21)

Other commentators have noted that the relationship has gradually become far
more conflictual over the last 30 or so years than it was previously.[1] Maltese, an

American political commentator, argues that, in the United States, a transformation in the deferential attitude of the printed press towards the administration came about in the 1960s when radio and television became a direct way of reaching the masses, over the heads of the newspapers, previously a vital and much esteemed go-between:

> As presidents became more adept at taking their message directly to the people – thereby performing an end run around intermediary interpreters – reporters became less willing to accept the strict 'ground rules' that presidents had once proffered for access. In the process, the adversarial aspects of the presidential-press conference were emphasized.
>
> (Maltese 1992: 5)

Moreover, in Jones' opinion, most politicians find the press conference a particularly difficult genre to handle:

> Most ministers and MPs make no secret of this, finding news conferences often extremely tiresome. They dislike the way some reporters hammer away at a minute point of detail or alternatively are only looking for quotes to fit a predetermined story line.
>
> (Jones 1996: 20)

They greatly prefer the live interview, which is brief, generally one-on-one and easier to manage. White House press secretaries, then, in meeting the press on a daily basis in a conference environment are taking on a task most politicians avoid whenever they can. They can be seen as a surrogate for the White House administration, paid to satisfy the press's liking for conference-style questioning.

The politicians' viewpoint is expressed by (then) Congressman Dick Cheney in an interview with Maltese. The latter begins by observing:

> Communications experts often note that the media are preoccupied with conflict. By the media's own definition, news is drama, and drama thrives on conflict.[2]
>
> (Maltese 1992: 1)

According to Mr Cheney, events, whenever possible, are represented by the media in terms of conflict:

> conflict between policy-makers over the implementation of the federal budget makes for a much more interesting story than one that concentrates on the dry details of the budget itself [...].
>
> (Maltese 1992: 1)

Besides, conflict is easier for reporters to cover:

> it's much easier for them, for example, to get into covering and focusing on an alleged personnel clash between the secretary of defense and the secretary of state over what the arms control policy is going to be than it is to talk about the policy itself, which most of them don't understand.
>
> (Congressman Cheney in Maltese 1992: 1–2)

This for the White House, however, is potentially extremely damaging:

> As a result of the media's preoccupation with conflict, good-faith debate within the administration is sometimes depicted as serious dissension among the ranks. Furthermore, stories about real conflicts increase the tension between those at odds and make the president look like a poor manager.
>
> (Maltese 1992: 2)

And so, in order to 'correct' such representation and maintain control of the 'public agenda', the White House:

> must not only minimize exposure of internal conflict but also aggressively promote the messages that it wants conveyed to the American people. Bluntly put, the White House must attempt to manipulate media coverage of the administration.
>
> (Maltese 1992: 2)

In this view of the world then, media manipulation is no more than self-defence, vital for political survival, as Mr Cheney argues: 'You don't let the press set the agenda. They like to decide what's important and what isn't important. But if you let them do that, they're going to trash your presidency' (Maltese 1992: 2). Thus, the press and the presidency have opposite, incompatible interests. The first needs to dramatize, the second to tranquillize and each wishes to wrest control of 'the agenda' from the other. The title of Jones' first chapter is 'Rules of Engagement', a clearly military metaphor, and the press briefing is one of the battlefields on which this civilized, rule-bound war is fought.

To complicate the issue, however, it is important to recognize that there are also pressures in the opposite direction, to make the press less hostile to politicians. Unhealthy pressures in the view of many journalists:

> Ministers, party leaders and backbenchers alike have grown accustomed to dealing directly with the staff of individual programmes. Producers are encouraged by editors and presenters to build up strong working relationships, and as a result they can end up being on far friendlier terms with individual politicians than some political journalists would either contemplate or tolerate.
>
> (Jones 1996: 21)

In addition, the competition among news outlets to interview senior politicians has become so great as to give considerable editorial power to those who decide who gets to be interviewed – generally political party bureaucrats and professional media managers. However, White House press briefings are relatively sheltered from this ill wind, being regular and frequent events and open to all accredited reporters. They cannot be used to reward favourable copy. They do, however, inevitably favour the Washington press – a long-standing bone of contention for the other US media outlets. Nevertheless, 'strong working relationships', in Jones's words, are built up between podium and press because they meet so often that both sides know each other well. The journalists are also generally well acquainted with each other.

This, then, is the background that helps to explain the two most striking – and almost paradoxical – features of the interpersonal relationship between the podium and the press in these briefings, their adversarial nature and the air of informality [that 'measure of amicability', as Mr McCurry puts it in example (2)] which suffuses them.

6.2   An antagonistic press

The press's antagonism can be observed in their continual attempts to detect or invent 'weakness in the administration' stories. As a means to investigate this I prepared a concordance of *you + *n't* in questioner moves.[3] In July 1977, the White House was trying to appoint Congressman Foley, ex-Speaker in the House, to the post of Ambassador to Japan. The appointment was taking time due to opposition in the Senate, which prompts one journalist to comment acidly:

(3)   Q: It's many months, the Speaker – the man who's been the Speaker, you can't even get a breakthrough on that?

To which Mr McCurry quips:

(4)   MR McCURRY: Get it right, not necessarily get it fast.

To the observation above that the media are preoccupied with conflict, we might add another: that they are obsessed with *strength and weakness*. In this perspective, even good-faith discussion with opposing parties may well be portrayed as weak government. The motivation for this fixation is the same: first, it adds drama to otherwise dull stories to talk of who is winning and who is losing, which 'dog' is 'top' and which 'under', and, second, it can make essentially complex issues easier for the journalist to understand and to recount.

6.3   A sarcastic press

The *you + *n't* concordance contained plenty of examples of sarcastic repetition:

(5)   MR LOCKHART: I don't know the details of this case.
      Q: You don't know the details of this case?

In general, any whiff of perceived weakness is likely to provoke a bout of sarcasm from the press, for example, on the Foley delay:

(6)   Q: [...] I wonder, how long does it take to find out if Mr Foley paid Social Security for nannies?

Or on the administration's failure to keep a good enemy down:

(7)   Q: You mentioned that Saddam Hussein has been in a box, a very tight box for quite a long time, but every six months or so he seems to act up. Is there any U.S. plan to try to keep him more firmly in this box?

As in this case, the podium's own statements (he had previously said: 'Since the end of the Gulf War, we have put Saddam Hussein in a very tight box. It's where he remains.') are a rich source for sarcasm. A further, interesting example:

(8)   Q: If I may follow up, during this time when everybody is talking about cutting budgets and fiscal responsibility and austerity in government spending, is the President the least bit concerned about these stories that Hazel O'Leary may have taken these trips with some amount of extravagance?

The choice of phrase 'is the President the least bit concerned ... ?' is highly marked, since phrases like *the least bit/ the tiniest bit*, and so on appear in a negative grammatical environment, as demonstrated by the following concordance from a corpus of the *Times* newspaper:

1   Not that the Goans are **in the least** bit anti-tourist. On the contrary, Sergio Carvalho
2   And I'm not even **the teeniest bit** rich or successful,
3   the traditional English craft fayre is, of course, **not the remotest bit** traditional.
4   we cannot accept that Sarajevo should be threatened even **the tiniest bit**'
5   none of its leaders appears in **the least bit** bothered,
6   I don't feel in **the least bit** embarrassed by it.
7   He is not in **the least bit** fazed by last year's Bombay stock exchange scandal
8   And Leicester would not have been in **the least bit** flattered had they scored three more tries.
9   I told him I didn't feel **the least bit** guilty about him paying since sterling was 10 per cent
10   On Anne Diamond: She wasn't **the least bit** hoity-toity. She was always having me back

In contrast, the question in example (8) has a positive polarity. The rhetorical effect is one of ironic litotes, understatement. The suggestion is that the President should be *much more* than *a tiny bit* worried and that he should perhaps take immediate action. The podium responds very carefully:

(9)   MR MCCURRY: Well, the President rightfully would be concerned about any examples of waste, fraud and abuse in the federal budget. But he also

knows that those missions that Secretary O'Leary traveled upon, returned for every dollar of taxpayer money spent, about $1,000 in private sector-generated activity that brings jobs and commerce here to the United States. That's why these delegations go abroad.

He rightly identifies two tiers to a trick question, of the 'have you stopped beating your wife?' variety. To the original question:

(10)   [...] is the President the least bit concerned about these stories that Hazel O'Leary may have taken these trips with some amount of extravagance?

he cannot answer *yes*, since this would suggest that Ms O'Leary *had* in fact been extravagant. Nor can he answer *no* since this would insinuate that the President was not at all *worried* about possible overspending by his representatives. Note the careful use by the podium in example (8) of the conditional '*would be concerned*', implying grammatically the non-factuality of the question's presuppositions.

The press has, however, not yet exhausted its rich sarcastic vein:

(11)   Q: [...] Using that argument, if she would have taken half as many people, she would have returned $2,000 for every dollar spent. (Laughter.)

6.4   Worldly-wise cynicism and devil's advocacy

This sarcasm is an indication of a pervading cynicism expressed by the press with regard to the administration's activities and motives. Time and again the podium will recount a White House event or proposal and the press will proffer a less noble motivation for it:

(12)   Q: Barry, the trip to California is still on next week?
MR TOIV: Oh, yes. There's a three-day trip to five states. The President's looking forward to visiting every one of them.
Q: He's looking forward to collecting money from every one of them for the Democratic party. (Laughter.)

For their part, the podium reformulates the journalist's comment in a more positive, if a little po-faced way:

(13)   MR TOIV: He's looking forward to helping some very good candidates in those states and also talking about some very important issues.

(Section 9.2 looks at the reformulation – and re-reformulation – of the other party's move.) On a further occasion, the podium joins in the humour and politely points out the questioner's cynicism:

(14)   MR BERGER: It was a NATO judgment. All of the 16 NATO countries
      agreed to that assessment, not just the United States. You know,
      deadlines are a double-edged sword. On the one hand, deadlines
      provide a –
      Q: Selling point. (Laughter.)
      MR BERGER: No. That's more cynical than I know you mean to be, Helen.
      (Laughter.)

On yet another occasion, the press want to know the motivation behind the
administration's use of language, in particular the neologism *visit and search*, meaning stop and inspect any vessels suspected of carrying fuel into the Federal
Republic of Yugoslavia:

(15)   Q: Joe, back on enforcing the oil embargo. Where did the phrase 'visit and
      search' come from?[…]
      MR LOCKHART: I don't know. I just started hearing it about a week ago.
      I don't know the origins of it.

Not satisfied with the podium's profession of ignorance, the questioner goes on:

(16)   Q: But it sounds like it's such a nice version of 'stop and search'.
      MR LOCKHART: Well, it does have a certain hospitable ring to it. But those
      who deal in this, I think, you know, it has a particular meaning.

And again, until the podium gives some kind of reply, even if it is too general to
be in any way informative:

(17)   Q: What is that meaning? I mean, it sounds like we're coming over to
      Sunday brunch. (Laughter.) What is the meaning that we should take
      from 'visit and search'?
      MR LOCKHART: The meaning you should take from either that phrase or
      any other phrase is that General Clark is in the process of, in an expe-
      ditious way, coming up with an operational plan for how we can cut off
      petroleum, oil and lubricant imports so that the important work of the
      allied forces is not undone.

It is hard to see what answer the questioner is looking for after Mr Lockhart's
initial 'I don't know'. In all probability the journalist simply wishes to discuss
the topic of White House spin, its attempts at language manipulation, and to
send a message to the administration that the press is vigilant and their linguistic
experiments do not pass unnoticed.

The above example is light-hearted enough, but this doggedness and refusal to be wooed is extremely noticeable (see Chapter 12, especially Section 12.3.5). It can border on bloody-mindedness when a questioner insists on painting the blackest picture possible:

(18)   Q: If you folks acknowledge, as you plainly do, that you were wrong about the amount of time that it would take [...] why shouldn't we believe critics who say this is a morass, they're not going to be able to get out, there is no exit strategy? What I'm saying is, why should we give you credibility [...] and not believe your critics [...]?

In other words, since you got it wrong once, why should we ever believe you again? The press see it as a vital part of their job to represent the other side, the opposing argument, as aggressively as circumstances allow. In fact, they see their role in democratic society as that of *devil's advocate*, automatically proposing the other side of the argument to test the administration's case, and they are protected in this role by the co-operative presumption of journalistic neutralism (Section 5.1). This entitles them to reformulate what the podium has said in a negative, even cynical fashion, to see how he responds. A concordance of the word *So* in questioner moves provided many examples. On the Kosovo crisis:

(19)   Q: But, again, has anyone ever said, well, we're now winning?
        MR LOCKHART: Everyone has said that to date this has been an effective air campaign and they're highly confident we'll reach our military objectives.
        Q: So the answer is no?

On the testimony of Mr Dick Morris in front of the grand jury, which contained an allegation of secret police operations in the White House:

(20)   MR McCURRY: [...] as he admitted to those of you who contacted him yesterday, he has no factual information to support that allegation. He just kind of made it up [...] He thinks he read it somewhere.
        Q: So you're saying this former top aide to Mr Clinton perjured himself in front of the grand jury?

Alarmed by the suggestion that he could be accusing Mr Morris of a serious legal misdemeanour, Mr McCurry quickly reconsiders:

(21)   MR McCURRY: No, I don't – haven't seen his testimony, so I don't know the nature of it. Normally, grand jury testimony is secret. I haven't seen the transcript of what he said, it hasn't been released – it's been seen by some and it's been reported on by some of you, but we haven't seen the nature of his testimony. So there's no way we can know.

The reformulation has clearly perturbed and confused him and has forced him to revise and soften his stance. Press antagonism and devil's advocacy has produced some very concrete results.

6.5   *Agents provocateurs* and laying traps for the podium

The press may, however, go still further. Not content with being devil's advocate, as in the two examples above, they can even become *agents provocateurs*[4] to try to tease or trick the podium into saying something he might regret. The technique works as follows. A pre-question is put to the podium:

(22)   Q: Does the President regard Paul Sarbanes of Maryland as a Senator of many good accomplishments, or not?

Mr Lockhart's instinct warns him that he is being set up for a fall:

(23)   MR LOCKHART: What's the trick here? (Laughter.) What did he say?

His intuition has not let him down, because the question is not about Senator Sarbanes at all but about whether Mrs Clinton, a figure much closer to home, is thinking of running for the Senate in Maryland rather than face a tougher electoral test in New York.

However, it is a tactic that rarely bears full fruit. The podium is aware of the possibility and on guard, as above. Moreover, it is so patently disingenuous that the podium can generally shrug it off with humour or accuse the questioner of sleight of hand and breaking the rules of neutralism.

However, in one case it can be potentially dangerous. This is when the pre-questions are meant to provoke a statement in the present which events in the future could belie. This was a rather frequent occurrence during the Kosovo crisis, when journalists would look for a concrete statement about US or NATO policy aims which could be compared to actual events and outcomes at a future stage. In the following case, the questioner wants a black-and-white statement that bombing will continue until all refugees are back in Kosovo:

(24)   Q: Does [your statement that it will go on as long as it takes] mean that the air strikes will continue until the refugees are back in Kosovo?
       MR LOCKHART: No. The air strikes will continue until we've met the objectives. And the objectives, as –
       Q: That's one of the objectives, isn't it?

Note the importance implicitly granted to the podium's words, almost as if he was accountable himself for NATO policy (Chapter 4 discusses podium accountability). The podium is in deep water, being unable to give a straight answer that *yes, bombing will go on until all refugees are back* in case NATO in the future decides to desist under some other conditions. Instead, in the extract below he talks in vaguer terms about 'until the objectives have been reached':

(25)   Q: Is the refugees returning to Kosovo a requirement of U.S. policy?
       MR LOCKHART: As part of our policy is, the people of Kosovo can live free of repression, and that doesn't –
       Q: And we won't stop until they can come back?
       MR LOCKHART: I have no reason to believe that the military campaign will halt *until the objectives have been reached*, and I've laid out as clear as I can what those objectives are.

The wrestling continues until an exasperated podium calls for a truce: 'Our objectives are clear […] Let's move on'. But the journalists refuse to let go:

(26)   Q: Can I try this one more time? Can this conflict end successfully, from the standpoint of the administration, if the refugees aren't back in Kosovo, safe with autonomy?

To which the podium's reply is a vaguer, somewhat rhetorical reformulation, but one which is almost an affirmative:

(27)   MR LOCKHART: I think part of living free of repression is being able to live where you live, not someplace else.

And he adds a plea for understanding: 'That's my answer, and I think that's as clear as I can be', but the questioner is not to be denied and still demands an unequivocal statement of position:

(28)   Q: If in the end, that's not what happens, your policy will have failed?

At this point, the podium takes a step back from the exchange itself to comment upon the questioner's tactics:

(29)   MR LOCKHART: Listen, I'm not trying to say that at all. I think what you're trying to do is, once again, find a way where I can set a marker where, at a certain point of time, you can say the policy has failed, and that's just not how we're doing this.

He claims that the questioner is being disingenuous, is not really interested in hearing an answer, only in setting a trap for him. He implies that this is not impartial conduct, that it is contrary to the rules of neutralism and violates the 'rules of engagement'. The questioner does not accept the reproof, however, and argues that this is legitimate journalistic behaviour:

(30)   Q: It's not bad for us to try to set a marker upon which to gauge whether or not this is worth it or not.

6.6 When the adversarial manner becomes a threat to co-operative neutralism

At this point, we can pick up a theme first broached in Chapter 5. As was seen in example (29), there are moments when the adversarial nature of the relationship appears to pose a threat to the conventions of neutralism, that is, the co-operative presumption of the journalist's neutrality. This generally happens when the podium has a sense that the journalist is breaking the rules of the convention governing this kind of briefing. Or it occurs at moments when the podium is feeling under pressure and irritated. One of the most frequent signs that he is losing patience is a critical comment on the question. The following are from a concordance of *question/suggestion/statement* in podium moves:

(31)   Q: Armey didn't try to blackmail the President in any way?
       MR McCURRY: A ridiculous question.
(32)   Q: For the last several weeks, the President has hurried away from the podium. It seems clear that he's been given advice not to answer questions. Does that interfere with his dialogue with the American people?
       MR McCURRY: Look, Scott, it's a disingenuous question. You know that the President is not in a position to comment on these things.
(33)   Q: Do you have any concern that Saddam Hussein may be taking advantage of the President's political difficulties at home?
       COLONEL CROWLEY: I think that kind of suggestion is absurd.

In the first of these, the podium feels that the question 'breaks the rules', because it is too vicious an attack on the individuals in question. Not only is Mr Armey, Republican leader of the majority in the House, accused of inappropriate and probably illegal behaviour, but, more seriously for the podium, the question contains an embedded presupposition (see Section 9.3) that the President has done something for which he can be held to ransom. Presumably the podium's response – 'A ridiculous question' – applies to both accusations.

In example (32), the podium implies that the convention has been broken because the questioner has asked a question (on the Clinton–Lewinsky affair), which cannot be answered, in this case, for legal reasons.

It is more difficult to see why the podium feels that the question in example (33) is out of bounds. He probably objects to the suggestion of presidential weakness, but, given the press obsession with strength–weakness, such suggestions are little more than par for the course. In fact, the questioner follows up by asking 'Why?' and the podium goes on to answer the question in a much more co-operative tone.

Note that in all these examples, the question is censured, not the questioner. This is the usual case, even when the podium is quite annoyed:

(34)   MR LOCKHART: First off, there are several things wrong with the question.
(35)   MR LOCKHART: It would take 10 minutes for me to unravel all of the deception that is in that question, so we'll do it another time. That sort

of ad hominem attack on Mr Hormel has come from various sources over the last year. It has no basis in fact –

Since one of the podium's strongest (and most useful) creeds is that, as indicated in example (35), *ad hominem* attacks are not part of briefing etiquette, it would ill behove him to criticize a questioner.

There are, however, moments when the podium, Mr Lockhart at least, makes an exception to this rule. He occasionally implies that the questioner is trying to trick him, and this in his view would count as breaking the rules of neutralism. He admonishes the journalist for their 'try', that is, their *attempt* to get the better of him. At times he does so good humouredly:

(36) MR LOCKHART: I think that's about the question you asked me a few minutes ago. I'll give you the same answer. Good try, though.

At other times his humour is less well disposed:

(37) Q: Some are saying that by attacking a residence, whether he was there or not, this was an assassination attempt.
      MR LOCKHART: Well, as Wolf said, probably the – some are saying that, the same some that Wolf referenced, and those some are still wrong. Try again.
(38) MR LOCKHART: Peter, this is a game that I'm not going to continue to play.

The accusation contained in the question in example (37) is serious and possibly deeply embarrassing for the NATO allies. Mr Lockhart's rebuttal is equally serious, even somewhat aggressive. In example (38), the journalist is openly rebuked (by name) for attempting to 'play a game' of beguiling the podium into saying something more than or different from his brief. Observe here how the *game* metaphor is not always positive or light hearted (Section 10.3.2).

6.7 Further debate about the rules of engagement: *fair* and *unfair*

In order to further examine the debate between the two parties over what constitutes permissible behaviour during these briefings, a concordance was prepared of *fair* and *unfair*. The question is frequently in the air. There is even a moment of repartee about it:

(39) Q: Joe, I want to go back at something. I think it's *a fair question* and maybe deserves a thoughtful answer, which perhaps we haven't received so far. (Laughter.)
      MR LOCKHART: Do I get to decide whether it's *a fair question*? (my emphasis)

Usually, however, it is a very serious point and provokes a good deal of protestation on both sides.

(40)　Q: My question, if I could ask it, is, is it appropriate and *fair* to make decisions about access to the President based on what you think we might ask him?

MR McCURRY: Sure, we do that every single day – every single hour of every single day.

Q: News manager?

MR McCURRY: Not a manager.

The press here is asking whether Mr McCurry feels it is fair that their access to the President should be based upon his decision about what kind of questions they might ask. Behind this general question is the fact that the White House has decided not to respond to questions about the Clinton–Lewinsky affair. Mr McCurry's reply implies that it is of course part of his job to focus attention on certain matters rather than others; the press call this being a 'news manager' but he rejects the appellation. He argues that they should concentrate on the real issues:

(41)　MR McCURRY: Look, we had an important event today about a federal budget surplus. You all can decide whether it was news or not.

whilst the press uphold their right to report what they please:

(42)　Q: Why can't there be two stories? (Laughter.)

Mr McCurry comes back with the humorous insinuation that the press has only been interested in the President's relationship with Ms Lewinsky:

(43)　MR McCURRY: Looking back over the last eight months, I would have been happy to have had two stories. (Laughter.)

The exchange then becomes more serious with a counter-accusation of denial of access to question the President, followed by the podium's refutation:

(44)　Q: You have not provided us a real opportunity.

MR McCURRY: I dispute that. We come out here every single day. We offer up all kinds of stories –

and his final open, rather testy, criticism of press obsession:

(45)　MR McCURRY: – and it's been Monica, Monica, Monica, Monica. And you know that, and I know that. I mean, you can't pretend otherwise.

Okay, good. Thanks.

At which point the press change the subject.

Both sides maintain that their own behaviour is fair whilst that of their interlocutor is not. The press argue for more open access and the right to ask more or less what it wishes, and maintain that any attempt to 'manage' their questions is unjust. The podium, on its part, accuses the press of irresponsible behaviour, of concentrating on a single issue and neglecting all other serious business.

6.8   Other criticism of the press

Elsewhere, the podium also admonishes the press for supposed unprofessional reporting [over the Morris testimony, see examples (20) and (21) in Section 6.4]:

(47)   MR McCURRY: No – I mean, we've seen the same kind of anecdotal reporting that's some of you are carrying in your own reports.

for being arrogantly over-sure of themselves:

(48)   MR LOCKHART: You very confidently sit there and tell us what we're doing and we're not doing.

for being tedious and repetitive:

(49)   MR TOIV: [...] I'm as sick of saying it as you are of hearing it, believe me.

for being tiresomely predictable:

(50)   Q: Can I just finish?
       MR LOCKHART: Yes, finish. It's not too hard to forecast where you're going, so why don't you just get to it.

for being generally ill-mannered and offensive:

(51)   MR LOCKHART: Well, if I got into what was insulting in the press, we'd be here all evening.

We have seen a number of examples of press sarcasm. The podium too is not averse to employing this technique occasionally:

(52)   MR LOCKHART: Those two issues had nothing to do with each other.
       Q: Nothing to do with it?
       MR LOCKHART: Nothing.
       Q: Coincidental? Totally coincidental?
       MR LOCKHART: Nothing to do with each other, which, I think if you looked in a dictionary, coincidental might work.

It must be stressed however that, despite these examples, the typical podium reaction to the contrariety of his audience is not tit-for-tat response, but the attempt to placate, to mollify and to gain sympathy (Section 7.5). It is not generally in the White House's interest for the podium to engage in all-out war with the press. But the 'contentious environment' [example (2)] is sometimes just too much for him.

6.9   Conclusion

It has sometimes been argued that the relationship between the official press and the political administration in the United States is too complicitous, that their interests are too intertwined. This argument is heard from both the left and the far right, though in rather different terms. The former maintain that the realities of press ownership militate against any real independence (see Herman and Chomsky 1999). The latter believe that the Washington establishment and a traditionally left-leaning media are in cahoots to deny middle America a voice to 'talk back' (see Davis and Owen 1998). Be this all as it may, the evidence presented in this chapter and in the rest of the book is that this is certainly not how it seems to the protagonists themselves. They perceive the relationship as highly adversarial and comport themselves accordingly. A close analysis of the greater economic and social implications of government–press relations is beyond the scope of this book. In the microcosm of briefings, whether or not the sides are suffering the most complete of delusions, the *rhetorical*, the *linguistic* combat is real enough. The globalization of news sources and the concentration of news media ownership in ever fewer hands is a growing preoccupation but it is still possible (as yet) for individual groups of journalists to engage the powerful in conflict, as they clearly do in these briefings.

Some final reflections on the relationship between the podium and press are expressed in Chapter 13.

7   Politics, power and politeness

7.1   Introduction and definitions

7.1.1   Politeness phenomena and face

Much of the linguistic behaviour outlined in the previous chapter can be interpreted using the socio-pragmatic theory of politeness phenomena, defined by Crystal as follows:

> *politeness phenomena*: In SOCIOLINGUISTICS and PRAGMATICS, a term which characterizes linguistic features mediating norms of social behaviour, in relation to such notions as courtesy, rapport, deference and distance. Such features include the use of special discourse markers (*please*), appropriate tones of voice, and acceptable forms of ADDRESS (e.g. the choice of intimate v. distant PRONOUNS, or of first v. last names).
>
> (Crystal 1997: 297)

The model of interpretation I will use here is that developed by Brown and Levinson (1987), who propose a kind of 'economics' of social relationships (Cherry 1988), in which politeness helps an individual to maximize their acquisition of 'goods and services'. These include all social wants, from tangible possessions through love and attention to privacy. Their theory evolves from the dual axioms that (model) human beings are: (a) rational entities and (b) driven by needs and desires. These axioms are interdependent: humans are rational precisely inasmuch as they are capable of developing strategies to achieve their goals (their needs and desires). Moreover, all normal adult members of society have, and recognize that other members have, what is known as *face* [a term borrowed from Goffman (1967) and from the English folk usage]. Face is defined as 'the public self-image that every member wants to claim for himself' and consists of two related types:

> *negative face*: the basic claim to territories, personal preserves, rights to non-distraction – i.e. to freedom of action and freedom from imposition

positive face: the positive consistent self-image or 'personality' (crucially including the desire that this self-image be appreciated and approved of) claimed by interactants

(Brown and Levinson 1987: 61)

Negative face, the desire for freedom from imposition and freedom of action is recognizable as more or less the kind of phenomenon we mean when we normally refer to politeness – we pay attention to another's negative face every time we knock on their door to request their permission to enter. Positive face is less straightforward, but it comprises 'the desire to be ratified, understood, approved of, liked or admired' by at least some others, presumably those we in turn approve of and admire. One important further step in the theory is that this positive face includes the desire to have one's *goals* thought of as desirable. Whilst the precise characteristics and delimitations of both types of face will differ from culture to culture, including of course the exact nature of goals generally thought worthy of approbation – the suggestion has been made that some societies give more weight to one type than the other – there is an assumption that face is a universal phenomenon. It is the consequence of the need for the human animal to cohabit with other similar animals in society and to cooperate with them in order to protect and pursue its interests.[1]

7.12 Threatening face

The theory, however, also asserts that face is an extremely vulnerable affair. It claims we pay vast amounts of attention to protecting and enhancing our own face and in ensuring that we do not threaten or even seem to threaten that of others, and we expect others to do the same for us. It maintains that even much of normal social interaction is potentially threatening to either or both the speaker's or hearer's face. Any act[2] which puts pressure on the hearer to do something – order, request, suggestion, reminding and so on – potentially threatens their negative face, as would any act (giving a gift, paying a compliment) which entails the hearer incurring a debt. Any act which could be construed as demonstrating a lack of care for the hearer's desires and goals is a potential threat to the latter's positive face, for example, criticism and disapproval but also contradiction, challenge, even interruption, or simply the failure to show alignment and agreement with their views (in Section 5.1 we mentioned how interlocutors in conversation generally act under a 'with me or against me' assumption).

Speakers put their *own* negative face at risk in a number of ways, including by expressing thanks or accepting an offer (thereby recognizing a debt). They risk their own positive face when, for example, they apologize or confess guilt or responsibility (thereby acknowledging some previous shortcoming).

We do not, however, treat all our interlocutors in the same way at all times. We adopt different politeness strategies according to context, and it is part of adult communicative competence (Hymes 1971) to judge which is the correct strategy for a particular situation. For example, greater indirectness in requesting is usually perceived as directly proportional to politeness. But speakers cannot always choose to err on the side of caution, to be hyper-indirect, if the circumstances are not right – they will be seen as joking, facetious or making a more serious request than they actually are (thereby arousing unnecessary suspicion or anxiety). Speaker 'strategies' are by and large unconscious, though they are to some extent open to introspection. They may come to the surface when communication breaks down and participants need to reassess them.

Brown and Levinson list three 'sociological variables' that speakers use in choosing the degree of politeness to use and in calculating the amount of threat to their own face:

(i)   the 'social distance' of the speaker and the hearer;
(ii) the relative 'power' of the speaker over the hearer;
(iii) the absolute ranking of impositions in the particular culture.

The greater the social distance between the interlocutors (for example, if they know each other very little), the more politeness is generally expected. The greater the (perceived) relative power of hearer over speaker, the more politeness is recommended. The heavier the imposition made on the hearer (the more of their time required, or the greater the favour requested), the more politeness will generally have to be used.

Twelve years after the first outline of Brown and Levinson's work in 1978, Kasper (1990) reported on intervening research on politeness. Several authors have questioned the universality of their theory, especially in regard to non-European societies, and a number of refinements have been suggested – that the effect of power and distance on politeness is not deterministic, that the importance of *affect* (e.g. whether or not the interlocutors like each other) be reappraised, that *rudeness* receive more attention (for example R. Lakoff 1989). Yet, on the whole, the edifice of their ideas of politeness as *strategic conflict management* has weathered the scrutiny of time and criticism very well. As Holtgraves (1977: 235) points out, however, most research into politeness 'has examined hypothetical politeness or the perception of theoretically generated politeness strategies' without availing itself of naturally occurring language data. The present study is, of course, entirely based on authentic examples. Moreover, Harris (2001: 452) notes that 'politeness has also been much less examined in relationship to institutional contexts and/or discourse types other than ordinary conversation'. What follows is hopefully a step in filling this gap.

7.1.3   *Power: a definition for briefings talk*

One of the concepts mentioned above needs further attention. The term *power* is one of the most confusing in linguistics. It is used to refer to a wide range of often disparate phenomena. It is used, in concomitance with the opposing term *solidarity* to describe the pronoun system of numerous European languages, in which – with some variation from language to language – the V-pronoun (from French *vous*) is used by inferiors to superiors and among strangers, whilst the T-pronoun (from *tu*) is used by superiors to inferiors but also generally amongst social equals and intimates [Brown and Gilman (1972) – note that the system is really an inter-mix of power and distance in Brown and Levinson's terms]. More in general, power is also discussed in sociolinguistics in many situations of bilingualism where one language variety is associated, historically at least, with a powerful social group (e.g. Spanish in Paraguay, Brahmin varieties in India).

Second, the term *power* is used in the description of social situations where the powerful are able to openly coerce the less powerful: the military, the family, many hierarchically organized workplaces [especially where the workforce is not union-ized or is perhaps composed of non-native speakers (Roberts *et al.* 1992)].

It is also, however, commonly used in the description of situations of interac-tion where coercion is much less direct, if a factor in the relationship at all. It has been used to describe the asymmetry in doctor–patient, job interviewer–applicant, counsellor–student relationships, the former in each case, of course, said to be the powerful agent. Roberts *et al.* (1992), among others, employ the more useful term *gatekeepers* to describe such figures, who control the public's access to some goods or service (often, in practice, information). The goal of the interaction between gatekeeper and client is – supposedly at least – to further the client's interests and well-being. Very frequently in, say, a doctor–patient relationship, the different *power roles* are used cooperatively, to get the work (of helping the patient) done. The concept of *power* in this situation, if it has any meaning at all, must be interpreted as being 'in control of the situation', as having the power of the initiative to do a number of things typical of gatekeep-ing. These include: limiting the possible topics of the interaction, prying into the client's private affairs, interrupting if he or she (the gatekeeper) feels things are wandering.[3]

Of particular relevance to this study is the fact that in most circumstances the gatekeepers are the ones who ask the questions. The work of the podium bears some resemblance to gatekeeping, in that he is controlling press and public access to information or other important resources. However, he typically *responds to* rather than *asks* the questions. Much as if a doctor, in order to find out what was wrong with a patient, confined herself to replying to their questions.

In any case, it might seem rather perverse to use indiscriminately the same term *power* in describing both coercive and gatekeeping interactions. Unfortunately, this is what frequently has happened in the field, although some pragmatists and con-versation analysts prefer to talk of *asymmetries* between participants. By this is meant 'differential access to such common speech acts as questions, directives, accusations, assertions' (Harris 1995: 122) and so on. Harris uses the example of questions in court, which are the prerogative of representatives of the institution and which 'appear to be used [...] as a mode of control, making it difficult for non-institutional participants (i.e. defendants, witnesses) to put forward proposi-tions of their own' (Harris 1995: 122). This, she suggests, makes it difficult for them to challenge the institution's view of the world and of 'truth' (i.e. what actually happened). Differential access to discursive resources clearly plays a major part in these briefings, but the cards are not stacked against the podium as respondent in the same way. He has resources of his own to call upon. In any case, what is meant by 'power' in the discussion that follows is power of initiative. In particular, the 'power' that the podium and press wrangle over is principally the power to set the agenda, and to decide to what degree it can be pursued, to choose which topics can legitimately be discussed, to control access to and presentation of information (see the more detailed discussion in Section 9.4).

We may generalize from these ideas as follows. In all forms of talk – but the phenomenon is often more pervasive and more constricting in gatekeeping institutional talk – the participant who exposes him- or herself, whose arguments, beliefs, state of health or of mind, personal background, job prospects, and so on, are the object of the talk is in a vulnerable position. The flow of information is asymmetrical – one person gets to know about the other but not vice versa. In terms of politeness, only one of the interlocutors is risking face, and this places them in a less powerful role. It has been argued that one way of tracing the power relationships in institutional talk is by counting the number of questions that are asked by each participant (Maynard 1991). The questioner role can be both a prerogative of superiority and also a way of maintaining it. It might therefore be expected that the journalists hold the whip hand in these briefings. However, things are complicated by the fact that it is not strictly the podium's own personal face which is at issue. In addition, as we shall see, he has at his disposal other discursive resources which help redress the balance.

Finally, *power* is used in some branches of the discipline, notably critical linguistics, in the description of how some, the *empowered*, use language as an instrument of control as well as communication in relation to the *powerless* (see Kress and Hodge 1979). Texts are one of the places where the conflict between the social classes is enacted: 'Language is both a site of and a stake in class struggle and those who exercise power through language must constantly be involved in struggle with others to defend (or lose) their position' (Fairclough 1989: 35). Critical linguists, inspired by Barthes' (1977) essay 'The Death of the Author', tend to concentrate on those kinds of texts which can be viewed as emanations from institutions of power, as the voice of those institutions rather than of individuals, for example, political speeches, police interviews, and see Bell (1996) on the multiple authorship of newspaper articles. They often believe that their own analysis can play a part in the class struggle by uncovering the hidden agendas and the mechanisms of persuasion used by the powerful in such texts. These briefings could certainly be seen from this perspective. However, the present work is far from indifferent to issues of individual involvement in the text. In fact, much of what is interesting about footing and politeness phenomena derives from the conflict between the institutional and personal voices of the participants. These texts are also an antidote to the impression given by many critical linguists that only they are vigilant over the language of the powerful. The journalists attending these briefings are as critical and as cynical about the administration's language and intentions, as keen to uncover hidden agendas, as any linguist could be.

7.2   Politeness phenomena in White House briefings

The questions to be posed in the main part of this chapter are: how do politeness phenomena affect the work being done in these briefings and what light can they throw on the way the podium and the press interact? The podium is both (a) an individual; and (b) a paid representative of other people's interests. What kind of politeness does he show? The journalists are: (a) individuals; (b) members of a large group interacting with a single individual; and (c) representatives of other people's interests. What is the nature of their politeness? Politeness phenomena have generally in the past been studied in fairly static circumstances, famously in encounters such as those between doctor–patient, teacher–pupil, management–worker and so on. My first reaction on reading these briefings was that, in common with political interviews, relations of power and distance (sociological variables (i) and (ii) in Brown and Levinson's list in Section 7.1.2) are unstable and subject to negotiation and competition. How do the parties vie to acquire, maintain and express power and distance?

7.3   Informality

One of the most striking features of these briefings is the informality of the atmosphere in which they are held. This is probably partly due to their routineness – they are held almost every day, sometimes even twice a day, whenever the political administration is in session. As Brown and Levinson remark, frequency of interaction is the main criterion of distance, which therefore in these briefings is very small. Relative informality is also common working practice in US and British professional circles.[4]

However, frequency of interaction is no guarantee of informality, let alone friendship. Brown and Levinson (1987: 16) mention the need to introduce a separate, independent variable of *liking* (or *positive affect*) in order, for instance, to distinguish an expression of admiration (compliment) from an attack (insult) in the form of an ironic compliment (Slugoski 1985: 96). Though there is no doubt that the atmosphere of the briefings is informal, whether there is genuine amiability is another question.

Address between the two parties is strictly first name: *Mike* and *Joe* for the two main podiums, *Helen, Wolf, Sam*, amongst others, for the members of the press. Only on a couple of occasions are journalists' surnames included, once as a humorous reproof [example (10) below] and once for clarity of reference:

(1)   Q: Mike, I've got a parochial question with the Watertown Daily Times in New York.
   MR McCURRY: A fine newspaper.
   Q: Thank you.
   MR McCURRY: You're the Alan Emory understudy then.
   Q: The new Alan Emory.

The various podiums also tend to refer to other members of the administration staff by first names, *shortened* first names on the model of *Bill* Clinton, even making a point of it (my emphasis):

> (2)   MR LOCKHART: [...] I think there have been very supportive statements made this morning [...] about supporting Lawrence, *Larry* Summers as the next Treasury Secretary.

Both the podium and the press regularly use colloquial language. This will be discussed in greater detail in Section 11.7, but a couple of examples will suffice here to give the flavour. Both sides talk of *you guys* and *you folks*, the press referring to the government, the podium meaning members of the press. Saddam Hussein is a 'junior league Hitler' (a phrase previously employed by both the President and the Vice President) and his Republican Guard are his 'cronies'. The people of Serbia are said to be 'fed up' with their government. Official business is familiarized, de-bureaucratized:

> (3)   MR McCURRY: We'll have David – David and Mary Ellen will be in a position to *run through* the schedule and brief on it later. Maybe you guys can just *jump up* and do that at the end.

with the use of terms like *run through* and *jump up*, whilst Congress is likely to *muck around* (a Britishism) over urgent business. In the same vein, Mr McCurry famously referred to his briefings as his 'gaggles'. Sometimes it is also tactically useful for the podium to talk about the President with familiar, non-bureaucratic language:

> (4)   MR McCURRY: [...] The President *dropped by* for about 15 minutes.
> (5)   MR McCURRY: [...] So they are going to *get together* and *chat*. (The President with Senator Dole).

A number of authors have commented upon the *informalization* of institutional language, the increasing use by institutions of informal forms traditionally reserved for more intimate relations in their dealings with the public. Fairclough views the practice with some suspicion:

> There is a deep ambivalence about the contemporary 'conversationalisation' of language, as we might call it, in its implications for power: on the one hand, it goes along with a genuine opening up and democratisation of professional domains, a shift in power towards the client and the consumer. But on the other hand, conversational style provides a strategy for exercising power in more subtle and implicit ways, and many professionals are now trained in such strategies.
>
> (Fairclough 1992: 4–5)

White House podiums are certainly to be counted among those professionals 'trained in such strategies'. Conversationalism is especially useful for the podium in creating a sense of complicity between themselves and the press, it 'implies a commonly held view of the world, a shared subjective reality that is taken for granted and does not have to be proved' (Fowler 1991: 57, following Berger and Luckmann 1976).

In the particular environment of political journalism, however, informalism may also be a result of the demise of the deferential manner of reporting of authority, as mentioned in the previous chapter (Section 6.1). It is partly to be seen as self-defence, the response of a more harassed, less self-confident political establishment to a more critical press. In fact, at times in these briefings, it has an air of desperation.

In sum, then, in terms of the sociological variables used to calculate politeness, these briefings take place against the background of an apparent assumption of low social distance and low power differential.

7.4 Threatening face

7.4.1 *Threats to the podium's face*

What then of the third of Brown and Levinson's sociological variables, the relative weight of request? Who, in other words, is making the weightiest demands in the interaction? At first sight, it might seem that the press are the ones with the greater requirements, after all, they are the ones who do the asking. But they simply demand information and it is the podium's job to supply it. The podium has a much greater need: the *complicity* of his audience in the preservation of his face. And the press are under no obligation to satisfy him on this score. If anything, as we have seen, their instinct, their duty almost, is quite the opposite. As Jucker says:

> It is clear that what is primarily at issue in news interviews is the interviewee's positive face. Thus the interviewee's face will usually be found to be threatened by the interviewer, and the interviewees themselves threaten their own faces if they can be seen to accept criticism or blame etc.
>
> (Jucker 1986: 71)

We have already seen that interviews are normally conducted under the mutual assumption of journalistic neutralism. In terms of politeness phenomena, neutralism involves the interviewee relinquishing normal rights and their face can be put under more pressure than in ordinary conversation.

Of considerable relevance to the present study is Jucker's examination of face-threatening behaviour in political news interviews. He analysed a corpus of 111 interviews from BBC Radio 4, recorded between 1982 and 1984. He suggests 13 ways in which an interviewer may threaten the interviewee's face, which are divided into five categories. A question may ask, encourage or force one or more of the following acts:

(A) *Future act of interviewee*
   1 Commit yourself to doing something;

(B) *Interviewee's opinion*

    2 State your opinion;
    3 Confirm your opinion (presupposing it is demeaning);
    4 Accept discrepancy between your opinion and your actions;
    5 Accept discrepancy between your opinion and reality;

(C) *Past action associated with interviewee*

    6 Accept that the reason for doing that action is demeaning;
    7 State that the action is demeaning;
    8 Confirm the action (presupposing it is demeaning);
    9 Take responsibility for the action;
  10 Justify the action;
  11 Take action against something;

(D) *Other's face*

  12 State that other's face is demeaning;

(E) *Interviewee's face*

  13 State that your own face is demeaning.

The list is ranked in increasing severity of threat. Class B events are mainly concerned with opinion and are less face-threatening than class C ones, which deal with concrete events. Classes D and E are more serious still because interviewees are asked to demean someone else's face (usually that of an ally) or their own face directly (Jucker 1986: 77–94). The word *demeaning* is used in the technical sense of 'liable to damage face (either one's own or another's, depending on circumstances)'. As pointed out by Best (1996), who compiled his own small corpus of news interviews conducted on the BBC Radio 4 *Today* programme, largely with the aim of replicating Jucker's work, the difference between nos. 1 and 11 is not clear. He interprets Jucker to mean: 1. Take action (against something which is not your fault); 11. Take action (against something that *is* your fault).

There are a number of differences between the genres of news interviews and briefings talk. The most important from the present point of view are the following. In the news interview, the person being interviewed directly, even though he or she may represent a party, trade union, pressure group or suchlike, is putting their own face on the line directly.[5] In the case of these briefings, it is the face, the reputation, of the administration which is in danger and needs defending (although, of course, the face of the podium is also involved indirectly). This means – and this is the second major difference – that the stakes are generally higher in the briefings situation. A politician may make a temporary fool of himself,[6] but the reputation of the entire administration of the United States both at home and abroad, in the eyes of both friend and foe – all in play in these briefings – is large beer indeed.

Best (1996: 4.43) makes out a case for inverting the order of acts 1 and 2 of Jucker's list of categories. In fact, although act no. 1 – 'commit yourself to doing something' – is not particularly threatening in the here and now, it could well become seriously embarrassing at some future moment, could in fact become an act no. 4 or 5 (accept discrepancy between your opinion and your actions). There are numerous examples in the briefings when the podium is asked to commit the White House to some course, especially during the Kosovo crisis, but he either hedges, evades or is vague in some way. Committing yourself to doing something is potentially more face-threatening for the podium than for Jucker's interviewees.

Another area of divergence is at the level of act no. 12 – 'state that other's face is demeaning'. If the face being demeaned is that of the President, this is the severest of all possible face-threatening situations for the podium:

(6)   Q: Mike, considering your answer to Pete's question, then why has the President made it a practice in recent days and in recent weeks, for that matter, to beat such a hasty retreat from the podium after he's made a statement. He almost knocks over people. He ran into the flag on his way out this morning. Has he become –
MR McCURRY: Oh, that's not true.

The President is accused not only of evasiveness but also of Keystone clumsiness, a charge the podium cannot possibly allow.

With these considerations in mind, then, we might hazard the following as a classification of threats to the podium's face in White House briefings, in order of increasing severity. A questioner may ask for, encourage or force one or more of the following acts, in order of seriousness:

1   State or justify your own opinion;
2   Admit you personally were wrong;
3   State or justify your client's opinion or action;
4   State or confirm your client's course of future action;
5   Admit disagreement among different clients;
6   Admit something your client *said* was wrong;
7   Admit something your client *did* was wrong.

7.4.2   Threats to the questioner's face

Best also notes that, although far more rare, face-threatening acts from the interviewee do occur. He lists two general types, attacks on the question and attacks on the questioner, which are sub-divided as follows:

(A)   *Attacks on the question*

1   The source of the information;
2   The relevance of the question to the subject in hand;
3   The appropriacy of the question to an interview context.

(B)   *Attacks on the interviewer*

1   Undermining of the interviewer's role;
2   Generalized attack on the BBC (the interviewer's institution);
3   Personal criticism of the interviewer.

Again, these are listed in ascending order of weight.

He reports that 'attacks on the question are much more common than attacks on the interviewer' (Best 1996: 4.51). This concords with the findings reported in the previous chapter (Section 6.6) concerning these briefings.

We can apply Best's findings to briefings discourse. Taking Group A first (attacks on the question), we have already seen ways in which the podium attacks 'the source of the information' (A1), that is, how he denies the accounts of sources (see Section 5.6.1). As regards attacking the 'relevance' or 'appropriacy' of the question (A2, A3), it is less common for the podium, compared with the kind of news interviewee in Best's study, to challenge questions in such ways, since briefings are wide ranging in topic and the press are fairly free to ask what they will. To this first group, however, we might add 'attacking the coherency of the question':

(7) MR LOCKHART: Because you're comparing apples and oranges here.

Similarly:

(8) Q: Why did the President wait until the Vice President unleashed his faith-based approach at the Salvation Army Center in Atlanta before bypassing the Senate and appointing Mr Hormel?
     MR LOCKHART: Those two issues had nothing to do with each other.

and 'attacking the propriety of the question':

(9) MR LOCKHART: It would take 10 minutes for me to unravel all of the deception that is in that question.

As regards Group B (attacks on the interviewer), first of all, since the roles of questioner and respondent are clearly defined in the institution of briefings, there is no attempt by the podium to 'undermine the interviewer's role' (B1) of the kind Best describes (1996: 4.521). Furthermore, there are no general attacks on 'the media institutions' (B2) any of the questioners work for, and any 'personal criticism of individual interviewers' (B3) is generally of the joshing type:

(10) MR McCURRY: When you need a good, bizarre question, boy, I tell you, it's really helpful to have Lester Kinsolving. (Laughter.)
(11) MR LOCKHART: Sam, if you're late, we aren't going to wait for you.

On one occasion only do we find an expression of dissatisfaction with the press as a group:

(12) MR McCURRY: No – I mean, we've seen the same kind of anecdotal reporting that some of you are carrying in your own reports.

But this is as rare as it is dangerous. It is less risky if the target is left unspecified:

(13) MR LOCKHART: I think the President uses his words carefully because there are many who would like to twist them around and turn them upside down.

Making lists of the type discussed in Sections 7.4.1 and 7.4.2 is always somewhat dangerous since the actual severity of a face-threatening act will always depend largely on context, on the relationship between interlocutors, on voice and gesture and so on. What we can safely say is that classifications of types of face-threatening acts and the perception of their relative severity will differ from one genre of talk to another, even genres as superficially similar as news interviews and briefings.

7.5 Positive politeness

7.5.1 The podium's search for complicity

The press, as we have seen on numerous occasions, generally assume the right to attack the podium's positive face. The podium rarely responds in kind. We have already mentioned how the podium attempts to blandish and conciliate the press – with varying degrees of success. These we might reinterpret in the light of the concept of positive politeness as follows.

Positive politeness ' "anoints" the face of the addresee [...] by treating him as a member of an in-group, a friend, a person whose wants and personality traits are known and liked' (Brown and Levinson 1987: 70), and has been condensed by R. Lakoff (1973b) into the maxim 'make your receiver feel good'. The three main strategies for doing so are as follows:

- claim common ground with the hearer, imply that their desires and yours coincide;
- convey that you wish to cooperate with the hearer to fulfil their wishes;
- fulfil the hearer's needs and desires.

Precisely because the third of these is not always possible or in the podium's interest, he must spend more time on the first two, emphasizing common concerns with the press and expressing interest in them and their affairs. One obvious way of doing so is to compliment the audience:

(14) MR BERGER: I wish I had the clip. This is actually in the Iraqi news service, which does show that the American journalistic profession is superior to the Iraqi journalistic profession. (Laughter.)

There are individual compliments on the incisive nature of a particular question (especially when the podium cannot or does not intend to give an answer) as witnessed in this extract from a sentence concordance of *good question*:

1   MR LOCKHART: That is a **good question** of which I do not know the answer. Let me look into it, and we'll try to post an answer to that.
2   MR TOIV: I'm sorry, Helen. It's a real **good question** to which I do not have the answer and you know who is the only person who has the answer to that question […]
3   MR McCURRY: Can you hold off for a second? That's a **good question**; we'll come back to it. Any more on Kosovo?

One of the ways of claiming common ground listed by Brown and Levinson is to stress membership of an in-group. The podium does this by extensive use of in-group jargon, language related specifically to the 'work we do' (inclusive *we*, that is, me and you). Such items include: *downsize -ing, empowerment -ing, a build-down, upcoming* as in 'her upcoming testimony' or even 'in his remarks that are upcoming' (this latter from the press). The common use of sporting jargon with a predominantly male audience is probably felt to be particularly group-building: *in the ballpark* (a rough approximation), *handicap in advance* (guess, estimate), *quarterbacking* (masterminding).[7]

The regular use of abbreviations for bodies and activities that both sides know about has the same in-group solidifying function:

(15)   MR McCURRY: […] He stated his own policy of seeking MFN renewal this year.[8]
(16)   MR McCURRY: […] By the way, just – at the end of last week, the Blue Chip revised its forecast. And again, it's more optimistic than either OMB or CBO, even the new and improved CBO.[9]

as does the routine use of first names we have already discussed earlier. These are particular examples of the role of *contraction* and *ellipsis* in positive politeness:

the use of ellipsis and contraction is associated with positive politeness […] Because of the reliance on shared mutual knowledge to make ellipsis comprehensible, there is an inevitable association between the use of ellipsis and the existence of in-group shared knowledge

(Brown and Levinson 1987: 111)

The podium's talk is also peppered with in-jokes. Often they are about some quality of an individual known to all:

(17)   MR LOCKHART: But I'd suggest you just give Jim Kennedy a call, who is a vastly under-used person here. (Laughter.)
(18)   Q: […] Will the President try to nudge a decision out of her in the interest of the party?
       MR LOCKHART: You've got to be kidding me. (Laughter) No.

Everyone knows that Mr Kennedy in example (17) is very busy and so the joke is ironic. In example (18), the 'her' in question is Mrs Clinton, who has a reputation for independent-mindedness.

They can even be directed at an individual member of the audience:

(19) MR LOCKHART: [...] Sam, if you're late, we're not going to wait for you. (Laughter.)

The complicity of a single member of the audience – in this case, Sam, who presumably has a reputation for tardiness – can be sacrificed to obtain that of the group. In general:

> joking is a basic positive-politeness strategy, for putting [the hearer] 'at ease' [...] Since jokes are based on mutual shared background knowledge and values, jokes may be used to stress that shared background or those shared values.
>
> (Brown and Levinson 1987: 124)

A further important way of manifesting positive politeness, of 'anointing the face' of one's interlocutor, is to show, to exaggerate even, an interest in their affairs and concerns (Brown and Levinson 1987: 103–7). We have already seen several occasions when the podium tries to soft-soap a questioner. All manner of attempts to involve the audience in small talk also fall into this category (Brown and Levinson 1987: 117–18). But this also explains a particular common feature of the podium's language, namely that the podium very often takes a good deal more time than is strictly necessary to answer a simple *yes* or *no* or *I don't know*. All things being equal, the more time spent on replying, the more interest shown in the questioner and his question. This, what we might term *phatic verbosity* in the service of politeness, is very probably not confined to the kind of text examined here. As a teacher I frequently find myself spending rather longer on responding to a student's question than it might actually merit in order to encourage the questioner and avoid giving offence. A simple example of a long-winded *yes*:

(20) Q: Those are Contact Group meetings?
      MR McCURRY: Those are Contact Group meetings.

A *no* when there is nothing much of substance to say:

(21) Q: Is the President at this point considering sending any administration official over to London or Ireland or Northern Ireland to participate in efforts to get this back on track – Lake or perhaps others?
      MR McCURRY: There are no definite plans that I'm aware of at the moment for US government officials to travel to work on that issue, in particular. Now, Senator Mitchell, who retains his position as a special advisor to the President and the Secretary of State on economic matters

related to Northern Ireland, has a previously scheduled trip to London,
but it's in connection with another subject. I believe the subject is
Bosnia, not the Northern Ireland peace process.

The length of the response here serves a dual purpose: to massage the hearer's
face but also to protect the speaker's. The podium takes a long time over a *no* to
a question of the type 'are you doing x?' partly to defuse any suggestion potentially inherent in such a question of '*why* aren't you doing x?' (in this particular
case 'why aren't you doing more to get this back on track by sending someone to
Northern Ireland?').

This must be interpreted in the light of one of Labov and Fanshel's discourse
rules, the *rule of overdue obligations*, which states that:

> If A asserts that B has not performed obligations in role R, then A is heard
> as challenging B's competence in R.
>
> (Labov and Fanshel 1977: 96)

In some cases, as in example (21), it may be enough for A to *imply* that B has
not performed their obligations, even simply by *asking whether or not* they have
been carried out, for A to be heard (including by B, the podium in this case) as
challenging B's competence.

Sometimes the politeness is directed not just at the questioner:

(22)   Q: One more on Africa. Does the President have any plans to go to Nigeria
            for Obasango's inauguration?
        MR LOCKHART: I think we have received an invitation to attend the inau-
            guration. I think the President is honored to get it. The President and
            the U.S. government has been very involved in facilitating the shift from
            military to civilian rule. I'm certain that a high-level and appropriate
            delegation will attend, but I know of no decision on whether the
            President himself will attend.

It is usual conversational practice to take longer over refusing (the dispreferred
response) rather than accepting (the preferred response) an *offer*, since it is
necessary to soothe any potential offence to the offerer's face (Levinson 1983:
307–8, 332–45). The podium takes time to charm the face of the Nigerian
government, who made the offer, as well as to pay attention to the question and
the questioner.

Long responses also allow the podium to indulge still another positive
politeness mechanism, namely, wherever possible to *seek agreement* and *avoid open
disagreement* with the interlocutor (Brown and Levinson 1987: 112–16). Part of
seeking agreement is the raising of 'safe topics', ones on which there is bound to
be common ground.

(23)   Q: Joe, a lot of people want to know what our exit strategy is. Can you shed
       any light on that?
       MR LOCKHART: Well, I think it may be the wrong way to look at this. Let
       me talk a little bit about what we believe the objectives to be. I think
       quite simply – and I'll talk in a little more detail – is that our objective
       is to stop the killing and achieve a durable peace that prevents further
       repression and provides for democratic self-government for the Kosovar
       people.

The questioner raises a question, about NATO's so-called *exit strategy*, which is
both impossible for the podium to answer (see Section 5.5) and which has also
been used in the past as a stick with which to beat the administration. The
podium moves the agenda on to the more congenial ground of ensuring the security and rights of the oppressed. Who could take issue with that? However, the
strategy of raising safe topics is rarely a wholly successful one. The press interpret
it as evading the question and seldom fail to return to the matter.

   Politeness, though, is not the only reason why long replies are common.
As Harris explains:

> in the context of a political interview we expect politicians to elaborate, even
> when asked questions which require a "yes/no" response.
>
> (Harris 1991: 82)

That is to say, elaborate responses in this context are appropriate to the situation
and serve specific functions:

> a politician is primarily concerned to get his/her message across to the over-
> hearing audience rather than attempting merely to influence the questioner.
>
> (Harris 1991: 82–3)

And therefore:

> politicians are likely to produce highly elaborated answers, and 'yes' +
> elaboration is equally common to 'no' + elaboration.
>
> (Harris 1991: 83)

However, the *situational appropriacy* of long responses for the podium cuts still
deeper. The press attend briefings with the expectancy, the need even, of producing copy at the end of the exercise. It is much more convenient for the podium
to prattle on (if the topic is safe, that is – dangerous ones are an entirely different
affair) and give them copy on his own terms rather than force them to make it up,
to use their fertile and none-too-amicable imaginations.

7.5.2   *The perils of bragging*

Since the administration is so frequently under attack, it is the podium's duty to
defend it, if possible to sing its praises. But there is a fine line between this and

being seen as boasting, as showing off. Moreover, according once more to Brown and Levinson (1987: 67), bragging, along with any kind of self-ostentation, is a direct threat to the hearer's face. Promoting one's own face is likely to diminish that of others in comparison and implies that 'the S[peaker] doesn't care about H[earer]'s feelings'. It is, in other words, one of the quickest ways of forfeiting common ground.

The podium then is often careful to temper the temptation to crow:

(24)   MR McCURRY: […] We clearly, *like any White House*, want to make sure that the very strong news on the economy today dominated the President's message today. We had – we've now created 15 million jobs since this President came to office in 1993. We've got the lowest unemployment rate in 25 years. We created 310,000 new jobs – *the American people did*, in the month of February. That is very good news and the President, *like most Presidents have before him*, wanted to make sure that you all focused on that very important message.

The podium is trying to switch topics from questioning about the Clinton–Lewinsky case to the safer ground of encouraging news on the economy. However, he is aware that taking the credit for good news can be seen as hubris and as an afterthought assigns some of the merit to 'the American people'. He also twice emphasizes that this administration is only acting as all others have done in wanting to talk about the positive things that happen under its aegis: 'like any White House', 'like most Presidents have before him'.

Where the podium is allowed a certain license to brag is when talking of the efforts and achievements of third parties, even if linked to the administration:

(25)   MR BELL: […] and very skillful negotiations by our lead negotiators […]
(26)   MR McCURRY: […] but I imagine that our embassy staff, being the very effective staff that it is […]

The press is also relatively indulgent to podium rhetoric when he is wearing his hat as champion of the Democratic party. After one particular bout of party-political grandiloquence, Mr McCurry, whose common touch rarely fails him, realizes he has thumped the tub rather hard:

(27)   MR McCURRY: Want a little bit more of that? (Laughter.)
       Q: No, that's enough. (Laughter.)
       Q: Maybe later.
       MR McCURRY: I don't think they're going to ask that question again.
       Q: Read that back to him.

Presumably, since the real destination of party-political tub-thumping is the opposition, the Republicans, the press feel that their own face is under no threat from this particular type of boasting.

7.5.3 *Common ground or no-man's land? – the impossible job*

How do the podium's tactics of using positive politeness to seek common ground and defuse antagonism with the press square with what Mr McCurry had to say, reported at the beginning of the previous chapter, about the adversarial, combative nature of their relationship?

(28) MR McCURRY: I am much too close to the combat that we've enjoyed here to make any profound comments […] look, this is a contentious environment, and it is, by design, an adversarial relationship.

Realizing it may have been inopportune to characterize his relationship with the press in quite this way, later in the same (his last) session, Mr McCurry specifies that the two sides in the 'combat' are the press and the President. He is asked the question:

(29) Q: Who does a press secretary work for? Does he work for the press? Does he work for the President?

To which he responds (after a little initial confusion):

(30) MR McCURRY: […] you work for both sides of this equation. I like to tell people, my office is perfectly situated as a geographic metaphor here in the White House – 50 feet in one direction is the Oval Office, and 50 feet away is here where we are dealing with you. And that's the role of the Press Secretary, to be equi-distant between two combatants in this adversarial relationship.

thus defining himself as a neutral in no-man's-land between the two armies. Not a comfortable situation, of course. A little later he also defines his mediation thus:

(31) MR McCURRY: Look, when you're in the middle of the – I like to say I'm the chum in the feeding frenzy.

He is metaphorically surrounded by ravenous sharks.

This is, in fact, a motif of podium talk. They very frequently depict themselves as: (a) man in the middle, referee and/or (b) being in a very difficult, almost impossible role, under torture even. In example (32), Mr McCurry appeals for press clemency over the question of court proceedings under seal:

(32) MR McCURRY: The lawyers here at the White House take that so seriously that they make me go through the kind of torture I'm going through right now because they can't discuss those matters outside court.

The podium portrays himself as an interrogation subject, a quiz-show contestant, facing the most awkward questions:

(33) Q: Joe, on China –
      MR LOCKHART: Sure. An easy one, China. (Laughter.)
(34) Q: Change of subject?
      MR McCURRY: Please. (Laughter.)

as often as not *trick* questions designed to catch him out:

(35) MR LOCKHART: I think that's about the question you asked me a few min-
      utes ago. I'll give you the same answer. Good try, though.
(36) MR TOIV: You got me on that one. (Laughter.)
      Q: Dinner for two. (Laughter.)

The press are infected by this victimism. During Mr McCurry's last briefing:

(37) Q: […] And also, you have this kind of 'free at last' sense today, and
      I wondered –
      MR McCURRY: Free at last? […] Does it show? (Laughter.)

He even playfully complains about his employers:

(38) Q: Well, have you seen reports that he will be going to Japan?
      MR McCURRY: I've seen those news reports. (Laughter.) See, even on my
      last day, they don't trust me. (Laughter.)

The 'they' who don't trust him is the administration. Elsewhere he complains about the 'gobblygook' (nonsense) he is sometimes forced to read out. The impli-cation is that he is in the same position, on the same side, as the audience.

These are very useful politeness strategies for the podium. In asking for the audience's clemency, one is implying that one's interlocutor is important and pow-erful but at the same time capable of goodness. It anoints their face in no meagre fashion. And judging from the good-humoured laughter which usually follows, it is very effective in winning over a vain press. Moreover, it invites sympathy and understanding, thus establishing complicity and common ground. In addition, by implying that the *real* adversary is elsewhere, it deflects antagonism away from him and defuses disagreement with him.

An extreme tactic in the search for compassion and complicity is that of apparent self-deprecation, of self-disparaging humour. Mr Lockhart is the main exponent:

(39) Q: Is the General in the doghouse here?
      MR LOCKHART: Here? There is no doghouse here; if there was, I'd live
      there. (Laughter.)

(40)   MR LOCKHART: [...] I'm not quite as dumb as I look, Jim. Close, but –
       (Laughter.)
(41)   Q: Joe, is The New York Times one of the papers that you read carefully?
       MR LOCKHART: Some days, but they use a lot of big words, so it's some-
       times hard to understand. (Laughter.)

This is, of course, linked to the concept of the 'difficult job'. The podium presents himself as out of his depth in this tough role. And it has the added bonus
of depicting him as 'a regular guy', no intellectual but smart enough to get by: an
attractive figure in US culture [note (1) to Chapter 4].

Self-deprecation is listed by Brown and Levinson (1987: 68) as one of the ways
a speaker can damage their own positive face, along with *inter alia*: confessions of
guilt, apologizing and emotional leakage. When, however, it is *humorous* self-
deprecation the phenomenon is more subtle. It increases the speaker's face by
depicting them as convivial and anoints the hearer's face by depicting them too as
congenial enough to enjoy the joke. Moreover, self-*effacement* is one of the main
characteristics of negative politeness.

Furthermore, when the podiums point explicitly to the difficulty of their role,
they are necessarily stepping outside that role for a moment to focus on it from
outside. In doing this they shift footing from that of a paid representative to that
of a harassed individual and invite their interlocutors to also see them thus. As
individual human beings they have altogether different rights, duties and potential strategies in terms of politeness, they can treat – and expect to be treated
by – the audience in an entirely new way. In particular, no longer in the role of
interviewee, they acquire more and better rights in terms of negative face.

7.6   Negative politeness

Negative face, we will recall, is the desire to be left in peace to pursue one's interests while negative politeness is attention paid to such desire, and can be summarized as 'do not impose'. However:

> Questions of any kind are an attack on the interviewee's negative face, in that
> they infringe upon the questionee's right to be unimpeded.
>
> (Best 1996: 4.31)

When the respondent is *paid* to reply to questions, or has otherwise volunteered
to fill the interviewee role, according to Jucker they relinquish normal rights to
negative face:

> The interviewee has undertaken to be publicly questioned on a certain topic
> and therefore his/her negative face is for the time being to some extent put
> out of force.
>
> (Jucker 1986: 73)

As mentioned in Section 7.4.1, this is the practice of interview neutralism. The interviewer/journalist has greater than normal power to impose on interviewee space, the interviewee/podium less than normal right to be free from imposition and attack.

7.6.1   *Syntactic clues to negative face threats*

However, this suspension of rights is only partial: in the quotation above the podium's negative face is said to be '*to some extent* out of force'. The question is: to *what* extent? Best argues that we can ascertain the severity of an attack on the interviewee's face by looking at the question syntax:

> The syntactic form which the question takes varies its negative face threat-ening potential considerably. Syntax forms a useful benchmark for measuring the extent of the attack on negative face, and is therefore important when considering whether a question is 'hostile and caustic'.
>
> (Best 1996: 4.31)

He looks at three constructions:

(1) *Polar yes/no questions and narrow* wh-*questions*; which he claims 'are attacks on negative face in that they attempt to pin the interviewee down, whereas the inter-viewee may wish to provide only the sketchiest of outlines' (Best 1996: 4.321). Narrow *wh*-questions include *who, where, when, which*, in contradistinction to broader *wh*-questions (*what, why, how*) which allow a wider scope to the response (Woodbury 1984, quoted in Jucker 1986).

(2) *Questions in the imperative voice*; for example: 'Remind us of the rule because there's always a bit of debate …'. The directness of the imperative 'obviously con-travenes the interviewee's right […] to freedom from imposition' (Best 1996: 4.323)

(3) *Moodless questions* (or *chipping in*); for example:

(42)   INTERVIEWEE: […] the reforms to our constitution, which Britain has
           needed for SO long, to bring our constitution up to date
       INTERVIEWER: including reforming the House of Lords?
                                                     (quoted in Best 1996: 4.324)

These are openly 'demeaning the interviewee's negative face' (Best 1996: 4.324)

Best (1996: 4.33) finds relatively more polar and narrow *wh*-questions in his data compared to Jucker's from 10 years earlier. Over this time he claims 'there is a net movement to polar questions' which leads him to conclude 'that interview-ers seem to be narrowing the range of possible responses available to their inter-viewee by the use of polar questions'. His data contains few examples of the broader *wh*- kind.

We can examine these findings in terms of the briefings. Taking the Q-file (which, if we recall, contains questioner moves only), we have a sample of 131 moves (some of which do not contain a question, either defined in grammatical or functional terms, and some of which conversely include more than one). The occurrence of *wh-* type questions is as follows:

'Narrow' wh-questions	'Broad' wh-questions
Who: 1	*What*: 24[10]
Where: 1	*Why*: 12
When: 3	*How*: 8[11]
Which: 1	
Total 6	Total 44

There is thus a clear preponderance of the broader type question.

As regards the polar questions, there are 14 occurrences of *do/does/did* (e.g. '*Do* you have a clear position on criminal liability?', 'It turns out, he wasn't really asked those questions. *Does* that trouble the White House?') and 14 occurrences of *is/are/was/were*: (e.g. '*Is* the census a non-negotiable item?', 'Joe, *was* it appropriate – along the same vein, *is* it appropriate for the President to be raising money...'). There are also four occurrences of *has/have* polar questions.

These results are not easy to interpret, since we do not have data we can compare them to on the relative proportions of 'narrow *wh-*', 'broad *wh-*' and polar questions in other genres of English. However, they do not seem to comfort the hypothesis, deriving from Best's findings, that broad type questions (those which supposedly give an interviewee plenty of scope in their response) are comparatively rare. Quite the reverse in fact; they are the most frequent type in this data. Of course, one explanation might be that the briefing genre is different from that of the news interview (studied by Best) in a number of ways. There are several journalists competing for questioning time and their questions may well be less prepared, more spontaneous, than that of a studio interviewer on air. The questions tend to sweep over a wider range of topics. There are many more questions put in a longer period of time.

In any case, these results suggest that somewhat different politeness principles are in force in this data and that the journalists do *not* always wish to tie the podium down to specifics. A longer reply is more likely to satisfy their need for copy. In a free-ranging response, the podium just might let something slip.

What does stand out very clearly in the briefings data, on the other hand, is the paucity of *indirectness* in the questioning, whether polar or otherwise. If we recall, indirectness is one of the main indications of the use of negative politeness, of reducing threat to face in a question, and its scarcity in the journalists' moves is significant. The following is one of the few examples in the Q-files:

(43)   Q: Mike, the Senate voted today on a State Department authorization bill and *I wonder if you could* comment on two aspects.

Any polite indirectness or hedging (see below) tends to be reserved for delicate, particularly face-threatening questions, for example:

(44) Q: Mike, that doesn't really answer the question, though. Because you're saying to them, *if what I'm taking is correct*, you're saying, you figure out whether you think it's a good deal [...]

Here, the questioner accuses the podium of failing to answer and needs to be a little cautious in their language.

These, however, are exceptions to a general rule of directness of questioning. The explanation of this lack of indirectness lies in both the journalists' license with interviewee face and also to the familiarity, the routineness of the situation (that is, the closeness on the sociological dimension of 'distance').

A second way of reducing the face-threatening weight of a question, according to Jucker (1986: 136–8), is to give a reason, an account, as to why one is asking. Jucker finds that 5 per cent of all the questions in his material include an account of some sort. In contrast they are relatively uncommon in the briefings corpus. The following are a couple of examples (found by concordancing *because* in the Q-file):

(45) Q: We ask because past Presidents have specifically insisted they have the right to deploy U.S. forces –
(46) Q: The question about the language is important because there is a move afoot to take the language, adjourn the trial, put the language before the Senate as a legislative body as opposed to a trial body. So would you object to that?

The *language* in example (46) is that contained in a Senate motion hostile to the President. There are two reasons for the relative scarcity of such accounts in briefings. First of all, there is an expectation (especially on the part of other journalists) that questions be kept short. Secondly, as we have seen, less care is taken in briefings to preserving interviewee face.

7.6.2 *Hedging and modality*

To recapitulate, negative politeness dictates: do not coerce, do not presume on the other's time, and if you must do so, give reasons, excuses and apologies: that is, *hedge* your imposition.

There are two ways of looking at the category of items known as hedges.[12] In politeness theory and discourse studies, in general, they are usually defined as words or phrases which *modify* the force of an utterance, either *softening* it:

> **hedge/hedging device**: an item that softens the force of an expression in some way, e.g. *sort of, if you see what I mean.*
>
> (Lombardo *et al.* 1999: 297)

or relaxing the requirement on the speaker to be *precise*:

> **hedge** (noun/verb) [...] a range of items which express a notion of imprecision or qualification. Examples include *sort of, more or less, I mean, approximately, roughly*.
>
> (Crystal 1997: 182)

In some way they tone down the illocutionary force of an utterance.

The second way of defining hedges is in terms of formal grammar, where hedging is related to modality, to modal space, defined as the speakers' room for manoeuvre between absolute *yes* and absolute *no* (Halliday 1985: 85–9; Thompson 1997: 57). When interlocutors are *exchanging information* (using statements and questions), as is often the case in briefings, the positive and negative poles are realized through, respectively, asserting and denying the truth of a proposition. In between these two poles, however, there lie degrees of indeterminacy involving the probability that something is true: *possibly / probably / almost certainly* and degrees of the frequency or usualness that something is true: *rarely / sometimes / usually* (O'Donnell 1990: 219).

When speakers make *offers*, the space between the absolute positive *will do it* and the absolute negative *won't do it* is defined as 'the degree of willingness or inclination of the speaker to fulfil the offer [...] ability/willingness/determination' (Thompson 1997: 57). Since, for our purposes, 'offers' includes 'promises', this scale is also clearly relevant to political language in general and our briefings in particular.

As regards *commands*, the degree of obligation can be modulated between positive *do it* and negative *don't do it*: the interlocutor may be *allowed / supposed / required* to do it. This dimension is probably less relevant to briefings discourse than the others.

In English, the two principal ways of expressing modality in the utterance are auxiliaries attached to the verb (modal verbal operators) and the broad set of items collected together under the general heading of *Mood Adjuncts*. For our ends, we will take the latter to be the equivalent in grammatical description of the hedging devices of discourse studies.

As regards their function, in particular their rhetorical and psychological function, hedges are closely associated with the expression of modesty. As Caffi (1999) reports, mitigation is mentioned as early as 86–82 BC. in the classical text *Rhetorica ad Herennium* whose *auctor* explains how it is used to avoid an impression of arrogance. The role of modesty and its opposite, boasting, in these briefings was discussed earlier. Furthermore, 'the rhetorical categories closest to [...] hedges are euphemism, litotes, understatement and periphrasis' (Caffi 1999: 906), all indicators of verbal restraint.

Other writers, however, have defined hedges in a slightly different way. We have so far said that hedges set a proposition as being somewhere in the space denoting *less* than 100 per cent true, necessary, possible *etc.*, hence definitions of hedging as 'softening', 'qualifying' and so on. But some have argued that utterance propositions often deal in terms of *expectations* and so it is perfectly possible for something to be *more* true, necessary, possible, and so on, than expected. Under this definition even intensifiers such as *absolute, truly, really, exceptionally* would qualify as hedges. Note that this broader definition 'is an extension of the colloquial sense of "hedge"' (Brown and Levinson 1987: 145).

7.6.3   Hedging in the briefings

In this section we look at the use of hedges for politeness purposes in both the podium's and the press's language. We have already looked at some of the most common hedges in this material: the podium's use of phrases like *I think, I believe, I doubt, I'm aware of* as truth or accuracy hedging mechanisms, that is, to declare '*to the best of my knowledge* what I'm saying is the case' (so-called *quality* hedges in Gricean terms, Brown and Levinson 1987: 164–5). The first two of these also have a negative politeness function, in that they reduce speaker imposition on hearer; they imply 'I am not *telling* you this, I merely think or believe it to be so'. Their use is so common on the podium's part as to be practically habitual. The following are the first four of the 32 occurrences in just one briefing:

1   But **I think** as the President and others said yesterday, keeping Kosovo as part of Serbia is what Milosevic wants most.
2   **I think** having said that, we are concerned about these statements because of the signal that may be received in Belgrade.
3   So **I think** he wants to recognize the work they do there, the sacrifices they make.
4   I was disappointed in some of the coverage of that, but **I think** he has spoken and he'll continue to speak.

These are very rarely responses to a 'Do you think that ...' question (which occurs only once in this particular briefing). They are instead being used as what Brown and Levinson (1987: 145) call 'hedged performatives' (G. Lakoff 1973), that is, items which modify the force of a speech act. Roughly half of them are turn initial and another part of their function is to give the speaker a moment's thinking time (see Section 4.3.1 on *discourse managing* I).

Still more imposition-mitigating is *I thought* which is used by both podium and press:

1   Q: I mean, it was a day for the President, **I thought** maybe he and his wife talked on the phone.
2   Q: **I thought** the President said it includes other than the air campaign
3   Okay. **I thought** this was pretty important stuff, though.
4   The report, **I thought**, was clear about the medicinal value of some of the compounds in marijuana
5   I think – I watched him this morning, and **I thought** he was pretty clear, but you can put any questions directly to him

This implies 'please correct me if I'm wrong'. The past tense of the verb in these examples is an instance of the *distancing* (non-temporal) use of this tense. Pastness, or distance from the here-and-now can be reinterpreted as distance from *reality* (see Thompson 1997: 185 for unreal meanings even in the present *i.e.* 'If I *had* a hammer'), or distance from the *speaker* (see Morley 1998: 89–93 on the journalistic use of the past for signalling the *reporting* of others' words or opinions). In using *I thought* in this way, the speaker distances themselves from the propositional content of their utterance for politeness purposes, allowing the hearer to challenge it should they so wish. This extra politeness technique is useful when the gist of an utterance is particularly face-threatening as in the following questioner turn:

(47)   Q: And related to that, this morning you were, *I thought*, a little less than unequivocal that U.S. troops had to be part of any NATO –

It is one of a series of hedges which the speaker deems necessary since they are telling the podium that they have been unclear or misleading. The tactic is successful since the podium's responding turn is apologetic (though note that the questioner's deference perhaps encourages the podium to interrupt – too much politeness can be risky):

(48)   MR LOCKHART: I didn't mean to be and that was my loose language [...]

If we accept the wider definition of hedges, that they may strengthen as well as soften the modality of an utterance, some Quality hedges (hedges on truth) can stress the speaker's commitment to the truth of their utterance, in other words, their *honesty*. Brown and Levinson (1987: 164–5) cite the hedging expression '*With complete honesty*, I can say'. A concordance of *honest – honesty – honestly* from the briefings threw up these examples:

1   I **honestly** don't know how often they talk, but I'm sure they talk fairly often.
2   I believe it is Kendall and Ms Seligman that he meets with, but I **honestly** don't know.
3   Well, I **honestly** don't know how the jurisdiction gets decided [...]
4   Do you know what that means?
    MR LOCKHART: I **honestly** don't know what that means.
5   Low turnout wouldn't mean much of anything, to be **honest** with you.
6   Q: I meant no pejorative there, Joe, in all **honesty**.

All but the last one are uttered by the podium, and four of these five are used to qualify *I don't know*. It is almost as if at times he needs to stress that he *really* doesn't know the answer as opposed to those times when not knowing something is an evasion. The final example, uttered by a journalist, occurs in a moment of tension when the journalist needs to defuse a particularly face-threatening move during which the podium has shown signs of taking offence:

(49)   Q: Joe, I want to go back at something. I think it's a fair question and maybe deserves a thoughtful answer, which perhaps we haven't received so far. (Laughter.)
MR LOCKHART: Do I get to decide whether it's a fair question?
Q: I meant no pejorative there, Joe, in all honesty.

A general comment on truth strengthening may be useful here. Other examples occur in the following exchange:

(50)   MR LOCKHART: [...] That sort of ad hominem attack on Mr Hormel has come from various sources over the last year. It has no basis in fact –
Q: No, he saluted these people –
MR LOCKHART: It has no basis in fact –
Q: It does, Joe.
MR LOCKHART: Well, having spoken to Mr Hormel directly on this subject, it has no basis in fact.

The phrase *it has no basis in fact*, used three times by the podium, is of course a truth-strengthening way of saying that 'Mr Hormel denies it'. It makes Mr Hormel's position more factual, more real, than a simple *claim* not to have said it. Truth-strengthening of a claim is extremely face threatening and is thus fairly unusual, a last resort. As here, it occurs when positions are radically entrenched, when each side is loath to accept the other's version.

Other Quality hedges are based on the concept of memory, for example:

(51)   Q: *If I remember correctly*, these negotiations – and please correct me if I'm wrong – were seen as a way to [...]

That is, they declare 'to the best of my *memory* (as opposed to *knowledge* as in the previous examples) what I am saying is correct'. The politeness function is clearly both negative and positive. They first of all lighten the imposition on the hearer by reducing speaker certainty, thus allowing the hearer to choose between believing and not believing what is said. Secondly, they anoint the hearer's face by implying that their memory is undoubtedly better.

7.6.4   *Quantity hedges: imprecision and evasion*

Another group of hedges relevant to politeness are *quantity* hedges, which give notice that the information given may not be as *much* or not as *precise* as possible or as expected (Brown and Levinson 1987: 166–7). These include: *roughly, more or less, or so, I should think, I can't really say more than that, I'll just say.*

It is, of course, quite normal in human communication to be less precise than is absolutely necessary. Sperber and Wilson (1995: 233–7) have termed this phenomenon *loose talk* and give the following example. In reply to the question 'how much do you earn?':

> I can choose between the strictly literal and truthful answer (a), and the less
> than literal (b), which I know to be strictly speaking false:
> (a) I earn £797.32 pence a month
> (b) I earn £800 a month
>
> (Sperber and Wilson 1995: 233)

The fact that in normal conversational circumstances most people choose the
latter is explained in terms of *relevance*, of optimal communicability. The second
answer gives as much information, and no more, as is appropriate to most conversational situations. The first would be appropriate (and relevant) when filling
out a tax form. The concept of loose talk is also used by Sperber and Wilson to
account for many other language phenomena, including metaphor and figurative
language in general (see Chapter 10).

The appropriacy of (b) is of course equally explicable in terms of politeness
phenomenon, since in normal conversation (a) would be overburdening the
hearer, thus threatening their negative face. But, in briefings the question of precision and lack of it is a much hotter issue than in conversation, and what would
be normal imprecision in everyday talk, could well be a podium tactic for evasion
and a bone of contention for the press. In other words, the podium might argue
that an utterance of his contained an element of imprecision merely out of
respect for normal conversational politeness requirements, but the press may fail
to accept this suggestion and push for further details. Looked at the other way
round, the podium may often be tempted to seek comfort in the many quantity
hedges supplied by the language in situations where he cannot, for whatever reason, be more exact.

The press, of course, are fully aware of the evasive possibilities of certain kinds
of language. At one point, Mr Lockhart is informed:

(52) Q: Joe, the Vice President has said flatly that there will be no ground
      troops. Is he a little off the reservation there?

He said so 'flatly', in other words, he did not hedge. The podium is happy to be
able to confirm:

(53) MR LOCKHART: No, I think the Vice President is articulating administra-
      tion policy.

The questioner can hardly believe their ears:

(54) Q: But he didn't use the word "intend" or "no plans" or anything like that.
      MR LOCKHART: The Vice President articulates the administration's policy.

In other words, a high-ranking figure in the administration has made a bald, on-
record policy statement without the safety-net of modality-altering hedges like *we*

do not intend or *there are no plans*, which both podium and press know are code terms meaning: it is not going to happen tomorrow, but in the future, who knows? Without these stock safety-devices the Vice President's statement will be nailed to the mast if there is a policy change, and the press are keen to point this out.

7.6.5   *One hedge, different uses: concordances of just*

It is interesting to compare the way common hedges are employed differently by the two sides. For instance, concordance evidence shows how the item *just* is often used when the podium adopts the footing of *relayer/spokesperson*. It lightens the burden of listening to official news and information: 'let me *just* bring you up to date', 'let me *just* add to that', 'let me first *just* do a quick read out'. It is also used to minimize the import of potentially controversial acts or statements carried out by parties the podium represents: 'We have *just* said, look, our views on tort reform are pretty well-known', or to minimize his own shortcomings, especially his evasiveness: 'I'm *just* declining to get into specifics on that'. It is used to soften disagreement with other bodies, especially 'friendly' ones (here the CBO): 'No, we *just* – we *just* don't think they're right'.

But *just* can also express a modal sense of firmness, of resolution, especially in combination with *not going to*:

1   I'm **just** *not going to* get into a debate about a report
2   I'm **just** *not going to* answer a hypothetical question like that
3   I'm **just** *not going to* get into that.
4   I'm **just** *not going to* walk down a speculative road here today
5   I'm **just** *not going to* get into drawing up a prescription on a daily basis
6   I'm **just** *not going to* go down the road and make decisions.
7   I'm **just** *not going to* get into details here,
8   No. It **just** means I'm *not going to* talk about a private conversation

or other future expressions, such as *going to* and *have to*:

1   where we're making the real decisions, and we're **just** *going to have to* wait until we get the process done.
2   they don't have the specific question to address. We'll **just** *have to* see what happens.

where the podium wishes to imply that his is the final word on the matter. The podium *does* have the power of the last word (Section 8.5), but often has to tussle with the press to use it.

Finally, expressions such as *let me just say* or *I would just say* are mixtures of a quantity hedge ('this is as much as I can say') and a firmness hedge ('this is all I'm going to say'):

1   Let me **just say** in response to – without commenting on the invest
2   Let me **just say** that we are certainly aware of those reports
3   So I would **just say** that the story is not accurate.
4   Let me **just say** this: We are in the second week of an air campaign

The press's use of *just* is very different, though similarly revealing of their needs and aims. It is used – like *if I may* or *if I can* – to justify an additional move, a follow-up taken by a journalist:

(55)　Q:　And *just* one other question on this.

or to excuse taking up time:

(56)　Q:　*Just* to follow up on Mara's question.
(57)　Q:　*Just* to nail this down.

and is politeness mainly directed to press colleagues. It also seems to be used to lull the podium into a false sense of security:

(58)　Q:　Well, *just as a matter of principle*, should a White House official lie to the American public?
(59)　Q:　And *just one other question about this*. Can the President imagine a deal that would both meet his objectives and also, when it's announced, boost the stock of the tobacco companies? (Laughter.)

It is often found, as above, to precede what turn out to be barbed questions, or to introduce a controversial or negative reformulation:

(60)　Q:　So adjournment – *just to be precise*, if I may – so adjournment without a verdict is acceptable to the White House?
　　　　MR LOCKHART:　I don't think I said that. I said […]

Sometimes it may be used to attack the face of someone the podium may be required to defend. After three Democratic party consultants were found to be working for one of the sides in the Israeli elections, the podium argues that they are simply trying to earn a crust. The press take him up:

(61)　Q:　So they're *just* trying to make cash. In other words they're *just* consultants making the cash and there's no connection with the White House?

There is an obvious tone of disbelief. We might call this a cynical or *demeaning reformulation*, which will be looked at more closely in Section 9.2.
　　Finally, they can turn the podium's *just say* expression round on him:

(62)　Q:　[…] What I'm asking you is do you have a strategy for what happens after the first round of bombs?
　　　　MR LOCKHART:　Again, I'm not going to get –
　　　　Q:　I'm not asking you to tell me what the strategy is, *just say* if you have one.

The questioner implies that they do not expect the podium to be over-precise but they do expect to be told *something*.

7.7   Conclusions on politeness in the briefings

7.7.1   *Different rights and practices*

Despite the atmosphere of informality and egalitarianism that pervades these briefings, the podium and the press enjoy very asymmetrical rights and employ very different practices as regards both types of politeness.

The podium's positive face and that of his clients is routinely under threat from questioners. His job is to defend his clients' face by the various techniques of denial, counter-argument, reformulation and generally placing positive spin on their past record and current ideas. The boundaries beyond which the press cannot go in their attacks is constantly under negotiation; any podium protest of being cruelly used is likely to meet resistance.

But such podium protests are rare, and are far more likely to take the form of censure of the question rather than the questioner. This is generally in line with: (a) an acceptance of the convention of journalistic neutralism; and (b) avoidance of open threats to the press's face. In fact, whenever possible, he assuages that face, claiming common ground in the hope of some degree of reciprocation.

The podium resorts to negative politeness more often than the press, employing it routinely when addressing his audience. It has a number of strategic functions. It reduces the distance between the two sides. The podium likes to offer rather than impose his knowledge and views, because he can thereby avoid the alienating role of authority figure. It also, as we have seen, allows him a certain imprecision in language which can be very convenient.

Negative politeness occurs less frequently in the press talk – the typical directness of their questions has already been mentioned – but it is found in two particular circumstances. The first is in claiming a turn at talk when other journalists might be wanting the floor. This is commonly realized with phrases like *if I may* (*follow up etc.*), *just* (*to follow this up*), and also *quickly, briefly*, for example: 'back on China just briefly', 'another subject quickly', 'to follow up just briefly, if I may …'. The second is when they are about to threaten face especially severely, particularly the face of the podium himself as opposed to that of his clients', for example, when a questioner's move could be construed as implying that the podium is failing in his duty. The particular kind of journalistic neutralism in play in these briefings does not seem to wholly excuse attacks on the person of the podium.

7.7.2   *Politeness in transaction and interaction*

One other key to interpreting the differences in press and podium politeness is to consider that the two sides are involved in rather different discourse activities. Two broad categories of discourse types have been proposed (Brown and Yule 1983; R. Lakoff 1989), that affect the quantity and quality of politeness: the *transactional* and the *interactional*. 'Transactional discourse types focus on the optimally efficient transmission of information'. These are task-focused where the 'need for truthfulness, clarity and brevity overrules face-concerns' (Kasper 1990: 205).

'Interactional discourse, by contrast, has as its primary goal the establishment and maintenance of social relationships' in which care for face is paramount (Kasper 1990: 205). In practice, individual texts can be placed along a cline from the entirely transactional to the totally interactional, and 'on the criterion of politeness investment, discourse types can be arranged on a continuum ranging from total lack of politeness in the most radical forms of transactional discourse to complete domination of the politeness over propositional information in the prototypically interactional discourse forms' (Kasper 1990: 205). When there are two separate participants in the discourse, as in these briefings, it is entirely feasible that one of them will give more importance to the transactional, the other to the interactional. The press are here primarily to do business, are interested in 'the efficient transmission of information' from the podium to their editors. Their concerns are with 'truthfulness' and clarity. The podium, on the other hand, has an interest in building and maintaining an interpersonal relationship with his audience and has thus to invest more time in politeness and the interactional aspects of discourse. He may even consciously or unconsciously seek to move the focus of the entire discourse towards the interactional end of the scale in order to avoid the transmission of too much information.

It is often claimed that the genre or discourse type 'exerts decisive constraints' (Kasper 1990: 205) on the linguistic behaviour of participants [see Saville-Troike (1989) for an overview]. But, on occasion, as the podium is seen to do in these briefings, they can make strategic choices about what type of discourse it is convenient for them to produce. This is another reminder that we should not be totally deterministic in our view of discourse: 'discourse is not only reflective of social relationships and entitlements but just as instrumental in constructing them' (Kasper 1990: 207). The preexistence of discourse types is, to a degree, constraining, but it is at the same time a resource to be exploited to advantage.

7.8 Epilogue

Finally, there is also one form of politeness which has barely been mentioned in this chapter: diplomatic politeness, hedging for political purposes:

(63)   MR LOCKHART: I think it would not be illogical for some in Belgrade to think that their statements that they have no intention of becoming involved in this are not rock-solid.

This – almost comic – turn is practically one hedge upon the heels of the last. The podium piles Pelion on Ossa in the attempt to mitigate the face-threatening import of a criticism of an antagonist (at that moment, 31 March 1999). This is a reminder that these briefings are political documents, available to a wider world, and that questions of politeness in them can be very serious indeed.

8 Conflict talk

8.1 Introduction: when discord is waiting to happen

The antagonism inherent in White House briefings can be seen as a specific case of the kind of 'conflict talk' discussed in the work of Grimshaw (1990) and Vuchinich (1990), who combine the sociolinguist's interest in discovering the rules of argumentational engagement with the conversation analyst's regard for the individual's participation in arguing.

'Verbal conflict' says Vuchinich, happens when 'participants oppose the utterances, actions, or selves of one another in successive turns at talk' (Vuchinich 1990: 118). It is 'unique among speech activities because participants overtly display and focus upon the fact that consensus on a matter worth talking about has broken down' (Vuchinich 1990: 119). Generally, this is perceived as a problem: 'Trouble often exists under such circumstances because consensus on many matters is a necessary prerequisite for successful verbal interaction. When consensus breaks down, stable interaction can be in jeopardy' (Vuchinich 1990: 118). But he recognizes that this is not necessarily the case: 'this is not inevitable as the conflict form can be used as an expression of sociability' (Vuchinich 1990: 118). In other words, argument can be a cooperative social activity creating bonds between participants or training participants in highly valued life skills.

Vuchinich was studying arguments in families. White House briefings are very different in that arguments are expected (especially from the press's point of view), verbal conflict to a large extent *is* the interaction. Lack of consensus, far from placing it in jeopardy, is the spur for interaction. However, as we have seen in Chapter 6, there can be moments of acrimony when the assumption of neutralism is under threat. In these moments, the 'trouble' talked about by Vuchinich earlier comes into being and has to be resolved before 'stable interaction' can continue.

The fact that differences of opinion are a normal expected part of these briefings means they belong to a very particular type of interaction: the *scheduled* argument. This is less perverse than might at first appear. Even in everyday life, particular moments and activities are propitious for quarrelling. Vuchinich's family dinners 'provide a regularly occurring setting in which complainants and offenders [...] will be together; [they] confirm the stereotype that Americans (at least) find the dinner table an optimal setting for disputes' (Grimshaw 1990: 286). Similarly, 'school lunches (Eder 1990) and after-school play (Goodwin and Goodwin 1990) also provide regular *opportunities* for disputes to occur' (Grimshaw 1990: 286). In more formal areas, the courtroom (Philips 1990) and labour and management meetings (O'Donnell 1990) are scheduled settings for potential and highly likely verbal battle. Grimshaw hypothesizes the existence of a dimension of avoidability–inevitability for disputes. Some everyday and some professional environments are settings where discord is 'waiting to happen'.

Grimshaw considers a number of issues relevant to conflict talk. These include: the *content* of such talk, the *orientation of participants* (similar to *footing*), the perceived *stakes* (what there is to win) and *outcomes* (who wins and who loses), how episodes of conflict are *closed*, the use of *affect/emotion* and *power* both as a weapon and as an outcome. We will briefly discuss each of these in terms of their relevance to the briefings.

8.2 Content of arguments

According to Grimshaw (1990), people argue about the following:

 (i)   things or 'rights' (toys or territory, authority or precedence, respectively);
 (ii) beliefs (ideologies, values, opinions);
 (iii) factual claims (usually historical);
 (iv) some combination of the above.

He goes on to observe that there is another kind of conflict talk which revolves around 'claims and negotiation of personal identities, that is, about what kinds of persons participants and their interlocutors *are* and about what the nature of their social relations should be' (Grimshaw 1990: 284). Whatever else they argue about 'it appears that *all* conflict talk involves *some* negotiation of identities and of the appropriate nature of interpersonal (i.e. structural, organizational) arrangements' (Grimshaw 1990: 284). In briefings discourse, this negotiation is evident in the press's questions about whom the podium works for (see Section 7.5.3), in complaints from both sides that the other party is not doing its job, not fulfilling its organizational obligations [as in example (1)] and in debate on whether or not this is the right place to be discussing a particular matter [see example (2)]. These complaints are rarely as completely personalized as, say, the grievances expressed during Vuchinich's family dinners or the accusations of racism in Labov (1990), since they tend to be mitigated by the parties' official roles, as here (found by concordancing *dispute/disagree*):

 (1)   Q: You have not provided us a real opportunity.
       MR McCURRY: I dispute that. We come out here every single day. We offer
         up all kinds of stories
       Q: I'm not talking about you, I'm talking about the President.

But there is the odd occasion when tempers are heated:

(2)   MR LOCKHART: You very confidently sit there and tell us what we're doing and we're not doing. I'm telling you that the place to discuss operational detail, to the extent that it can be done, is at the Pentagon and not here.

The utterance act in the first part is accusation: Mr Lockhart is charging the questioner with arrogance.

The press too can become equally heated. In particular, there is a more than usual 'displayed lack of consensus on some feature of the social world' (Vuchinich 1990: 119) over questions of exactly what was said, especially by the podium. These become a sort of institutional version of the 'I did not say that' – 'yes you did' type argument (see Section 9.1 on the importance of the form of words actually used). At one point a questioner objects to mentions of 'strong indications' (of a settlement) being referred to in the same breath as 'air strikes', as they seem contradictory:

(3)   Q: For you to stand there, though – I mean, you've never done this before, saying that there are strong indications before. But you –

The podium attempts to defend himself by pointing out what he actually said:

(4)   MR LOCKHART: I said there are indications. Others in the room have said strong.

But his language remains the object of acrimonious scrutiny:

(5)   Q: Okay. Well, but it's still a serious situation when you say, indications, and you're still talking air strikes. But you're cautiously looking at ending this thing. How can you seriously sit here and say 'indications' and 'air strikes' in the same breath?

The podium, incidentally, refuses to be drawn and responds with the routine statement: 'because we've made very clear what we need to see to bring this conflict to an end'.

8.3   Three types of argument: ideational, interpersonal and textual

Argument in these briefings – and very probably all argument – falls into three main categories. The first type concerns factual claims (whether an event happened in a certain way) and opinions (when the podium's and the press's interpretation of events is at odds). The second kind is more interpersonal and revolves around an *accusation* of some sort and takes the form of attack and defence and possible counter-attack. This second kind can be further divided into dispute over roles and dispute over the actual words used. We can, thus, talk in Hallidayan terms of these three types of argument: (i) *ideational*, over factual claims; (ii) *interpersonal*, over participant roles; and (iii) *textual*, over the form of language. In real life, of course, any single argument is likely to range among all three of these.

Finally, Vuchinich points out that 'American English provides many different illocutionary structures for accomplishing oppositional turns at talk. These include disagreement, challenge, denial, accusation, threat, insult'. The first two, disagreement and challenge, are important in disputes about facts and opinions. The middle two, accusation and denial, are especially relevant in interpersonal debate over identity and role. The last two, threat and insult, are also clearly inter-personal but are not relevant to the kind of argument under discussion here. There are no real threats in these texts, although one occurs in jest:

(6)   Q: Have we given any thought to where we're going to put these 20,000 –
        MR LOCKHART: We've given a lot of thought to it, we just haven't come to
        a final conclusion.
        Q: – suggested that they put them in Arkansas. (Laughter.)
        MR LOCKHART: I will pass that suggestion on with your name on it.
        (Laughter.)

Whenever insults are found they are also generally joshing and used to relieve the tension.

8.4   Participant orientation: self or the collectivity

Returning to Grimshaw's thoughts on *participant orientation*, a distinction is made (following Parsons 1951) between self-orientation and collectivity-orientation:

> Parsons asserted, quite logically, that all human behaviors are directed to maximization of own self-interests or those of the collectivity: he was not unaware that social actors may have stakes in defining the two as isomorphic.
>
> (Grimshaw 1990: 288)

In other words, parties may claim to be speaking for a group, for society, for moral good sense (using ideological arguments) whilst their main interest is actually simply in 'winning' an argument. It is also common practice, he points out, for speakers to 'claim a collectivity-orientation while assigning a self-orientation to their opponent', thus commanding the nobler, less selfish, moral high-ground. As a corollary to this, it is a feature of conflict talk, relative to other kinds of interaction that:

> participants [do] not accept the roles (and orientations) assigned to them by their opposite parties – they are likely to assign, and claim for themselves, roles the reverse of those claimed and assigned by opponents.
>
> (Grimshaw 1990: 288)

We have seen in Chapters 3 and 4 how participants try to project the other party in a particular role or footing and how such attempts are resisted. However, not all of these issues are as important in these briefings as in other kinds of verbal conflict. That the podium represents various 'collectivities' (the White House, his political party, etc.) is normally tacitly accepted by both sides, and the only occasion when the press' claims to represent large groups (their readership, the American public and so on) is challenged is when the assumption of neutralism (Chapter 5) is under threat.

We have looked elsewhere at the footing of both podium and press as representing collectivities (Chapters 3 and 4). We have not yet dealt sufficiently with Grimshaw's other motivation in arguing: self-interest, the very personal desire to win.

8.5   Winning an argument

Employing the terminology of game theory, arguments, in general, can have two possible outcomes: zero-sum or non-zero-sum. A zero-sum resolution is one in which there is a complete winner and a complete loser. A non-zero sum decision, which includes the winner–winner or even loser–loser[1] scenario, allows the possibility of compromise. Which outcome a 'player' is willing to settle for, whether they want absolutely to win or are willing to accept compromise (their 'level of commitment' or 'outcome priorities'; Grimshaw 1990: 288–9) will generally depend on their perception of what is at stake. If, for some reason, a player feels that winning is vital to them, they are likely to continue the conflict and refuse the other party's offer of compromise (perhaps not seeing it as compromise at all). Outcome priorities can, of course, shift during the course of a dispute 'as new information becomes available, as alliances shift, as ennui replaces passion' (Grimshaw 1990: 289) and so on. However, there are also cases 'in which individual (or organizational) priorities are both initially clear and robust over time' (Grimshaw 1990: 289). By and large, these briefings are one such case, since both the press interest (to find out more) and podium motivation (to reveal only what he wants to) tend to remain the same.

Vuchinich (1990) studies the way antagonists close verbal conflicts in extensive family interaction data. He detects four principal formats of conflict termination:

1   *Submission*: in which 'one participant "gives in" and accepts the opponent's position' (Vuchinich 1990: 123).
2   *Dominant third-party intervention*: in which 'an on-going conflict involving two or more participants can be "broken up" by a third party' (Vuchinich 1990: 125).
3   *Compromise*: in which 'a participant offers a position that is *between* the opposing positions that define the dispute [...] if the concession offered is accepted [...] the conflict can terminate'.
4   *Stand-off–withdrawal*: in which participants simply 'change the speech activity and drop the conflict form' either by changing topic (*stand off*) or retreating from conversational activity (*withdrawal*).

In his data, the last of these was by far the most frequent – 66 per cent of conflicts terminated in stand-offs compared to only 26 per cent in submission or compromise. His explanation is that:

> In a stand-off no one must lose face through submission. In addition, opponents do not have to make concessions or engage in the delicate negotiation of a compromise position [...]
>
> (Vuchinich 1990:134)

Submission may be relatively simple but involves considerable loss of face. Compromise entails less face loss but is hard to organize. The stand-off is a draw with no outright winner or loser, is achieved spontaneously and leaves face more or less intact.

The briefings offer a similar picture. Submission is even rarer given the importance of face to both sides. The only clear example of the podium submitting is in the 'baloney' episode (see Section 4.3.5):

(7) Q: – and therefore, I really would like to tell you something – what is this baloney? (Laughter.)
     Q: You said it better than he could say it. It's baloney.
     MR LOCKHART: Sometimes it's hard to spin baloney into anything else.

Note how the press gloat in their victory:

(8) Q: What he just said is good.
     Q: What did he say?
     Q: He said it's hard to spin baloney into anything else. Thank you. (Laughter.)

There are few clear examples of questioner submission. However, this may well be a feature of the way briefings are organized. Even if the podium were to 'win' an argument, there is little pressure on the journalist to express their submission verbally. Silence would be enough to get them off the hook since someone else is bound to be ready with another question, as in the following case. The journalist has just complained about lack of communication from the White House. The podium responds by taking the press to task for only being interested in scandal:

(9) MR McCURRY: – and it's been Monica, Monica, Monica, Monica. And you know that, and I know that. I mean, you can't pretend otherwise. Okay, good. Thanks.
     Q: What's the President doing this afternoon?

Thus, possible questioner submission is transformed into stand-off by a change of subject. To this extent the journalist's face is less vulnerable, less open to outright defeat (and public humiliation) than the podium's.[2]

In Chapter 7, we saw how the podium uses politeness techniques to deflect antagonism. It also appears from the data that his level of commitment to winning outright is generally lower than that of the press, he is much more willing to compromise. Many of his asides could be taken as the first move in compromise-seeking:

(10)   MR TOIV: I'm as sick of saying it as you are of hearing it, believe me. (Laughter.)

A response move from the press indicating the acceptance of compromise is rarely explicitly forthcoming. However, we might interpret the laughter in example (10) in this fashion.

The press often seem to have different outcome priorities and seek victory much more assiduously. This can take the form of 'going after' the podium, asking the same question over and over: 'Is it fair to ask the question this way ...', 'Joe, that said ...', 'But Joe ...', 'But if it isn't enough, though?' (Note how *that said* and *but* are often ways of suggesting that the reply is less than satisfactory). Nevertheless, except in particularly dire circumstances (i.e. when the whole audience is seriously hunting for him, as in the 'baloney' case), the multiple nature of his audience enables him to eventually switch questioner, which, if he is lucky, will bring forward a new topic and so allow him a stand-off draw.

However, this is not always successful. If the attempt to change topic fails, he can alternatively achieve a draw by withdrawing, that is, 'retreating from the conversational activity' (see above):

(11)   Q: So you're saying, even if the President didn't want him to, he'd continue –
        MR McCURRY: Anything else?
        Q: What was the answer?
        MR McCURRY: Same one I gave now.
        Q: You wouldn't repeat it for us now, would you?
        MR McCURRY: Nope. (Laughter.)

This tends to be a last resort – his job, after all, is to respond to questions – and he will normally attempt other forms of evasion first (Chapter 12).

Finally, the podium's role – and command of the microphone – usually allows him to have the last word, which is not the same as winning, but makes withdrawing a more attractive proposition. In the following, the questioner wants to know whether the podium agrees with the proposition that President Clinton 'has a very horny appetite' (the episode is quoted in detail in Section 5.3). The podium attempts to treat it as a joke:

(12)   MR McCURRY: Is that a medical diagnosis, or was that a – (laughter).

But the questioner is both serious and aggressive, forcing the podium to give a more sobre if ironic reply:

(13)   Q: I wonder, would you agree, disagree, or give that an icy 'no comment'?

MR McCURRY: I'm not familiar enough with Angie Dickinson to know whether she's been in a position to render such an astute and explicit diagnosis, but I doubt that she has any informed ability to make that decision.

Anything else –

After several more exchanges, the topic is terminated as follows:

(14) Q: What do we do? How can we regard this now, Mike? What can we do about it?

MR McCURRY: I'm sure you'll find something.

This is a potentially threatening exchange with the double attack, first on the President, then on the podium's personal face implicit in the questioner's 'I wonder, would you agree, disagree, or give that an icy "no comment"?'. Mr McCurry first tries to change the subject – 'Anything else' – but when this fails he eventually withdraws from the conflict by avoiding the question 'What can we do about it?'. But the withdrawal is barbed, hinting that the questioner is not impartial. 'Getting in the "last word" does not win a conflict but it does show that you haven't given in or submitted' (Vuchinich 1990: 133).

The process of disengagement, as can be seen, is generally not an easy one for the podium. A concordance of the phrase 'anything else' shows how it is frequently used in the attempt to change the subject, but by itself it is rarely successful:

(15) Q: So what you're saying is that unless he agrees to a deal, the refugees will never be able to go back to Kosovo?

MR LOCKHART: No, I'm not saying that. And I think we've been around enough on this.

Do we have anything else?

Q: Hang on, let me take a stab at this. Unless he agrees to deal, they'll never go back with NATO escort?

He will generally be forced into some more explicit expression of his refusal to answer, as in the response to the last question in example (15):

(16) MR LOCKHART: Listen, I can't go down – but that's – we have laid down conditions for NATO involvement now and those are the conditions.

The phrase 'Next question' was also concordanced and found to have a similar function and a similarly low success rate:

(17) Q: Back on the contempt order, how do you answer those who say that this vindicates the House Judiciary Committee and Ken Starr?

MR LOCKHART: I don't. Next question.

Q: Why not?

> MR LOCKHART: Because I don't.
> Q: You have no quarrel with that?
> MR LOCKHART: No, I just said I'm not answering them. We've been through this before and I'm not interested in revisiting that old ground.

Again, the podium is forced to make his evasiveness plain. Forcing the podium to put his evasion *on record* presumably entails a greater loss of his face.

In another instance, on the occasion of a question which juxtaposes Mr Clinton's youthful draft evasion with his desire for a military solution to the Kosovo crisis, the podium tries several times to achieve a stand-off or withdraw:

(18) MR LOCKHART: Next question.
> Q: Next question – you're ashamed of this, Joe? Is that what you're saying?
> MR LOCKHART: Lester, I don't have time for this today. Next question.
> Q: You don't have time for it, okay.
> MR LOCKHART: And you can put that in your report. That doesn't bother me.
> Q: I will. Oh, I'm delighted to.

Notice how the questioner draws attention to the podium's attempts to change the subject by echoing his words 'next question' and 'you don't have time for it'. The questioner feels his face is damaged, he clearly feels offended and cheated. There can be a thin distinction indeed between withdrawing from an argument and treating the questioner and their question with contempt. In fact, speaker withdrawal is probably inherently face-threatening for the hearer, which partly explains why the press frequently ignore 'anything else' or 'next question' type ploys.

Except when the press themselves offer it:

(19) Q: Change of subject?
> MR McCURRY: Please. (Laughter.)

The laughter occurs partly because the podium's difficulties are being highlighted, but also because one of the podium's stock ploys is pointed out explicitly. The tension of antagonism is allayed for the moment.

8.6 Affect and emotion: instrumental or expressive

Lester, the questioner in the draft evasion example (18), is a 'high-risk' questioner. His questions are highly antagonistic behaviour which threatens both his interlocutor's face but also, as we have seen, his own, since the risk of retaliation is so much the greater. His gladiatorial style is something of an in-joke for those present:

(20) MR McCURRY: When you need a good, bizarre question, boy, I tell you, it's really helpful to have Lester Kinsolving. (Laughter.)

Lester's fate also shows how an overwhelming commitment to a zero-sum outcome, to winning, is not always the most successful tactic. In game metaphor, he overplays his hand; his use of 'power talk' (Aitchison 1999: 118–9) misfires.

From another perspective, Lester's commitment is too 'honest', too 'expressive'; it is often more fruitful to use affect more 'instrumentally' (Grimshaw 1990: 291–3). It is impossible to know what the journalists and the podium *really* feel about each other from these texts. However, there is evidence that some of the press feel genuine respect and affection for Mr McCurry, which is expressed on his leave-taking. This itself enhances his 'power', in the sense it allows him to do things, say things, which otherwise would be of higher risk: 'some users [...] may be successful because of extraneous considerations of sympathy or even physical attractiveness' (Grimshaw 1990: 307). Mr McCurry certainly qualifies on the first of these;[3] whether on the latter we will leave to individual taste.

8.7 Conclusion: power and *claims* to power

In a good deal of research into institutional talk, notes Hutchby (1996: 17), asymmetries of power 'are considered unproblematically related to the participants' institutional identities'. The claim is often made that institutions are 'characterized by [...] hierarchical relations of power between the occupants of institutional positions' and so agents act in ways which allow them to 'exercise the power which is institutionally endowed upon them' (Thompson J. 1984: 165 quoted in Hutchby 1996: 17). This is far too static a framework to be useful in analysing these briefings. We need an approach, like that proposed by Hutchby (1996: 17), which sees asymmetry and power 'as oriented to, and produced by actual talk, rather than being predetermined by a theoretically established context'.

Power in the sense we have already defined as control of the initiative and the ability to pursue one's interactional interests (Section 7.1.3) is, in this more dynamic approach, not just a *resource*, a *weapon* to use in achieving one's ends but also a *stake* in the briefings game, an *end* in itself.

The players command different resources from the start and throughout. The podium can to some extent control access to the floor by choosing the questioner (if more than one wishes to speak). However, to deny an individual access throughout an entire briefing would undoubtedly invite censure. He has a certain ability to refuse topics, though, as we have seen, this is often quite hard in practice. He can, within reason, judge the length of time he takes to reply, include or exclude as much detail as he sees fit. He has what we might call 'possession of the microphone', his voice is quite simply physically louder than anyone else's, which gives him more power to interrupt and to resist interruption:

(21) MR LOCKHART: Helen, let me tell you, we've been very clear about what they need to do, and that this isn't a negotiation.
      Q: But that's flat. I mean, that's –
      MR LOCKHART: Let me finish, please. The United States is [...]

These powers help redress the podium's position of vulnerability as the party whose thoughts and opinions are at issue, who exposes their face to risk by answering questions about themselves, which, as we have mentioned elsewhere (Section 7.1.3), is typical of the less powerful participant in many institutional situations.

The resources available to questioners, to the journalists, are as follows. They can set the topic agenda by their questions, which is undoubtedly one of the most important prerogatives and emblems of the powerful. However, each individual journalist's power in this sense is very limited, since their agenda can be turned down. They also have strictly limited rights to follow-up (Section 3.2.2), since hogging the floor is contrary to briefings etiquette. Moreover, individually they are vulnerable to joshing. Being made fun of in front of an audience is, as we all know from experience, extremely face-threatening. As a group, however, things are very different. If the entire press troupe decide that a topic is ripe for discussion, the podium is well advised to pay it attention.

Beyond this, we are in the realms of *claims* to power. We have already noted that the overriding ethos is one of equality, and it is probably the case that when power between *roles* is set at a minimum, there will be considerable competition among the *individuals* occupying those roles for more power to control events and further their interests. Moreover, 'power among putative equals results [...] from differences in competences' (Grimshaw 1990: 306). Whoever plays their cards better will tend to gain dominance, and these cards generally consist of verbal expertise (or *communicative competence*) and claims of dominance. Power can be evoked by claims of institutional authority, such as when the use of *we* claims a group membership from which an opponent is excluded, or as when the podium claims to represent, say, the President, or when the press claim to speak for the American people. 'Each of these and other power-claims will be variously credible and variously subject to counter-claim and challenge' (Grimshaw 1990: 307). Power may be claimed by a certain style of talking (O'Barr 1982), though, as we have seen with Lester, this is risky if taken too far. Power may be claimed by asserting superior knowledge especially, in the case of these briefings, if the press does so in a situation where the podium is supposed to be the one supplying information. Lack of knowledge on a subject is potentially face-threatening for the podium, which partly explains why some of his responses take a long time to say nothing. Finally, unscrupulous participants may succeed in conflicts with more principled ones by using subterfuge. We have seen occasions where questioners attempt to lay a trap for the podium (Chapter 6). Again, this is risky in terms of face and only the journalists indulge; the podium has too much to lose. It rarely succeeds and there is often an ensuing debate about whether or not it constitutes permissible behaviour.

At all times the loss or increase of face consequent upon 'losing' or 'winning' is a temporary, non-definitive affair.[4] On the occasion of the Clinton–Lewinsky affair, the press felt that their power was so low that the briefing format itself was at risk. Or at least they *claimed* to feel this way in order to swing the agenda-setting power back their way. But normal service, normal battle, was soon resumed.

As we have said earlier, much work in Discourse Analysis has concentrated on institutional texts where the power relations are particularly asymmetrical and exist prior to the actual talk itself.[5] Critical discourse analysts indeed are interested in the social and political implications of these very asymmetries (Van Dijk 1993). The present study, however, is a salutary reminder that power, even in institutional settings, is not always so straightforwardly uneven. Although it would, of course, be very foolish to argue that asymmetries of power do not exist in institutional and even in everyday relationships, they are often best viewed, except in extreme circumstances,[6] in terms of 'differential distributions of discursive resources' (Hutchby 1996: 17). These differences in resources 'enable certain participants to achieve interactional effects that are not available (or are less available) to others in the setting' (Hutchby 1996: 17). But participants will strive to use the resources available to them to best effect. As Foucault (1977) maintains, where there is power, there is resistance to it. Here, we have seen the ways power can shift and the ways claims to power are proposed by one side and resisted by the other. Certainly, in the sort of conflict talk we find in briefings, power exists to be claimed and exists to be challenged.

9 The form of words

In this chapter, we will look at the very considerable importance that both the press and the podium give to language, to the precise form of words used in both the questions and, especially, the responses. Further to this, we will see the several ways in which language shapes the nature of news itself and how different versions of language, different formulations of words, are used to propose competing accounts of reality. We need, however, to begin with a short consideration of the nature of journalism and how journalists themselves see their job.

9.1 Words and the truth

9.1.1 The objectivist view and the pursuit of truth

One conception of what journalists do, reported by Fowler as being prevalent amongst newspeople, is what we might call the 'objectivist' view:

> He or she collects facts, reports them objectively, and the newspaper presents them fairly and without bias, in language which is designed to be unambiguous, undistorting and agreeable to readers. This professional ethos is common to all the news media, Press, radio and television, and is certainly what the journalist claims in any general statement on the matter.[1]
>
> (Fowler 1991: 1)

Fowler goes on to challenge this view and we will turn to his arguments later (Section 9.4). Here, we must ask how the objectivist theory can apply to the briefings. News interviews, press conferences and briefings are all news-making events. Journalists produce copy for their papers or reports for their programmes out of them. But what are the 'facts', the objective events in an interview or briefing to be reported 'without bias'? The answer is, of course, that there are none: there are no fires, no strikes, no one marches into battle or meets a sticky end, nor do any of the other staple 'newsworthy' events happen.[2] The newsworthiness is in the language itself, in the actual utterances made by the podium and reported by the press. An unusual turn of phrase, a controversial comment, any hint of verbal dissent between members of the administration are all likely to make copious copy. It is words themselves which make the news. However, as we pointed out in the Introduction, the press are doubly involved in the briefings process. They both help shape the event itself by contributing the questions and report it in their stories at the end: they are counsel for the prosecution and jury all in one.

Whether we believe in it or not, however, one part of the objectivist theory which is of practical use is that it encourages reporters to get their facts right, to check whether things actually happened and how they happened. In terms of briefings, one of the preoccupations of the political journalist is to ascertain whether certain words were actually spoken and by whom. Conversely, it is often a priority of the podium to set them straight on such matters.

An epistemological correlative of the objectivist theory is that journalists are engaged in 'the pursuit of truth'. The podium for their part is there 'to tell them the truth'. Mr McCurry makes this idea explicit on the day of his last briefing when asked who he works for:

(1) MR McCURRY: That's where your first and only obligation is – it's to the truth and at helping the American people.

The following is a concordance of the occurrences of *truth*[3] in the briefings corpus:

1 as opposed to those who're pursuing something other than a search for the **truth**.
2 if there is no **truth** in what *The Times* reports, why have we ordered 9,000 new purple hearts?
3 and some recognition of those who know the reality, who know the **truth**, who don't believe the propaganda and the lies
4 It represents an unmasking of the **truth** that the world has long known
5 it speaks volumes for the Milosevic regime that those who represent dissent and speak the **truth** and recognize reality have no place in their government
6 as opposed to those who seek to perpetrate something other than the **truth**.
7 your first and only obligation is – it's to the **truth** and at helping the American people.
8 He went out and told the **truth** about the performance of the economy, 1993 –
9 some in some circles in Belgrade who understand the **truth** about this regime, that understand that NATO is united
10 in Belgrade, in Yugoslavia who understand what the **truth** here is
11 Somebody gave me one, which, to tell you the **truth**, I didn't get a chance to read.

All of these are uttered by the podium except line 2, and even this is pre-emptively quoting him. The podium in particular is committed to the concept of truth. It is something for which to *search* (line 1), which one can *understand* (lines 9 and 10), which can be *unmasked* (line 4), and therefore presumably also *masked*. It is a fairly robust tangible entity. There is also the suggestion of a definite dichotomy truth–untruth [which may be falsehood (line 6) or hiding of the truth (line 4)]. Moreover, it is something that one can *tell* (lines 8 and 11) and *speak* (line 5). When, as in these briefings, the words are the events, truth lies more than ever in the form of words.

9.1.2   *True words but only words*

To continue this investigation, the concordance of *words* itself was compiled (42 occurrences), from which it emerged quite clearly how *words* are seen (or projected) as both emblems of transience or, on the contrary, the very embodiment of truth.

Words can be contraposed, negatively, to deeds: 'and I think that certainly actions are more important than words'. And again:

(2)   MR LOCKHART: Because I think we have some *words* which need to be more fully clarified. They are only *words*; they are not actions. We've seen *words* before.

What is more, *words* can be synonymous with *rhetoric, bluster*, even *petulance* (line 17):

(3)   COLONEL CROWLEY: What we've heard today from Iraq is a great deal of rhetoric. We've heard this bluster before. We've seen this petulance before. But at the end of the day we'll judge the situation by Iraqi actions, not by Iraqi *words*.

On the other hand, there can be nothing 'truer' than the exact words. If truth resides in language, then, the argument would go, the precise words must be the precise truth. Especially when the words come from the mouth of the President:

(4)   MR LOCKHART: His *words* are his *words*, the policy is the policy and hasn't changed.

The President, for his part, selects his words conscientiously and so they can be utterly relied upon:

(5)   MR McCURRY: The President chooses his *words* very carefully when he addresses this and says what he wants to say.

They can neither be added to, nor need any interpretation:

(6)   MR TOIV: He will testify truthfully and completely, and I have no way of elaborating on his *words*.

It is others, enemies or opponents – like the Iraqis in example (3) or the Yugoslavs in example (2) – whose words are unreliable, do not correspond to the truth.

There are also unnamed antagonists, maybe even in the press, lying in wait to distort the presidential truth:

(7)   MR LOCKHART: I think the President uses his words carefully because there are many who would like to twist them around and turn them upside down.

The universe the podium likes to depict, then, is a black and white one. The White House – candid and honest, weighs its words 'carefully' as in example (7) and the following:

(8)   [...] the President said he was using his words carefully on no intention to send ground troops

which, as vehicles of truth, should be listened to equally carefully:

(9)   MR LOCKHART: I think you should go back and look at the words carefully [...]

It finds itself faced with those for whom talk is cheap [who use 'only words', see example (2)] and who do not hesitate to hide or deform the truth.

The press, on the other hand, inhabit a more sophisticated world in which the possibility of a distinction between *words* and *meaning* – where the two can exist on separate planes and where the first is not always coextensive with the second – can be convenient:

(10)   Q: Mike, leaving aside whatever *words* you want to, the thrust of this agreement is that 49 percent of the territory [...]
(11)   Q: You said this morning that you did not see any reason why it should not be made public. Maybe those were not your exact *words*, but we were talking about what issues might be there that needed to be under seal.

We will look at this representation of affairs, the divergence of language and meaning, in greater detail below.

9.1.3   *The exact* word(s) used

Even if they believe in a distinction between words and meaning, this does not imply that the press is not interested in the actual, exact words used. Far from it. The following examples are edited from a concordance of *word/words* in the context of *use/used/using*. The press may ask for language to be specified or confirmed:

(12)   Q: Joe, the German Defense Minister *used* the *word* 'genocide'. Are we *using* the *word* 'genocide' here?

(13) Q: […] he thinks what happened to him was something that others did, his political opponents did, and he's not – what was the *word* he *used*, Bill? Not ashamed of it or – not a badge of shame.

They want to know why specific terms were used:

(14) Q: Joe, you keep *using* the *word* 'cautious' –

(15) Q: […] Last week administration officials were *using* the *word* 'alarmed' by it.

or why they were *not* used:

(16) Q: Joe, some of us were given guidance yesterday […] that he was going to cooperate with the investigation. He didn't say that. And I'm wondering, the *word* 'cooperate' was *not used*. And I'm wondering why that was.

(17) Q: But he *didn't use* the *word* 'intend' or 'no plans' or anything like that.

or they can refer to the language used by a third party, especially when critical of the administration:

(18) Q: Mike, two publications today, the Post and the Times, both *used* the *word* 'paranoia' to describe the way the President feels about the issues that are raised by current accusations […]

This interest in terminology is, of course, partly due to the fact that the use of particular expressions can have important legal, political or diplomatic implications, as is made clear by the reply in the following:

(19) Q: […] Are we using the word 'genocide' here?
MR LOCKHART: Let me check, because I think 'genocide' has some legal ramifications to it.

The difference between Congressional *support* and *approval* is not just semantic but also legal:

(20) MR LOCKHART: […] if that happened there would be plenty of time for debate and for consultation and he would seek their support.
Q: Well, he did not say approval then?
MR LOCKHART: No, approval – I think the whole idea of approval and authority raises a series of constitutional questions –

There is considerable debate over the use of the term *partition* (in the context of Bosnia-Hercegovina):

(21) MR McCURRY: You've used a word that's not a correct word to use in connection with this agreement today. That's the word, 'partition'. A partition would be dismembering a unitary state and dividing the entities among other nation states. That is very specifically what the parties have agreed not to do.

And missing out a word can have major repercussions in the real world:

(22)   Q: When you say it would be a NATO force, you mean a NATO-led force?

Elsewhere, the administration is chaffed about inventing neologisms to put positive spin on their practice of controlling shipping into the Balkans:

(23)   Q: Where did the phrase 'visit and search' come from? [...] it sounds like it's such a nice version of 'stop and search'.
       MR LOCKHART: Well, it does have a certain hospitable ring to it. [...]
       Q: What is that meaning? I mean, it sounds like we're coming over to Sunday brunch. (Laughter.)

There are, however, other reasons why the press are interested in the exact language used. Citing a third party or quoting administration language back at it is an excellent way to introduce a hostile question (see Chapter 5 on attribution):

(24)   Q: [...] Last week administration officials were using the word 'alarmed' by it. If so, does that mean that perhaps there could have been more efforts taken to safeguard them, in fact, –

9.1.4 'It speaks for itself' – 'No, it doesn't. That's why we're asking'

Occasionally, the two portraits of the world – the podium's simple one of truth versus untruth and the press's search for truth beyond the words – come into conflict, generally over whether an utterance does or does not need further explanation or interpretation. The podium may claim that what they or their clients have said *speaks for itself*:

(25)   MR LOCKHART: I think that the statement that the President and the First Lady released speaks directly to that and it *speaks for itself*.

A repetition or tautology will have the same function:

(26)   MR LOCKHART: Jim, when I say that I haven't heard any discussion it means I haven't heard any discussion.

The press, however, are likely to challenge such claims:

(27)   MR LOCKHART: The statement *speaks for itself* –
       Q: No, it doesn't. That's why we're asking.
       MR LOCKHART: It *speaks for itself*, and I'm not going to get into the details of any private conversations.

Similarly, the podium very often claims that what they have said is *clear* [often premodified by *very* (58 occurrences) or *quite* (four occurrences)], that is, it needs no further words:

(28)   Q: Joe, it seems to me the NATO spokesman said over the weekend that if Milosevic just stopped hostile activities on the ground, that that would cause the air war to cease. Is that right […]?

MR LOCKHART: I didn't see that. And I think we've been *very clear* on what needs to be done. I didn't see that remark, but I think we've been *pretty clear* on what we believe needs to be done.

It is frequently used (as above) as an attempt to say that this is the final word on the subject, and that the topic should be changed. Predictably this does not always work:

(29)   MR LOCKHART: Let me leave it to the Russians to speak for themselves. I think what we've said on this is *quite clear*.

Q: Can I just clarify that point, Joe? [a further question follows]

The podium seems to try this tactic most often when discussing military policy and developments during the Kosovo crisis. His hands – and his tongue – are obviously tied by *raison d'état* on these matters. There is much debate, for instance, on the precise definition of 'permissive environment':

(30)   Q: Joe, I don't understand your reluctance to answer the question of what constitutes a permissive environment.

The podium has not actually been asked to define it, before this point, at least not in this briefing. The questioner defines it for him:

(31)   Q: It seems to me a permissive environment is one where you have permission to come in. Anything else would be an invasion force, right, in a hostile country?

The podium offers an additional scenario:

(32)   MR LOCKHART: Well, there's an environment where the Serbs and Milosevic don't have the ability to impose their will.

but the questioner retorts:

(33)   Q: That's not permissive.

The podium tries to take refuge by claiming clarity:

(34)   MR LOCKHART: But I have been *clear*, and my language has been *clear* here, that there is no intention of putting any NATO-led ground troops into Kosovo unless it's a permissive environment.

The journalist, predictably, ignores the clarity claim:

(35)   Q: So, basically, just to nail this down, Joe, what you're saying is
that a permissive environment would have to win the agreement
of Slobodan Milosevic or whoever happens to be in power in
Belgrade.

The exchange goes on until it is eventually put to rest, for the time being, by the
podium's submission of a definition of *permissive environment*:

(36)   Q: What do you mean by the words 'permissive environment'?
MR LOCKHART: It is an environment in which the U.S. troops are not
posed risk. It's one – subsequent to some sort of deal.

In the same vein, the podium professes to be deeply suspicious of *interpretation*,
which is, at the very least, antithetical to *the facts*:

(37)   Q: Should we interpret the fact that the President and Mr Yeltsin did not
discuss the security force makeup or the command – should we interpret that as saying they agreed to disagree on this issue –
MR LOCKHART: I would encourage you to try to limit your *interpretation*
and just let the facts play out.

Facts, of course, *speak for themselves*. Interpretation can *twist* them:

(38)   Q: And then today, he kind of appeared to indicate that this might be
a possibility. Is it correct to *interpret* this –
MR LOCKHART: I think the President uses his words carefully because
there are many who would like to twist them around and turn them
upside down. His words are his words [...]

Indeed, a polite, conflict-avoiding way of saying 'you're wrong' is to concede
someone their own *interpretation*:

(39)   Q: The President himself helped raise this the other day by suggesting
that he was changing his position, which you say he isn't.
MR LOCKHART: Well, Sam, you may have *interpreted* that way and
that's your right to do that, but he was not changing his position and
he was accurately articulating his position.

It is almost as if words are prior to, independent of, any meaning which might be
given to them:

(40)   MR LOCKHART: [...] I know how enticing it is to take a glib statement and
make it mean something and take it out of context [...]

Finally, there are a couple of occasions when the press turn the podium's oft professed predilection for straight-talking back on him, using *just* and *simply*:

(41)   Q: I'm just asking you a straight question. Does it take Milosevic saying, yes, I accede to ground troops, or not?

(42)   MR LOCKHART: Well, Helen, you're now accusing me of withholding something that might be to our advantage about making peace, so I can't figure out what the charge is here.

Q: I'm not accusing you, I'm simply asking why it was suppressed. (Laughter.)

Note the ironic suggestion that 'accusing you' is the podium's false, jittery interpretation of a *simple question*.

9.1.5   Different philosophies, different interests

To conclude this section on the relation of words to the world, we might mention Stubbs (1996: 157–95) who, inspired by Williams' (1976) work on cultural keywords, imagines the possibility of constructing a dictionary of 'focal' or 'pivotal' words that are descriptive of a society's culture. He cites Firth's (1935) proposal to study lexis such as *work, labour, employ* and Kress's (1994) examination of the noun *poverty*, while he himself looks at many items including *culture-cultural, nation-nationalist*. The aim here is less ambitious, but a concordance study of the keywords *truth* and *words* has revealed a great deal about the different cultural attitudes of the podium and the press to the work being done in briefings.

It is obviously tactically opportune at times for the podium to argue that his statement, even if minimally informative, is all there is to say on the matter, that his words are clear and speak for themselves and that everything else is mere interpretation. The more he has to say on delicate, dangerous topics the more he risks drowning in deep waters. Conversely, for the press, it is convenient to keep the podium talking as long as possible on such topics. To this end, they regularly suggest that there is further information, further meaning to be achieved beyond what the podium has so far supplied. This is not to say that they always openly accuse the podium of reticence, of holding back. They often prefer to intimate that words can be better defined, statements expanded, the distance between words and meaning ever more gradually diminished. In both cases, we must conclude that the kinds of philosophies the two sides hold as regards the value of words and their relation to truth are strategic, a product of their professional interests.

This study attempts to show how an analysis of the lexico-grammar of texts can help to explain social discourse – how different points of view can be expressed by stylistic choices and how such choices can embody different ideologies. All this does not necessarily imply that these embodiments are always conscious, but they exist all the same. As Stubbs (1996: 93) remarks: 'ideology need not function at the level of conscious or intentional bias. But ways of expressing things are not natural [...] other choices could be made, and [...] reality could be differently presented'. In these briefings it *is* differently presented by the two sides.

In Section 9.2, we will look at occasions when forms of words – and the interpretation of the world they present – are at their most competitive, that is, at the phenomenon of reformulation.

9.2 Reformulation

9.2.1 Definitions

Reformulation is the rewording of a piece of information uttered previously. It can serve a number of functions, as we shall see. It can be divided into two principal categories: *self-reformulation*, the rewording of something you have said yourself; and *other-reformulation*, the reworking of someone else's words.

Quirk *et al.* (1985: 1311) contemplate only the first of these, self-reformulation, and see it as a lexico-grammatical phenomenon. They define it as 'a rewording in the second (defining) appositive of the lexical content of the first (defined) appositive'. In other words, when a reworded concept is placed in apposition to its original utterance, we have a reformulation. They envisage four types, reformulation:

(a) based on linguistic information;
(b) based on factual knowledge;
(c) providing a more precise formulation;
(d) for revision.

The first, linguistic reformulation, consists in proposing a synonymous expression in apposite position:

> This is what is sometimes referred to as *an intentional terminological inexactitude*, in other words *a lie*.

A number of typical phrases said to introduce linguistic reformulation are listed, including *in other words, in words of one syllable, put (more) simply*.

The second, factual reformulation, gives further details:

> *The Nordic countries*, or *Denmark, Finland, Iceland, Norway, Sweden ...*

The following example is given of the third kind, reformulation for precision:

> They started going to *church, the Catholic Church*

And this example for the last sort, reformulation for revision:

> *All families*, well (at least) *those who can afford to*, will be going away for their holiday.

Typical phrases to introduce revision include, *that is (to say), or rather, I mean*. Of these, only *I mean* is found in the briefings (see Chapter 4).

The most common self-reformulation expression in the briefings is *in other words*. It is used predominantly by the journalists (of 20 occurrences, 19 are by the press) and it is not restricted to linguistic reformulation, that is, to simply proposing a synonym. In fact, it is not generally used to go over the same ground a second time. On the contrary, its chief functions include: to ask the question again from a different perspective:

(43)   Q: Joe, Strobe's talks with President Ahtisaari, will they follow more talks between Ahtisaari and Milosevic? *In other words*, will the envoys return to Belgrade and so forth?

to highlight an aspect of the question:

(44)   Q: I'm asking what is the evidence in Kosovo that he is somehow not being able to carry out his will? *In other words*, refugees are still being expelled.

to add extra background information to the question:

(45)   Q: I'm thinking of that report that indicated that there was a reduction in the map-making, *in other words*, there were two map-making organizations that were pooled together and they ended up using maps that were outdated for this tragedy.

to summarize the gist of the question:

(46)   Q: Are the ceilings in the new NATO states as a group in any way proportionately lower or different from ceilings in the longer-term NATO nations of the group? *In other words*, I'm really asking, are you trying to [...] address Russian concerns?

Other expressions used for self-reformulation include: *what I'm saying is, what I'm trying to get at is*:

(47)   Q: Why did it take longer than anticipated – and *what I'm trying to get at is*, what were the concrete goals during the period just ended and what factors militated against realization of those goals?

The main use of self-reformulation by the press, then, is for question clarification. It is usually spontaneous in the sense of being offered by the questioner when they sense something else is needed, but it can also be the result of solicitation:

(48)   Q: Do you know if it will be accompanied by a personal appearance?
       MR LOCKHART: What do you mean, personal appearance?
       Q: I mean, *in other words*, will one of the White House lawyers actually go –

Self-reformulation, as can be seen, is a feature of co-operation in talk. The speaker tries to help the listener out by not *presuming* too much shared knowledge, *creating* it instead. When unsolicited it can be interpreted as a kind of pre-emptive negotiation of meaning. Classifying it as co-operative does not of course mean it cannot be used antagonistically, to ask a hostile question:

(49)   Q: [...] why shouldn't we believe critics who say this is a morass, they're not going to be able to get out, there is no exit strategy? *What I'm saying is*, why should we give you credibility when you say it's not a permanent fix and not believe your critics who say it is?

9.2.2 Other-reformulation

Our main interest here, however, is in other-reformulation. The rephrasing of another's turn can be of three types in these briefings:

1   the podium reformulates a question;
2   a questioner reformulates a podium response;
3   the podium counter-formulates a questioner's reformulation.

In an article entitled 'Reformulating the question: a device for answering/not answering questions in news interviews and press conferences', Clayman (1993) deals with the first of these, taking the majority of his examples from US presidential press conferences. He analyses the use of reformulation of the question by respondents as a method for evasion or for shifting the questioner's agenda in their favour. He then looks at the ways in which these attempts are in turn resisted by questioners. He also lists a number of the prevailing features of other-reformulation. In general, he notes, 'the reformulation occurs within a discrete unit of talk which is syntactically disjoined from the ensuing response'. In other words, where reformulation occurs, the respondent usually takes time off – before launching into their actual response – to rephrase the question in a sort of preface to the response. Moreover, 'subsequent talk initially builds upon the reformulation rather than the original question' (Clayman 1993: 164), hence, its potential for avoidance. However, those that are most 'dangerous', in Clayman's terms, those most likely to pass unnoticed, are 'embedded' reformulations where there is no separate passage containing the reworked version. For example, and perhaps most commonly, assertions of agreement to a part of the question may actually serve to ignore other parts. Summarizing the question may also be a way of glossing over the threatening parts and altering the emphasis.

Nevertheless, Clayman does recognize that reformulation can be innocuous, a mechanism for meaning negotiation:

> In some instances, reformulations appear to be produced straightforwardly in the service of a kind of clarification. The need for clarification can arise when the question is particularly complex.

> (Clayman 1993: 165–6)

If other-reformulations was *never* innocent, it could, of course, not be used as a technique for evasion.

Towards the end of his study, Clayman concludes that agenda-shifting reformulation of the question is fairly infrequent, but is likely to be found more often in press conferences than news interviews since the existence of multiple questioners prevailing in the former mean less likelihood of a follow-up. Conference reporters may, therefore, be more inclined to ask complex, multiple-component questions – the sort that tempt reformulation – and they have less chance of challenging any eventual agenda shift. However, the more intimate atmosphere of the particular sort of briefings under scrutiny here and the fact that, as we have seen, individuals can and frequently do take follow-up turns, militate strongly against any obvious skulduggery by the podium, and blatant agenda-shifting reformulation of the type uncovered by Clayman rarely goes unchallenged. If a response is deemed incomplete or ambiguous, the journalist generally has few logistical problems in asking for clarification or reposing the question. Any obvious attempts to digress from the question agenda are unlikely to succeed. There are, in fact, numerous occasions when a questioner tells the podium that they feel he has not properly answered their question and these will be dealt with more fully in Chapter 12, on avoidance.

9.2.3   Reformulation of questions by the podium

One of the most frequent kinds of podium reformulation of a question is an innocuous and fairly routine long-winded rewording to simply say 'yes':

(50)   Q: – is that the same thing he told the White House?
       MR LOCKHART: I haven't checked, but I'm certain that what he reported to the news media is the same that he's reported to us.

There is often a reluctance to give a very short 'yes, it is' or 'no, it isn't' style answer. This can partly be explained as politeness – responses longer than necessary charm the hearer's positive face (see Section 7.5.1) – and partly in terms of situational appropriacy: politicians are expected to supply lengthy responses in news interview situations (see Harris 1991). The reformulation can be a repetition of part of the question as a pre-text to the response:

(51)   Q: Joe, repatriating nearly a million Kosovars would be a monumental task, requiring countless vehicles, bridging equipment, engineering battalions, on and on. *What should we make of the fact* that none of that is being assembled?
       MR LOCKHART: I think *what you should make of it is* there's important work going on now, that General Clark was [...]

although this can sound either patronizing or defensive.

Repetition of part of the questioner's turn, however, can also be used to challenge it, especially when the formulaic *not a question of* is used, as in these examples (from a concordance of *a question of* with context words *not, *n't*):

(52)   Q: Joe, that said, is the White House confident that the President *did enough* to prepare the American people for how long this is likely to take [...]
MR LOCKHART: [...] This is ***not a question of** did you do enough*. We will continue to speak to this in a variety of forums [continues]

(53)   Q: I'm really trying to find out what hasn't worked or what are the factors –
MR BERGER: I ***don't*** think ***it's a question of** what hasn't worked*. I think it's a question of it takes time. It takes time [...] for the habits of peace to take hold.

In example (52), the podium challenges a suggestion of presidential shortcoming that he failed to 'do enough' on some issue. In example (53), Mr Berger challenges the presupposition in the question that 'some things have not worked'.

The podiums must constantly be on their toes, on the lookout for damaging question presuppositions (the context here is the decision to issue an ultimatum to President Milosevic):

(54)   Q: Joe, there's obviously support within NATO for this decision, but there were emergency meetings in most of the European capitals yesterday, and the Europeans are not exactly happy campers over this result. [...]
MR LOCKHART: Well, I would suggest that your characterization of them not being 'happy campers' is a result of what President Milosevic is doing, not as a result of any split in the unity.

The podium is willing to admit that the Europeans may not be *happy campers* (i.e. 'overjoyed') but goes on to offer a different interpretation of its cause (*what President Milosevic is doing*) from that implied by the questioner (*a split in the unity*).

The challenge is signalled by the phrase *I would suggest*. A concordance of *I would* in the context of *dispute, question, quibble* (and synonyms) gives us other examples:

(55)   Q: Joe, going back to – displaced people, I think at the NATO briefing today they said there may be as many as 750,000 inside of Kosovo who have been driven from their homes [...] Do you feel any pressure because of this pending crisis to change your strategy [...]?
MR LOCKHART: *I would question* the foundation of the question that somehow leaves with NATO the responsibility for what's going on. NATO did not ethnically cleanse a million people out of the country. NATO did not close the border and force them back in [...]

Once again the podium challenges what they see as an erroneous presupposition – that somehow NATO is to blame for the refugee crisis – and proceeds to give his version. However, on this occasion the questioner is not satisfied with the challenge:

(56) Q: Well, how is that an answer? I mean, NATO is not responsible for the refugees that went across the border either, and we're doing everything we can to help them.

The questioner claims that the podium has not answered the question about strategy change and has used the presupposition challenge to indulge in a spot of political rhetoric. This is one occasion on which the podium comes close to attempting the kind of agenda avoiding or agenda shifting which Clayman outlines (see Section 9.2.2). Notice that he does not succeed.

These damaging presuppositions embedded in questions and the podium's reaction to them are very noticeable features of these texts and of most other forms of modern news interviews. The phenomenon is treated at length in Section 9.3.

It can be seen from these examples that the podium employs a number of formulae to indicate his disagreement with the questioner's view of events. These include *it's not a question of …* , *I wouldn't (don't) accept (the premise) (that characterization)*, *I would question, dispute, reject (the foundation of the question)* and similar.

The next example is slightly different. The podium challenges the use of a single word – *party* – and offers his own alternative – *commemoration*:

(57) Q: Did the President consider at any time asking NATO to call off the party this weekend, to call off the *party* – the celebration?
      MR LOCKHART: No. I mean, *I would quibble* a little bit with the question because it's not a party. It's a *commemoration* of 50 years of what we believe is the most important alliance we have, NATO.

What he is reformulating here, however, is the tone of the question rather than any fact, hoping to replace its levity with a touch of *gravitas*.

9.2.4 *Reformulation of responses by the press*

Rephrasing by journalists of the podium's responses is the richest and most complex source of examples of the phenomenon of reformulation in these texts. This is because response rephrasing is a necessary, inalienable part of modern news interviewing. In analysing the cohesion between questions and their preceding responses, Jucker (1986, which develops Blum-Kulka 1983) divides interviewer 'next moves', that is, moves after a response, into two major categories – those following a response felt by the interviewer to be 'supporting' and those felt to be 'hedging' the original question. If he or she decides it was supporting, the interviewer 'either extends the topic or shifts to a new topic'. Alternatively, if they feel the response was non-supporting (i.e. did not answer the question fully) 'he/she produces a "reformulation" or "challenge" ' (Jucker 1986: 126). In other words, they either move on to new ground or move back to cover the old. The difference, according to Jucker, between a reformulation and a challenge is that the first is more 'cooperative', the second more 'probing'. Here, we shall treat both types as variants of topic reformulation. To Jucker's analysis we might add that, since the decision is entirely up to the questioner, there may well be occasions when the choice as to whether a podium response is supporting or not is taken on tactical grounds.

There are a good number of signals by questioners that their turn is a reformulation of a previous turn. These include: *just to be clear, just to be precise:*

(58)   Q: So adjournment – *just to be precise*, if I may – so adjournment without a verdict is acceptable to the White House?

is it fair to say:

(59)   Q: So is it – excuse me. *Is it fair to say that* the President's position is the same as it has been since the beginning of the air campaign?

is that correct?: is it correct to say … ?

(60)   Q: So the Central European countries will, in fact, have relatively lower levels of hardware permitted than others, *is that correct*?

you're not disputing that:

(61)   Q: So *you're* also *not disputing*, then, that the British might have differences with us about something that might happen two or three months down the road?

plus a number of variations upon *are you saying that … ? Is what you're saying … ?* and so on. Notice that all these expressions are very likely to be preceded by the word *so*. The examples discussed below were garnered principally from two concordances: one of *saying* with *you* as context word and the other of *so* preceded by the context item *Q*.

9.2.5   The functions of response reformulation

There is no shortage of examples of simple innocuous press reformulation to check on facts:

(62)   MR LOCKHART: Houston and Austin. There will be a lunch and dinner fundraiser. We may have another event that could be added to the schedule – it tells me here not to rule it out.
      Q: So it might be an overnight?
(63)   Q: So you feel the caps should stay, no change at all in the caps?

This kind of recapitulation is, of course, utterly innocent and a normal feature of conversation. However, it can be turned into a useful weapon. At times confirmation questions are actually feelers put out to detect weak spots or they prepare the ground for hostile questions:

(64)   Q: So is it – excuse me. Is it fair to say that the President's position is the same as it has been since the beginning of the air campaign?
        MR LOCKHART: That is correct.
        Q: So there was a false impression created that he was ruling out ground troops?

Note again the damning suggestion that the President might have had a change of mind ('the dreaded sin of flip-flopping' – see Foreword). See also examples (4) and (39).

Also very frequent are reformulations that summarize the gist of a podium's response:

(65)   Q: So simply put, the level of cooperation from the White House depends on what the Committee wants to do?
(66)   Q: Aren't you saying that, in effect, this is going to take a lot longer than you originally anticipated?

Expressions of the type *simply put, in fact, in effect* and *basically* function as indicators of gist. Like the ones above, this kind of reformulation is generally provocative to some degree.

These examples need to be considered in the light of Jucker's division of post-response moves into topic-developing or topic-reformulating types. It is sometimes very difficult to decide whether a gist-clarification move falls into the first or second of these categories. Consider the following, where the topic of debate is the intricate, technical one of a treaty stipulating the details of decommissioning of military equipment. A question is posed:

(67)   Q: So the Central European countries will, in fact, have relatively lower levels of hardware permitted than others, is that correct?

This is, in fact, checking the gist of what has been said concerning the Central European countries several turns previously. A more immediate topic was the situation of Germany. A gist question, which concentrates on part of the topic, can be seen as *shifting* the topic onto that detail rather than just recapitulating. In the move, which precedes example (66), the podium has spent some time emphasizing the painstaking nature of NATO's so-called air campaign, of which the following is a short extract:

(68)   MR LOCKHART: [...] We have a sustained, systematic, phased air campaign that we believe, over time, can methodically and systematically take away the weapons that Milosevic uses [continues]

The follow-up question 'Aren't you saying that, in effect, this is going to take a lot longer than you originally anticipated?' may in a sense be a gist question, and is certainly signalled as such (with *in effect*), but it shifts the topic from both the President's policy (the topic of the original question) and the meticulousness of the air campaign (the main topic of the response) to concentrate entirely on the time factor implied by such circumspection.

Rather than *gist* we might talk here of *upshot* reformulations, but it is often difficult to distinguish the two. In any case, as was pointed out in Section 9.2.1, reformulation is rarely used solely to cover old ground or, rather, even old ground can be refocused in a number of ways and thus influence the development of topic.

This Janus nature of such questioning is not simply a feature of these texts, it is inherent in the language. A question frame like *are you saying* … and its variations[4] can be used to mean 'does what you have just said have the *sense* that … (followed by a reformulation)' or to 'does what you have just said have the *implication* that … (followed by a new proposition)'. The word *say* itself is systematically ambiguous[5] in this sense. Occasionally, there is some signal that one or the other is intended, for example:

(69) Q: Right. But are you saying you want Gingrich to exert leadership now?

The combination of *right* (meaning 'I understand what you just said') together with the topic changing signal *but* indicates that the question is a new proposition. In the following:

(70) Q: Joe, it sounds like you're saying some thought is being given to sending someone back to Belgrade. Is that true?

it sounds like and *is that true?* signal an intention to check comprehension. The point is, however, that the existence in the language of sets of devices, which fail to distinguish between forward-looking upshot questions and backward-looking gist questions, implies that the distinction itself in natural communication is often of little importance; both types of question are meant to shape the progression of topic in the discourse.

There are also a fair number of examples of unreservedly hostile or provocative reformulations of a response. They are meant simply to depict the administration in a negative light to provoke a response of some sort:

(71) Q: So the level of White House cooperation at this point is uncertain?

or they are 'leading' questions, designed to elicit some policy statement, which may be taken down and used against it at some later date:

(72) Q: So when Robin Cook says that it doesn't necessarily take a peace agreement for ground forces to go in, that's our policy as well?

(73)   Q: So you're saying that you could foresee a circumstance where Serb forces might be beginning a withdrawal from Kosovo, but NATO would continue to bomb?

or perhaps they do both:

(74)   Q: So you're saying this former top aide to Mr. Clinton perjured himself in front of the grand jury?

Here, both the former aide and, by association, the President are cast in a bad light, whilst any acquiescence to an accusation of perjury could have legal consequences. This *agent provocateur* technique has been discussed in detail in Section 6.5.

A particular kind of *agent provocateur* reformulation has been commented on by Heritage (also quoted by Jucker 1986: 133):

> The interviewer is invited to agree to a characterization of his position that overtly portrays him as critical of, or in conflict with, some third party [...] the interviewer's formulation probes his described position by testing how far he is prepared to go towards characterizing his position in overtly conflictual terms.
>
> (Heritage 1985: 110)

We have seen a number of instances of this technique in these briefings where it is used particularly to portray the podium or his clients in conflict with some other official source [the British in examples (61) and (72), a 'former top aide to Mr Clinton' in example (74), the White House contradicting itself in example (64)]. In Chapter 5, we discussed the press predilection for attributing contentious opinions to 'friendly' sources.

However, as we saw in Section 9.2.4, it is those questions which have a negative presupposstion or implication embedded in them that are likely to be the most damaging. Sometimes, this embedded criticism can be very hard to defend against:

(75)   Q: So the White House is not feeling any pressure from the American people, per se, to wrap it up?

As well as the direct question about *feeling pressure*, the question contains the implication that the White House is not doing enough to *wrap it up*. The podium's response manages to address both:

(76)   MR LOCKHART: I don't think so. I think the President believes, and I think the American public believes that we're doing this for the right reason and we should stay at it until the job is done.

But in the following example, the podium is less skilful:

(77)   Q: Joe, so you're now saying that air defenses have been weakened enough
to go in and –

MR LOCKHART: I think you can draw conclusions based on what he has
said and what the NATO military leaders have said.

The 'now' in the questioner's phrase 'so you're *now* saying' implies a contradiction
with some previous statement – 'flip-flopping' again – and the podium's response
fails to scotch the suggestion.

9.2.6   Counter-reformulation

When faced with a press reformulation of their words, the podium has a variety
of possible response strategies. He can simply reject it:

(78)   Q: Well, basically, almost how you're saying this, it's basically saying that
he's for Africa, leave it alone, this is none of your concern, stay with
Africa. That's what it almost sounds like you're saying.

MR LOCKHART: No, I prefer to leave it in what I said.

Note that this exchange is possible because of the ambiguity inherent in *say*,
which the press use in the sense of 'mean', but which the podium uses to signify
'the words I used'.

Very often the podium will reject the new version by denying he said such
a thing:

(79)   Q: So adjournment – just to be precise, if I may – so adjournment without a verdict is acceptable to the White House?

MR LOCKHART: I don't think I said that. I said, I think the time has come
to go, now, to take a vote […]

As in this example, the podium frequently reiterates his own version in preference
to that offered by the journalist, that is, he reformulates the reformulation
[(80–86) from the concordance of *I'm saying*]:

(80)   Q: If they refrain from launching a new offensive but still don't sign the
peace agreement, you're saying they're still going to get hit?

MR LOCKHART: I'm not saying that. I'm saying that he faces some tough
choices, and he's going to need to make them.

In this case, there is both a signal of disagreement, of rejection of the questioner's
version – 'I'm not saying that' – and also a signal of 're-reformulation' – 'I'm saying that …'. The presence of this latter creates a deliberate echo effect: 'So you're
saying …' – 'No I'm saying …'. What is striking, however, is that the former, the
explicit signal of rejection of the press' version, is as often as not lacking:

(81)   Q: You're saying that all of the suggestions about Chinese espionage are
simply allegations and that the administration is not convinced that

there has been any actual act of espionage by the Chinese against the U.S.?

MR LOCKHART: I'm saying that there are allegations, there are investigations that are ongoing and it would not be appropriate for me to comment on ongoing investigations.

This does not happen by accident but by strategic design. The following podium counter-reformulations contain no explicit signals of agreement or rejection. Is the reply a *yes* or *no* to the question?:

(82)   Q: So you're saying the trip is not canceled, but postponed?

MR McCURRY: I'm saying that the President remains strongly of the opinion that a trip to that region is both desirable and in the best interests of the people of the United States [...]

(83)   Q: If all they presented him is a longer-term, 30- to 45-day CR,[6] are you saying he would veto that?

MR McCURRY: I'm saying that we've got an interest in getting things done. And if it helps to get things done to have a very short duration continuing resolution that helps get things done [...]

The issue is further confounded by the fact that podium counter-reformulation is not confined to occasions of disagreement. If the press reformulation is deemed correct and non-threatening, the podium will often reformulate it in turn:

(84)   Q: So are you saying there's hope?

MR LOCKHART: I'm saying that we wouldn't be involved in the process if we didn't think there was hope of moving this forward to a peaceful settlement.

We have already mentioned the tendency to spend time on affirmative responses (Section 9.2.3) for politeness. This type of reformulation, however, is rarely signalled as agreement as such; it is the press's responsibility to interpret them.

It is clearly tactically convenient for the podium to avoid outright 'yes' or 'no' to difficult or leading questions. His counter-reformulation usually restates the original proposition in more general terms, which allows him to avoid committing himself to the more particular original one. In example (82), the trip is described as 'a good thing' but we are none the wiser as to the specific question of whether it will take place. In example (83), the general principle of getting things done promptly is lauded, but any decision on a veto is deferred to a later date. This tactic is perhaps most clearly illustrated in example (85), where the podium avoids commitment to specific courses of action such as resolving the refugee problem (whose outcome at the time was uncertain) and rebuilding (which would involve considerable expense) in favour of more general noble proposals such as 'promoting democracy':

(85)   Q: [...] you're saying there are two things. One is to get the refugees back; that's the first goal. But then, the longer-term goal, rebuilding Southeastern Europe –

MR LOCKHART: What I'm saying is, short-term, we've made very clear what they need to do. Long-term, we have had a long-term policy of promoting democracy within Serbia.

Alternatively, if you want to avoid being pinned down, you can actually answer *yes* and *no* in the same response:

(86) Q: Right. But are you saying you want Gingrich to exert leadership now?
      MR LOCKHART: I'm saying it's not our position to dictate who does, but we accept the wisdom and the judgment of Representative Gephardt when he says the Hill is in chaos right now.

The podium sidesteps any accusation of interference in Congressional affairs, but manages to confirm the suggestion that the Republican leadership (represented by Mr Gingrich) is indeed weak.

9.2.7 Countering sarcasm in reformulations

To conclude, we have so far looked at the podium's reaction to fairly straight-forward reformulations of his original statements. But open hostility is not the only danger for the podium in press rephrasing: they can also be glib to the point of sarcasm. Indeed, there is a particular type of hostile reformulation that has the underlying sense: 'So (you really expect us to believe it when) you're saying…?', a kind of sarcastic disbelief:

(87) Q: So you're saying that no one at the White House was informed about that deposition by those four people? Right? It's simply sealed within those four. They didn't tell you, they didn't tell anybody else, they didn't tell Bruce Lindsey?

It has the further advantage of being *defeasible*, that is, the questioner can always deny they ever meant to call the podium a liar ('I was just asking a straight ques-tion'). This illocutionary attack on the podium's veracity means that he is in the difficult position of having to defend himself as well as find a suitable reply to the question. What tactics does the podium adopt in such cases? One way of defus-ing sarcasm is to ignore it, as in the following (the topic is problems of security in the light of alleged espionage at US nuclear labs by Chinese agents):

(88) Q: So people came to him and said, gee, there are kind of some problems and maybe we ought to worry about them?
      MR LOCKHART: No, I don't think that's how it happened, Jim.

or the podium can reformulate the reformulation removing the glibness:

(89) MR TOIV: Oh, yes. There's a three-day trip to five states. The President's looking forward to visiting every one of them.

> Q: He's looking forward to collecting money from every one of them for the Democratic party. (Laughter.)
> MR TOIV: He's looking forward to helping some very good candidates in those states and also talking about some very important issues.

or he can enter into the spirit and good-humouredly turn a barbed reformulation back on the questioners (the topic is Democratic consultants found to be working for one side in the Israeli elections):

> (90)   Q: So they're just trying to make money. In other words, they're just consultants making the cash, but there's no connection with the White House.
> MR LOCKHART: Well, I mean – pursuing your craft, and being compensated fairly for it is something that everyone in this room understands – (laughter) –

9.3   Questions within questions: embedded propositions

9.3.1   *Embedding disputable propositions*

As we have seen, some of the most difficult questions for the podium to manage are without doubt those containing what Harris calls 'disputable propositions' when these are somehow 'either embedded in questions or in assertions prefacing a question' (Harris 1991: 81). She gives, among others, the following examples (original punctuation):

> (91)   INTERVIEWER: what's the future if uneconomic pits continue to be around – won't that in the end undermine the mining industry
> TRADE UNION LEADER: well – as you know Miss Chalmers it must be that you're listening to your own propaganda because for the last 40 minutes I've been explaining to you that the NCB in Britain is the most efficient and technologically advanced industry in the world
> (92)   INTERVIEWER: I ask you Prime Minister why you haven't applied real consumer power to parents in education by giving them real parent power
> PRIME MINISTER: we have to some extent – by doing assisted places – and they're very important

(Harris 1991: 85–6)

The first strongly implies that there actually *are* uneconomic pits around, and the second definitely presupposes that the Prime Minister has *not* 'applied real consumer power' in education. In both cases, the interviewee picks up on and challenges these implied propositions.

As she points out, they often act as accusations and are all the more insidious for being covert, almost undercover. The interviewee or respondent is faced with the choice of tacitly accepting the accusation or challenging the question. They might even fail to notice it. To make matters worse, if a respondent challenges the question too often they can give the impression of being evasive and uncooperative. The best solution is usually to call attention to one's disagreement with the question and propose one's own alternative version of events, a process that generally involves a certain amount of reformulation.

It is also the case, however, that all questions (indeed all meaningful utterances) rely on presuppositions, often quite a number, and so their appearance in an interview question does not necessarily imply a covert attack on the interviewee. Moreover, the questioner may simply have a different set of facts from the respondent:

(93)　Q: On Korea – what are you planning to highlight tomorrow? Will the President – has there been any consideration of the South Korean request that the U.S. consider lifting sanctions?

　　　　MR McCURRY: Well, there has not been a request by the Republic of Korea to lift sanctions on North Korea. There have been some suggestions that President Kim Dae Jung has an interest in raising that issue and exploring it with President Clinton during their state visit tomorrow.

The question takes for granted that South Korea has made a request that the United States consider lifting sanctions. The podium, according to his lights, corrects this. But the process by which this information is presented as granted is an interesting one. The disputable proposition 'that South Korea has requested the US to consider lifting sanctions' has become embedded inside the main question ('has there been any consideration …?') by being transformed into a nominal form 'the South Korean request'. This nominalization (Section 0.3.2) has the double consequence of both factualizing, reifying, the proposition by presenting it as already known, uncontentious information, and also making it harder to prise out of the rest of the question for special consideration.

Similarly:

(94)　Q: Mike, can you fill in the details on the reprimand that Hazel O'Leary got from Leon Panetta? And does the President intend to talk to her about this?

The proposition 'Leon Panetta reprimanded Hazel O'Leary' is nominalized and factualized in *the reprimand*, which is then embedded in a prepositional phrase. The rest of the question ('And does the President …?') builds on this presupposition. The podium at once disabuses the questioner:

(95)　MR McCURRY: No, I can't because that's not the nature of the conversation she had with Mr Panetta. Mr Panetta met with Secretary O'Leary

> yesterday to review her upcoming testimony on the Hill, to, one, give
> her support for the job she's been doing [continues with praise of
> Secretary O'Leary]

The 'nature of the conversation', he declares, far from being a reprimand, was
a commendation.

In the following, the nominalization of disputable propositions is instead used
tactically, to insert criticism of the podium and clients:

(96)   Q: The Senator from Virginia, John Warner, says the lack of a U.S.
exit strategy from Bosnia puts the U.S. on the brink of disaster
right now.

The nominalized 'lack of a US exit strategy' is embedded both structurally – in
being thematized (see the next paragraph) – and rhetorically as attributed to
another speaker. Nevertheless, the podium manages to dig it out for rebuttal:

(97)   MR McCURRY: He is wrong that there is no exit strategy. We have a mission plan with clear mission objectives [continues]

The questioner implies that John Warner actually said: 'The lack of a United
States exit strategy from Bosnia puts the US on the brink of disaster'. According
to information structure theory in systemic linguistics (Brazil 1985; Halliday
1985), utterances generally convey some *given* information (ideally, knowledge
shared between speaker and hearer) and some *new* (to the hearer) information. In
normal, unmarked circumstances, the given comes first (as *Theme*) and the new
follows (as *Rheme*). In the implied statement above, 'the lack of a US exit strategy
from Bosnia' is very probably being presented as given information, as shared
knowledge. By definition, given information is supposed to be uncontentious.
Passing disputable propositions off as shared knowledge is particularly disingenuous and is likely to be met with a challenge.

Another way of embedding a contentious proposition is to place it inside a subordinate clause [as in example (53): 'I'm just trying to find out *what hasn't
worked*...']. As we have already seen in example (91), subordinate *if* clauses are
frequently used in this way, for example:

(98)   Q: If Gerry Adams can't, in effect, deliver something from the IRA, at
least a commitment to peace, then what exactly is the U.S. trying to do
in talking with him?
        MR McCURRY: We don't accept the premise of that question because he
has been an important contributor in the discussions that have
occurred to date and we hope he will remain so.

The illocutionary sense of the *if* clause is 'given this premise to be the case', and
the question follows in the main clause. Once again, the proposition is presented

in the guise of given information. The podium is forced to formally refute the truth of the premise.

Still another way of embedding is to slip the contentious proposition into a list and hope it will pass unnoticed:

(99)   Q: Do you think that the practical effect of what you did in October by putting in the monitors and trusting Milosevic has tied NATO's hands –

MR LOCKHART: Mara, it's not a question of trusting Milosevic. If we trusted him, why would we put in monitors? We put in monitors to verify the agreements we've made.

the questioner equates 'putting in the monitors' with 'trusting Milosevic' (the use of the linker *and* between the two propositions allows the ambiguity of 'you did *a* and then you did *b*' and 'you did *a* which meant/caused/implied *b*'). The podium's rejoinder instead reformulates the two as mutually exclusive, as opposites in sense.

A reporting verb like *refuse* carries within it presuppositions, which a questioner can employ to effect:

(100)   Q: The White House supposedly refuses to intervene to try to resolve the tobacco dispute. Is that true?

MR McCURRY: We have not intervened at any point in the process. We have monitored the discussions the parties are having and we hope […]

The use of this verb presupposes a deliberate intention on the part of the actor (the White House in this case), and also strongly implies that whatever the actor is *not* doing they *should* be doing. Note how the podium reformulates the concept removing *refuses* and along with it these hostile insinuations.

The verb *say* can also convey unwelcome associations:

(101)   Q: But as it's retested again in the District Court using those new criteria, will the White House continue to say that it is complying?

MR McCURRY: Absolutely, because they are […]

The question wishes to hint at the world of difference between the White House *saying* it is complying and its actually doing so. The podium once again is forced to address the hidden accusation openly. The podium has in essence to respond to two questions, the concealed question: 'Is the White House complying?' (reply: 'they are') and the question frame: 'Will the White House continue to say?' (reply: 'Absolutely'). Harris comments that 'one of the features most noticeable in political interviews is that many of the questions […] contain a frame (such as *are you saying, are you arguing, do you accept, is it your view*, etc.) followed by an embedded proposition'. This 'provides the politician with the choice of responding to the frame (*yes I am* or *no I'm not* saying that) rather than the proposition directly'

(Harris 1991: 91). In the briefings, we find the following example where the frame rather than the embedded question is addressed:

(102)   Q: Have we given any thought to where we're going to put these 20,000 –
        MR LOCKHART: We've given a lot of thought to it, we just haven't come
        to a final conclusion.

although here the effect seems either tart or comic. In fact, the press pick up on the comic tone (hardly appropriate to the subject, which is the rehousing of refugees):

(103)   Q: – suggested that they put them in Arkansas. (Laughter.)
        MR LOCKHART: I will pass that suggestion on with your name on it.
        (Laughter.)

Even seemingly innocuous adverbs such as *now* [example (77) and discussion] and *suddenly* can have hidden perils:

(104)   Q: Some of our allies are saying that suddenly the U.S. seems more com-
        mitted to being involved and finding a solution. Is that the case?

The insinuation of 'suddenly' here being that the United States was somehow lax or remiss previously. The podium could also choose to protest the vagueness of the attribution 'some of our allies', but as we have said, challenging the question too often can create a bad impression. Instead, he reformulates the concept, removing the negative implication, emphasizing present energy and commitment:

(105)   MR McCURRY: I'd say that based on the President's direction, we are
        taking steps to try to stimulate the dialogue and accelerate the dialogue
        to bring about an end to the conflict, if that is in fact possible.

Unfortunately, his positive spin is completely ignored:

(106)   Q: What specifics might cause them to say that?

The 'them' refers back to the 'allies' of the original question, as does 'say that' (that the United States has been tardy).[7] The response has been treated as empty rhetoric and utterly disregarded.

   The final example of inserting a damaging presupposition to be discussed here is the 'have you stopped beating your wife?' manoeuvre (the topic is a supposed rift between the President and Senator Jackson):

(107)   Q: Did the phone call mean that they've kissed and made up?

The presupposition being they were at daggers drawn before the call. If the podium answers either *yes* or *no* he admits there was a tiff at some juncture and the press can launch a 'dissension in the administration ranks' story. The podium, however, discerns the danger:

(108)   MR LOCKHART: If you persist in believing that they needed to kiss and make up, I'll let you go on with this. But I think I've addressed that several times.

In her discussion, Harris goes on to observe that, when a disputable proposition is embedded in this way, challenges are not always to the presuppositions themselves of a question. The interviewee often feels authorized to challenge what she calls 'the illocutionary force of a question as a "request for information"' (Harris 1991: 81). In other words, if the question is felt to be a trick one, they may call into doubt whether the interviewer is simply doing their job (in terms we have used before, their *neutralism*). One of her examples is as follows:

(109)   INTERVIEWER: [...] are there any circumstances you can think of – such as confidentiality – which would justify any minister apparently concealing a matter such as this from the House
          MINISTER: well – you are making the accusation of concealment [...]

This kind of challenge seems to be far more common – and when it occurs it is more aggressively achieved – in Harris' data of news interviews than in these briefings. Her other examples include responses such as 'I cannot tell you – and you know that in asking the question', and see also example (91). Podium attacks on their questioners are rarer and certainly less belligerent. In the following, he implicitly indicates to the journalist 'the President cannot tell you – and you know that in asking the question' but in a rather more urbane fashion:

(110)   MR McCURRY: Look, Scott, it's a disingenuous question. You know that the President is not in a position to comment on these things.

9.3.2   *The utility of embedded propositions*

The placing of contentious information in the background, in, as it were, the non-questioning part of the question, causes problems both for the respondent and for the process of communication itself. The podium more often than not has to go back to 'correct' the question, and occasionally the questioner. Time and energy is spent on repair of the breakdown in fluent communication. But the press, at least, rarely see it as time wasted. All communication, including questions, has to be based on *some* presuppositions. *Something* has to be taken for granted about the universe in a question; there is not world enough and time to check every background fact. When the contentious presuppositions are innocent, ingenuous, not part of a hostile strategy, then their challenge or correction is so much the better – new, more precise information can take the place of the old, erroneous one. Where, on the other hand, they are disingenuous and hostile, they are being used by the journalist to put the podium and his vision of events to the test. They contain an alternative representation of the world, all the stronger for being 'fixed' and factualized as uncontentious, background, and shared, and the podium must react or suffer the consequences.

9.4   Conclusion: competing representations of the world

In her study of interrogation – of suspects by the police and witnesses or the accused in the courtroom – Harris notes how questions can be used to portray the world in a certain way. They can constrain 'the truth' in ways favourable to the powerful and hostile to the weak and in a manner that the latter find especially difficult to challenge:

> Not only is it difficult for the less powerful to raise validity claims relating to the 'truth' of the utterances of the more powerful participant but questions are particularly resistant to truth claims interactively, i.e. it is difficult for a defendant or suspect to raise a truth claim about a proposition which is structured into a question.
>
> (Harris 1995: 129)

The situation in these briefings is, of course, very different and the podium is far from being powerless. Nevertheless, he frequently has to defend himself from a hostile vision of events embedded in questions either implicitly or more explicitly in a reformulation. The press, for their part, seem to use their questions to put the institutional version of events to the test and also, if possible, to provoke controversy. In other words, they also constrain 'the truth' in ways favourable to them.

In examining the phenomenon of reformulation in briefings, we have seen how 'the truth' in this form of discourse consists of, exists in, the form of words chosen. As we pointed out in Section 0.6, although these briefings are news-making activities, no newsworthy 'events' occur outside the words themselves, and the 'facts' which are the topic of debate are largely non-verifiable and must be taken on trust. But the words project representations of the world, and the point at issue in these briefings is *which* representation of the world, *which* truth, will prevail – the official, institutional version encoded by the podium or the provocative counter-interpretation of the press meant to put the former to the test? And if the press is the final adjudicator then why do they not always favour their own account? The answer to this last question is that each individual journalist may well do so, but everyone else in the room has a choice between the official version and that single journalist's alternative view.

Moreover, the press, of course, often suggest a second interpretation of events without necessarily totally believing it, in order simply to test the podium's reaction. In fact, which account of reality is accepted is rarely a question of profound belief. Despite protestations to the contrary (especially by the podium – see Section 9.1), news-making is less a question of getting at the objective truth [after all, in the journalistic 'web of facticity', i.e. the mixture of a little observed fact with a great deal of hearsay (Tuchman 1978), the truth is essentially unknowable], more a question of arguing a case. As in a court of law, both sides present their own case and argue against any others with the eventual prize of having their version *inscribed on the record*. The aim of the whole exercise is this: to have your interpretation become the officially accepted one, the one for broadcast and publication. This final agreed version may in the end be the result of compromise, of considerable negotiation – hence reformulation and counter-reformulation of a case may go on for several turns, especially over issues where much face is at risk. The dual role of the press, as both presenters of one side and eventual final arbiters of matters – in the analogy used previously, as counsel for the prosecution and jury – further belies any pretence of objectivity. However, the podium's possession of information and control of source give him immense authority with which to argue his case. The press need their devil's advocacy, their scepticism and their power as composers of the final version of the news to resist and test that case.

10 Metaphors of the world

In this chapter, I attempt to isolate some of the particular metaphors and motifs used systematically by the podium and the press in the hope that this may shed light on the way they see – or profess to see – both the political world they move in and the business of briefing they are engaged in. One thing there is no shortage of are studies, and not just linguistic ones, into metaphor. My excuse in offering yet another is that here corpus techniques are used to analyse authentic spoken texts and the particular lexis the two sides employ is analysed critically to show how metaphor can be a strategic rhetorical weapon.

10.1 Genre-typical systematic metaphors

The isolated employment of a particular metaphor by a speaker/author is generally of limited interest to the discourse analyst. In contrast, the repeated use of a metaphor or set of metaphors may well be highly significant.

As noted by Lakoff and Johnson (1980), many everyday metaphors relating to the same topic can be grouped together into a mega-metaphor on a semantic basis. One of their examples is the group of metaphors such as *is that the foundation for your theory? his argument collapsed, we need to buttress the theory with solid arguments*, which add up to a mega-metaphor of the form THEORIES ARE BUILDINGS (the use of small capitals is their convention). Similarly, metaphors like *his ideas have come to fruition, we need to nip that idea in the bud, the seeds of these ideas were planted in her youth* are all part of a larger systematic metaphor IDEAS ARE PLANTS. The authors call such sets of metaphors 'systematic metaphors'.

However, Lakoff and Johnson (1980) do not investigate the question of genre. Certain metaphors will abound in one kind of speech or writing and be practically absent in another. In fact, it will be argued here that one of the characterizing features of a genre is the kind of metaphor found therein. Elsewhere, I have written about the specific metaphors of business journalism (Partington 1998: 107–20). In this chapter, we will look at the use of metaphors in the White House briefings corpus (*WHB*) and, since it is only possible to judge whether a certain use of metaphor is typical of a particular genre by comparing it with others, the corpus of political interviews (*INTS*) will be used as reference.

10.1.1 *Lexical clusters*

The first stage was a study of the relative frequency (keyword) lists described in Section 0.5. Items of interest in these lists were concordanced and also analysed using the *WordSmith* 'cluster' tool. Clusters, also known as 'lexical bundles' (Biber and Conrad 1999; Biber *et al.* 1999: 990–1024), are simply sequences or strings of words (for *WordSmith* from two to a maximum of eight items), which occur with some frequency in the set of texts the software is asked to process. They 'usually do not represent a complete structural unit', but neither do they occur, as it were, 'by accident', since they very often have 'important grammatical correlates' (Biber and Conrad 1999: 182) and, more relevant to this study, they also frequently have meaning correlates in that they reveal typical ways of saying things and, therefore, typical author/speaker messages. This is best illustrated with an example. Intrigued by the presence of the word *intention* in the keyword lists, I prepared a list of the four-word clusters of the item from the *WHB*:

N	Cluster (4) INTENTION	Freq.
1	have no intention of	12
2	they have no intention	7
3	that they have no	5
4	intention of becoming involved	4
5	no intention of becoming	4
6	we have no intention	4
7	becoming involved in this	3
8	has no intention of	3
9	he has no intention	3
10	intention of using ground	3
11	no intention of using	3
12	of becoming involved in	3
13	of using ground troops	3

An indication thus emerges both of the word's predominant grammatical environment in these texts, which is in negative expressions, especially *no intention of*, as well as its function, that is, to state that *they* or *we* have *no intention* of *becoming involved in* something, in particular of *using ground troops*. Add to this the simple fact that *intention* occurs 43 times in *WHB* but only eight times in *INTS* and just 10 times in the million-word *WSC*, and the importance of this message for the administration becomes very clear.

10.1.2 *Orientational metaphors in politics*

In Section 0.5, we noted how a good number of prepositions or adverbial particles are relatively frequent in *WHB* compared to other genres. Here, I will argue that the presence of certain prepositions and adverbs can be indicative of genre-specific metaphor.

In particular, the items *toward(s)* and *forward* were comparatively very frequent in *WHB*. Lakoff and Johnson discuss at length what they term 'orientational metaphors', which are based on movement in space, and frequently involve prepositions or adverbial particles. For Lakoff and Johnson (1980: 14) they are important because they 'arise from the fact that we have bodies of the sort we have and that function as they do in our physical environment'. They are the leading proof for these authors that metaphors are the result of experience and are therefore basic, natural features of thought and action. They include UP–DOWN, IN–OUT and FRONT–BACK metaphors. *Forward* and *toward(s)* are expressive of the latter, of front or forward movement.

The most frequent lexical collocates of *forward* and *toward(s)* in the briefings texts are forms of the verb *move*, of which *move* and *moving* are both themselves in the keyword lists. The most frequent four-word clusters of *move* confirms the close association:

N	Cluster MOVE (4)	Freq.
1	as we move forward	9
2	to move forward with	7
3	continue to move forward	4
4	going to move forward	4
5	move forward with this	4
6	how we move forward	3
7	in the right direction	3
8	that we can move	3
9	to continue to move	3
10	to try to move	3
11	try to move the	3
12	we can move forward	3
13	we move forward in	3
14	we need to move	3

The briefings clearly contain a systematic metaphor concerning moving forward, which seems to be of the type PROGRESS IS FORWARD MOTION, with the variation MOVING FORWARD IS NECESSARY. Obviously, these metaphors are not restricted to this genre, but these briefings are dominated by them. They are the podium's familiar litany, his call to action. The administration must at all times be seen to be making *progress*, to be moving or *headed* in *the right direction* (see cluster 7 above), on whatever issue is under discussion. The press sees immobility as stagnation, as culpable lethargy and so the administration must project itself as being in a state of perpetual motion. The centrality of the metaphor to these briefings is brought still further home if we compare the first 10 clusters of *move* found in *INTS*:

N	Cluster MOVE (4)	Freq.
1	move on to the	8
2	let me move on	7
3	me move on to	5
4	to move on to	4
5	we'll move on to	4
6	let's move on to	3
7	and we've got to	2
8	I want to move	2
9	let me move onto	2
10	let's move to now	2

Move is thus an interviewer's item in these texts and refers to movement on to another topic.

So much forward motion will often (though by no means always, since it is a good thing in itself) have an aim, a destination. The items *objective(s)* and *goals* as well as *reach* are all in the keyword lists. Note how many of these metaphors have some sort of semantic prosody (Section 0.3.3).

And if FORWARD MOTION is necessary and a good thing, then what is bad? Going *backwards* of course (my emphasis):

(1) MR McCURRY: And we don't want to go *backwards*.
(2) MR LOCKHART: [...] some critics are saying that the administration is *back-pedaling* for not inviting the Reverend Jesse Jackson to the event yesterday.

And even going slow, slowing down, is to be avoided, just as any obstacle which *bogs down* the forward momentum:

(3) MR LOCKHART: [...] and we shouldn't let it get *bogged down* in trying to have another debate, because that inevitably will *slow down* this process.

The obstacle here, interestingly, is 'debate'.

Another orientational metaphor that is important in these briefings, especially their diplomatic aspect, is that of CLOSENESS–DISTANCE, in which CLOSE IS COOPERATIVE and has a favourable prosody. A *close ally* is expected to be reliable. *Close ties*, whatever brings people *closer together*, and especially events that cause others to move *closer* to 'our position', are all jolly good things. Whether or not the reverse holds, that is, whether distance is something bad, rather depends on the situation. When Republicans are found *backing away* or even *backsliding away* from an agreement or commitment, distance is clearly undesirable, as it is when diplomatic positions *move apart*. But 'keeping the guns *away* from criminals', 'to take *away* the tools of these atrocities' are devoutly to be wished. Whether *to walk away* is good or bad depends on what is being walked away from: consider *trouble* and *responsibilities*.

Numbers 3 and 9–11 in the *WHB* cluster list for *move* talk of *trying* and *continuing* to *move forward*. These are clues to the existence of an *effort* motif. The frequency lists include *try, continue, continuing, ongoing, effort(s), step(s)* and *work, worked*. The top 10 four-word clusters of this last are a good illustration of the motif:

N	Cluster WORK (4)	Freq.
1	the work of the	9
2	to work with them	8
3	continue to work with	7
4	will continue to work	7
5	to be worked out	6
6	we continue to work	6
7	and we will continue	5
8	that we are working	5
9	the work that we	5
10	to continue to work	5

Perhaps the best picture of this motif comes from the clusters of *done*, also found in the keyword lists:

N	Cluster DONE (4)	Freq.
1	needs to be done	12
2	to get this done	7
3	get this done this	4
4	this done this year	4
5	we want to get	4
6	and it's being done	3
7	done a good job	3
8	getting the work done	3
9	has to be done	3
10	that needs to be	3
11	the president has done	3
12	to get it done	3

The White House, the administration, believes in *getting 'the work' done*, in *doing 'what needs to be done'*. A view of the world is projected, through the repeated use of the same expressions, in which a hard-working presidency is unstinting in its continuous efforts. What precisely the work and the efforts entail and the exact nature of the objectives are frequently left unspecified. What is important is the projected image of industry: Seest thou a man diligent in his business? He shall stand for President.

10.2   **Projecting metaphors and motifs as a strategy**

Lakoff and Johnson (1980), then, talk of systematic metaphors existing 'in the language'. Here, instead, we see the *creative, strategic* use of particular metaphors and motifs to create a picture of the world, a picture favourable to the speaker and to their clients. These metaphors or motifs are not necessarily newly created for the occasion. They can be fairly old, familiar and clichéd, like MOVING FORWARD IS PROGRESS, but they are called up and reactivated to serve in the present circumstance. For the podium's purposes it is perhaps even better if they are well-worn and easily recognized. They are thus sustained by the wisdom of ages.

Projected images of self and statements about the world can be retrieved by looking, not only at prepositions, but even sometimes at conjunctions. The word *until*, present in all three keyword lists, was concordanced and clustered, with the following results:

N	*Cluster* UNTIL *(4)*	*Freq.*
1	campaign will continue until	5
2	air campaign will continue	4
3	this military campaign until	4
4	until we've met our	4
5	bombing will continue until	3
6	continue until we see	3
7	met our military objectives	3
8	this campaign until we	3
9	until we see the	3
10	we will continue this	3
11	we've met our military	3
12	will continue until we	3

The podium repeats time and again the message that the military campaign, the bombing, will continue *until* its objectives are met. The statement is so strong because it is meant for foreign and enemy as well as home consumption. By comparison, in *INTS* there is only one cluster of any length involving *until*, which was entirely due to David Frost's regular salutation: 'until then, top of the morning to you'.

As the list of *until* clusters shows, the administration is keen to project itself as firm, stalwart, resolute. Similarly, it is always perfectly *clear* in what it says, as the clusters of *made*, present in the keyword lists, confirm:

N	Cluster MADE (4)	Freq.
1	the president has made	13
2	I think the president	10
3	have made very clear	7
4	think the president made	7
5	decision has been made	5
6	made it very clear	5
7	made very clear what	5
8	the president made clear	5
9	we have made very	5
10	made it clear that	4

It is clearly strategically beneficial for the administration to project itself as both *resolute* and *clear* in what it says, given the press alertness for any sign of tergiversation.

10.3   Lexical keywords

10.3.1   Semantic sets

Most of the items concordanced so far have been grammatical words (or semi-grammatical, such as *made*). There are also many *lexical* items in the keyword lists that indicate how the participants project their view of the world. The appearance of a single item by itself is usually of limited interest, but when whole semantic groups appear, a picture of how the world is seen by the participants begins to emerge.

The lists are full of words indicating mental processes: *tell, know, seen, looking, talking*. Following on from this last process, the briefings world is a wordy one, one that is full of talk, witness: *talk/talked/talks, discussion(s), discussed, statement(s), conversation, speak, negotiations, dialogue, articulated, expressed*, among others. The administration depicts itself, predictably, as an honest one which *honors* its *commitments, agreements*. It is also *humanitarian* and appalled by (its opponents') *atrocities, crimes, repression, genocide*. It is divided between *peace* (*peaceful, peacekeeping*) and *conflict* (*bombing, strikes*), the resolution of which contrast is to be brought about by *diplomacy*, and the above-mentioned *dialogue*, etc.

If we return to the *clear* group of words, the items *clear, clearly* and *clarify* are all significant in the lists. However, concordance evidence shows how they are used differently by the two sides. The podium uses *clear* extensively to insist *our position/ our message/my language is clear*, etc., as well as *we/the President has made clear our/his position* (see *made* clusters above). *Clarify*, on the other hand, is commonly employed by the press, as in *just to clarify one point.../can you clarify ...?* and so on. The word *clearly* is used by both sides as a rhetorical instrument to make an argument, perhaps even to pass off as uncontroversial parts of the argument that are not necessarily so:

(4) MR LOCKHART: A near cease-fire is *clearly* not sufficient to meet those conditions [...]

(5) Q: I suppose if the President had wanted to say, to stop, he could have found the word 'stop', but he didn't. So, *clearly*, we've not, I take it, committed ourselves to preventing all the killing in Kosovo?

The podium also uses it to insist on his own plain-speaking, for example, 'I have explained it as clearly as I know how', 'we've laid down our conditions clearly' (to President Milosevic). The item *clarity*, on the other hand, seems to be utilized by the podium to avoid answering the question or at least to avoid going into too much detail:

(6) MR LOCKHART: So I think, for now, our view is that it is prudent to be cautious. Again, we need more *clarity* [...]

(7) MR LOCKHART: I think if you listen to the important part of what I'm saying here about a cautious – being cautious and understanding, that the need for *clarity*, the need for details, the need for seeing implementation.

As so often, this last move fails to deter the questioner, who returns with a sarcastic echo of the podium's words:

(8) Q: Joe, pending *clarity* and detail and implementation, are Chernomyrdin and Ahtisaari singing from the same page [...]?

Note the rather clichéd metaphor *to sing from the same page*, meaning to be in accord, to issue the same public message.

10.3.2 *Concordancing items from the frequency lists*

A good number of other lexical items found in at least one of the relative frequency lists reflect systematic metaphors or motifs. The item *fair* was found in one list and we have already remarked on the running debate on what is *fair* and *unfair* behaviour (Section 6.7). Other examples are *strong*/*strength*, which, when concordanced, were found to collocate frequently with *economy*:

1 the numbers reflect the combination of the **strength** of the American economy –

2 that changes our fundamental view on the **strength** of the U.S. economy.

3 the Congress wants to see done, to keep our economy **strong** and growing into that 21st century.

4   want to make sure that the very **strong** news on the economy today
      dominated the President's message
5   We have low inflation. It is a **strong** economy, but that doesn't mean [...]
6   Indonesia as a **strong** and growing economy in the Asia Pacific region
7   – there's **strong** consumer spending going on in our country –
8   The U.S. economy remains strong. We have **strong** growth, as evidenced by
      the latest GDP numbers
9   education and the American people so we can have a **strong**, growing
      economy in the 21st century
10   The important thing is that the fundamentals in the economy are very
      strong.

In actual fact, the item *strong* was only found in one list, but *economic* and *fiscal* were found in more than one. Concordancing the briefings corpus for *econom** brought to light the collocation with *strong/strength* which were then concordanced themselves, the results finally edited to produce the lines above. This process illustrates how text-analysis tools can be usefully employed in combination.

As Henderson (1982) and others have pointed out, a number of systematic metaphors are common in economics writing, including THE ECONOMY IS A PLANT, A MACHINE and A PERSON. A closer look at the concordance above also reveals the presence of *growing/growth* and concordancing these items in turn show how they are used overwhelmingly in the sense of economic development, expressing THE ECONOMY AS A PLANT, for example:

1   The economy is **growing** robustly
2   This period of economic **growth** and development [...]

Instead, *fiscal* (30 occurrences in all) collocates intensively with *discipline* (11 times) and *(ir)responsibility* (four times), along with, predictably, *year* (14). The first two seem to be expressing THE ECONOMY AS A PERSON, though it has clearly become a cliché, a dead metaphor (see Section 10.3.3).

On economic metaphor, in writing about the White House politics and propaganda, Kurtz (1998), on several occasions, uses the metaphors of *buying* and *selling* to refer to persuasion: *sell a line, buy a story* and so on The only real traces of this in the corpus are the following:

(9)   Q: Do you *buy* the premise of that question?
(10)   MR BERGER: You know, deadlines are a double-edged sword. On the one
          hand, deadlines provide a –
       Q: *Selling* point. (Laughter.)

The metaphor seems to be something like DEBATING IS BARGAINING, for which PERSUASION IS SELLING and BEING PERSUADED IS BUYING are sub-variations.

Another metaphor – or, rather, set of metaphors – which have been noted in the previous chapters, are those associated with games and sports.

(11) Q: Joe, why did the President wait until the Vice President unleashed his faith-based –

MR LOCKHART: You know, in boxing, there's a three knockdown rule. (Laughter.) Anybody want to –

Q: Joe, why did the President –

MR LOCKHART: Has anybody got a towel? (Laughter.)

The podium portrays himself as a boxer who has taken too much punishment (too many trenchant questions) and wants to give in (to *throw in the towel*). This is part of the *impossible job* motif noted in Section 7.5.3, which gains him sympathy and simultaneously compliments the press on their assiduousness, although here they may well also be a touch of irony.

Although the concordance of *sport** proved to be unrevealing, that of *game* was most intriguing:

1 MR LOCKHART: Peter, this is a **game** that I'm not going to continue to play.
2 this is a continuation of a **game** of cat and mouse that Saddam has played for a number of years
3 is there any legitimacy to that, or is that just a Washington blame **game**?
4 the end **game** is clearly articulated in the Washington communique
5 the NATO allies have a different view about the end **game**, which is not yet here?
6 he didn't see an end **game**, he didn't see how bombing strikes alone could work
7 I'm not certain that there's any difference on the end **game**;
8 is perfectly within fair **game** as the President articulates his case.
9 he does not give any of his detractors the satisfaction of keeping him off his **game** because he knows that in the end
10 Is it a losing **game**?
11 I'll let others do – play that **game**, get into that business.
12 It's unfortunate that we've come to this late part in the **game** with so much work left to do.
13 and it's part of the **game** playing that may seem fun to some,
14 are the NATO allies prepared to modify the **game** plan, the air strikes, in advance of verifiable withdrawal?
15 the President's meeting with the Joint Chiefs of Staff this afternoon, the **game** plan for going forward?
16 to agree to the Rambouillet accords at this stage of the **game**, after the bombing, do you?
17 we're not willing to play this **game**. We will continue to keep the pressure on Saddam.
18 I wouldn't necessarily draw any firm conclusions about who's going to win this **game**.

Literal references to 'real' games have been edited out. *Game* is involved in a number of metaphors. The clearest, perhaps, is CONFLICT AS A GAME OF CHESS indicated by references to the *end game* (lines 4–7), that is, the strategy a player adopts in the attempt to force a checkmate, to find a victorious outcome. NATO and the Yugoslavian Republic are thus depicted (by the press, the metaphor is introduced by a questioner) as involved in a chess game in which – at the stage these references date from (May 1999) – NATO has the upper hand but whose outcome could still turn out to be a stalemate. A month earlier, the prospects were still less rosy from the podium's point of view. The context of lines 10 and 18 are as follows:

(12)   Q: – or their oil refineries, but they seem to have this facility to be able to get back on the air. Is it *a losing game?*

   MR LOCKHART: I wouldn't necessarily draw any firm conclusions about who's going to *win this game.*

A *losing game* in chess is an erroneous strategy that will lead almost inevitably to defeat. The prospects of NATO failure at this moment clearly seemed very real.[1]

In lines 14 and 15, we find mention of the *game plan*, once again in the context of the Kosovo crisis and again initiated by the press. The phrase probably originates in American football, but is fairly common and certainly a dead metaphor as used here. In lines 12 and 16, 'this late part in the game', 'this stage in the game' are equally conventional (the first refers to negotiations with Congress, the second to Kosovo).

Another common metaphor, this time elaborated by the podium, is BRIEFINGS ARE A GAME (lines 1, 11 and 13). Used in this sense, *game* always collocates with *play, playing* and has a very unfavourable prosody – others wish to play a game, implies the podium, whilst I am here to do serious business. The particular game itself is presumably similar to that of *the game of cat and mouse* played by Saddam Hussein (line 2) and that Washington is *not willing to play* (line 17).

The euphonious *blame game* (line 3) seems created for the nonce (and has been discussed in Section 5.6.2 as an attempt to create a dissension-in-the-government-ranks story). In line 9, we find *to keep him off his game*. The origin is golf where one's *game* is one's usual proficiency. To put someone *off their game* is to distract them, usually in order to cheat, which the podium claims none of the President's *detractors* have managed to do.

Finally and rather oddly, line 8 talks of the President being *fair game:*

(13)   MR McCURRY: [...] And so the President, reminding this Democratic audience that they stood on behalf of an economic program that is working exceedingly well for this country, is perfectly within *fair game* as the President articulates his case.

The prosody is as confused as the syntax. The *game* here is the ancient usage relating to hunting and generally *fair game* is used to describe any legitimate 'object of pursuit, attack or abuse' (Webster's *Encyclopedic*), an odd expression for the podium (though not others) to associate with the President.

It is probably wise not to read too much into the presence of game metaphors in this genre. A concordance of *game* from *INTS* also throws up examples, some of which are quite similar:

1 a dangerous **game** for someone who wants to be seen a future Prime Minister
2 the Church of England said 'well the basic, the end **game** or the basic aim is to scrap the Reformation
3 to cat and mouse **game** where he, okay withdraws, suspends the onslaught
4 the public will say that he's back in that old **game** of guy who spends a lot of money I'll get him into the Lords
5 flinging money around for political gestures, that that's what you are in the **game** of doing?
6 well the trouble is it's difficult to get on with the **game** without much of a ball to play with
7 they were really looking ahead and wanting to see the **game** develop
8 we ought to stop worrying about whether the pitch has been marked out properly and get on with the **game**.
9 'We've got fed up with this **game**, we're taking our ball off the pitch'?

Game metaphors are probably quite frequent in political talk in general. After all, Anglo-American political systems are largely seen as conflictual (see Section 6.1), and there are limitless grounds for a metaphor CONFLICT IS A GAME (see Goffman 1967: 244–5): both, for example, have winners and losers, both require strategies and choices in their conduct, both are essentially unpredictable. And indeed, the inverse is at least as common, GAMES are often described in terms of CONFLICT. The greater frequency in *WHB* than *INTS* may well be because the topic of discourse is more frequently war, but even the metaphor WAR IS A GAME is conventional. Note, however, that it is almost always the press that depicts the Kosovo conflict in this way. The podium needs to be more circumspect in his choice of tropes.

10.3.3 Collocation and dead metaphor

A last reflection concerns the nature of well-worn and dead metaphors. What may be a fairly new or striking metaphor to outsiders can often, in contrast, be dead and transparent to the point of invisibility to people working in a sector where the metaphor is common. How does someone who is not a member of a particular discourse community know if a given metaphor is alive and still figurative for that community or is defunct and literal? The answer is to examine the way the metaphor collocates. Henderson (1982) notes the frequency of what are usually called 'mixed metaphors' in economics texts, and several are also found in these texts. One example is the use of the word *momentum*, related to the metaphor we have already noted MOVEMENT AS PROGRESS. The phrase *build on the momentum* – an obvious mixed metaphor, since *momentum* can *build up* but hardly be *built upon* – occurs four times. In addition, we find 'there's some momentum coming out of the end of 1998 ...'. *Momentum* has become a dead metaphor, simply a stylistic alternative to *progress*, and no longer collocates as a figurative entity in keeping with its original sense of movement. This is as good a definition as any of dead metaphor: an item which has ceased to collocate, in a particular genre, with the set of items it collocated with in its earlier sense.

A particularly interesting instance is the following:

(14)   Q: Is it possible that that's going to *jump-start some wheels turning*?

The speaker here seems to run together two fairly dead or dying figures: to *jump-start* [literally an engine, figuratively almost anything which has stalled, e.g., *negotiations (Newspaper corpus), an economy, a conversation (BNC)*] and to *set, start* or *keep wheels turning (BNC)*. Entwining the two is almost comic, and shows how the overused expressions have lost their figurative power in the mind of the speaker. But since there is clearly a link between starting an engine and starting the wheels, the effect is also to somehow revitalize the two dead metaphors in the mind of the hearer.

10.4   Conclusions

The discussion above has tended to concentrate largely on the metaphors and motifs employed by the podium rather than the press and I have tried to show how the choices he makes are not necessarily arbitrary or innocent. He is far from being the only politician to have these skills. Garton *et al.* (1991) study a number of British political contexts in which systematic metaphors, consisting of a variety of sub-metaphors interacting among themselves, develop an ideological force and are used to present an argument. When employed in this way they become ideological *scripts*. The more common-place and natural-seeming (like CONFLICT IS A GAME), that is, the more common-sensical the script sounds, and the more powerful it is. The authors cite the *bully* script. Just as the school bully has to be stood up to, so Britain must stand up to the Soviet Union – and not relinquish its nuclear weapons. Much of political debate, they argue, is based on such scripts, and politicians, especially at election time, encourage the press to adopt scripts favourable to them and unfavourable to their opponents. A good deal of the debate in these briefings can be seen as a negotiation between the two sides over whose scripts to adopt.

The main indications of a particular press-speak in the keyword lists are discourse-management items, for example, *follow* (as in *may I follow up on that ....?*), *back* (*going back to what you said earlier...*). This is essentially because it is the administration which projects positively and deliberately its view of the world, whilst the press normally confines itself to questioning this world-view and, as a consequence, will use much the same vocabulary. In fact, the 'insider' press – the Washington press corps, the professional White House journalists – is often accused by the 'outsider' press – the non-Washington papers and the so-called 'new media' (Davis and Owen 1998), such as talk radio and electronic newsletters – of being too close to authority and of thus sharing its world and world views. The evidence from the vocabulary as studied here would be seized upon by some to justify the claim.

My own view is that this sharing the same vocabulary is largely inevitable precisely because it is the administration's world view which is at issue. It is adopted by the journalists, but only for the purposes of testing, of inquisition. On occasion, moreover, we have also seen that some press-initiated metaphor – for example, WAR AS A GAME, if adopted by the podium, would prove extremely embarrassing. Thus, even the metaphors used by the press can be a trap for the podium.

None of the metaphors discussed here is exclusive to briefings talk. In fact, most of them are well-worn, clichés even, and taken individually they are certainly not diagnostic of this particular genre. Taken together, however, they are. Of all the systematic metaphors and motifs that could be used, only a certain limited number are actually employed. And, as Wilson points out, those that get chosen tend to get repeated:

> In looking at how politicians employ metaphors it is quite clear that repeated metaphorical themes abound, and in one sense this is not surprising since the arguments which politicians present are not always necessarily new or different. Nevertheless, it would be possible to convey the same arguments with different metaphorical themes, yet this does not seem to be a preferred option.
>
> Wilson (1990: 130)

This selection among the possibilities and the combinations, frequency and 'weight' of what is selected – the particular importance given to FORWARD MOTION or to CLOSENESS or the special role of the language of TALK, the particular use of *until* to convey RESOLUTENESS and so on are in, all probability, unique to these texts. In addition, the particular *relations* that exist between the dominant metaphors/motifs of a text are equally diagnostic of its type, as here; for example, the relation between the MOVING FORWARD metaphor and the EFFORT metaphor. In other words, if one can list the systematic metaphors of a (long) text, define their relative importance and the relations between them, it should, ideally, be possible to predict the type of text, the genre or sub-genre it belongs to. Metaphor can, thus, be as diagnostic of genre as vocabulary or syntax.

11 Rhetoric, bluster and on-line gaffes

11.1 Definitions

The word *rhetoric* can, of course, have a number of meanings. It is defined as the 'arts of persuasive discourse' (Cockcroft and Cockcroft 1992: 3), that is, following Burke (1969), the use of words by human agents to form attitudes or to induce actions in other human agents. In this sense, it implies the activation of the *directive* function of language 'seeking to affect the behaviour of the addressee' (Cook 1989: 26, following Jakobson 1960). In terms of speech act theory, studying rhetoric means studying the perlocutionary force of utterances, that is, the effect speakers intend them to have on their audience.

In real life, as is well illustrated in these briefings, attempts to influence and convince others are likely to be met with suspicion and resistance; the more blatant the attempts, the deeper the suspicion. Such resistance to rhetoric is anything but new:

> The success of rhetoric rapidly drew upon itself a counter-attack, recorded in Plato's *Gorgias*, where Socrates deplores the skill taught by sophists (teachers of rhetoric) as a mere 'knack' to disguise falsehood or ignorance as plausible truth.
>
> (Cockcroft and Cockcroft 1992: 5)

For Plato himself, the rhetorician is a 'speech-rigger' (*logodaedalos*) (Cockcroft and Cockcroft 1992: 20). The irony is of course that, according to the definitions given above, Socrates' own methods of persuasion were just as 'rhetorical'.

On a theoretical plane, according to the social psychologist Billig (1987), all argument is likely to be opposed at some level by the audience because rhetorical practice is largely dialectic. As Cockcroft and Cockcroft summarize: 'every argument, every generalization, invites an exception or a counter-proposal from the individual (or group) invited to listen, whether or not their response is openly expressed'. Rhetoric is thus a dialogue and even when there is no overt response from the audience, a persuader must attempt to forestall all possible counter-arguments. In the briefings, of course, the audience does respond openly and the dialogic nature of proceedings is quite apparent. By Billig's lights, then, both sides, podium and press are not only doing their jobs but engaging in standard rhetorical, dialectic activity.

On a more mundane level, rhetoric is likely to be resisted on two related scores: that it is manipulative and that there is somehow a deficit between rhetorical argument and 'the truth'. The second of these is embodied in the stance Plato attributes to his *maestro* in the quotation above, and 'Plato's view can be recognized today in the contempt frequently expressed for "mere rhetoric"' (Cockcroft and Cockcroft 1992: 5). In Section 9.1 we have looked at how 'just words' are contraposed to 'reality', to deeds and the like, in the briefings (when this thesis is a rhetorically convenient one for the speaker, of course). We have also seen that the press is acutely aware of the manipulative intentions of the podium's discourse. As language professionals they are well equipped to contrast it and engage him in rhetorical dialectic. Their own attempts at using language for strategic purposes are, moreover, documented in various places in the current work.

Rhetoric of course has yet another sense, equivalent to 'grandiloquence' or the use of high-sounding language. This meaning presumably derives from the scholarly (and pseudo-scholarly) associations that rhetoric acquired after the codification of its persuasive techniques and language *tropes* or figures. *Rhetoric*, in this sense, is an 'over-the-fence' word, that is to say, it is used to describe what *others* do, is only applied to an outsider group, and is often roughly equivalent to 'bluster':

(1)   COLONEL CROWLEY: [...] What we've heard today from Iraq is a great deal of rhetoric. We've heard this bluster before. We've seen this petulance before.

And yet, as we shall see, it is often the language of the podiums themselves which appears grandiloquent, blustering and long-winded. At other times, in complete contrast, as noted elsewhere (Section 7.3), there is frequent recourse to slang and informalisms. Speech style in this sense is closely connected to footing. High-flown rhetoric is generally restricted to the podium as Democrat or as representative of the United States of America, whereas informal style is used to project the podium as plain Mike McCurry or Joe Lockhart.

All these definitions of the term are intermingled in the rest of this chapter, which is mainly concerned with an examination of the more apparent rhetorical techniques used by the podiums in their attempts at persuasion. The lion's share will be concerned with their grand language but a word will also be spent on their 'descent' into colloquialism. In passing we will mention the odd gaffe they make. The use of particularly lofty or inflated language can have its risks, especially when it is produced spontaneously and without planning, as so often here. More than once the podiums' desire to be eloquent leads them into saying more than they intended or something they regret. Eloquence is probably best prepared in advance. Given the on-line nature of these briefings, podiums would often be best advised to keep things simple.

11.2   Discourse analysis and rhetoric in history

In some areas of modern discourse analysis, and especially in the politically motivated branch known as critical discourse analysis, rhetoric enjoys a very evil reputation. Command of the techniques of persuasion is seen as one of the principal ways in which the powerful both express and reinforce their power over the powerless, for example in situations such as the courtroom, the doctor's surgery or, most noticeably and dangerously, in the mass media.

Although this may *frequently* be the case, it is not *necessarily* the case. The relationship between rhetoric and power has not always been a cosy one. In many periods of history, rhetoric has been subversive of authority – Giordano Bruno, Thomas Paine and the pamphleteers of the seventeenth and eighteenth centuries spring to mind – and office has always been most wary and intolerant of rhetoric and orators it could not control. Moreover, as Cockcroft and Cockcroft point out, the very need for the organs of state to avail themselves of persuasion, of the arts of rhetoric, has tended to coincide in history with periods of relative freedom (for some sections of society at least). It is no coincidence that it first enters the arena of history with Greek democracy. After all, absolute, despotic, coercive power has little need of rhetoric.

In these days, much attention is paid to the phenomenon of *spin-doctoring*, the tailoring of news and information on its release to the public to cast a favourable light on the institutions of authority. The White House Office of the Press Secretary, which hosts these briefings, is often (somewhat unfairly) seen simply as an organization for government spin. But the term would appear to be little more than a new name for an old game. Persuading people to accept your version of events, of the truth – in competition with other versions (see Section 9.4) – is at the very dialogic heart of rhetoric. And just as Socrates was alert to the efforts of the doctors of sophistry, in the kind of public dialogue embodied in these briefings we have our modern defences against the doctors of spin.

11.3   Parallelism and patterning

11.3.1   *Lexico-syntactic parallelism*

Probably the single most striking rhetorical device to be found in the podium's language is the use of lexico-syntactic parallelism (or *isocolon*). A simple example is:

(2)   I think **everyone agreed to** that; **everyone agreed** that **there must be** a follow-on force, **there must be** U.S. participation, **there must be** participation on the ground in Bosnia.

Parallelism is normally defined as the repetition of a syntactic structure within a short space of text or period of time. Its function in persuasion is well documented:

> The persuasive effects of syntactic structures can be developed by using various kinds of parallelism to add emphasis, clarity, balance, and cumulative *weight*.

> (Cockcroft and Cockcroft 1992: 129)

When used properly it can convey 'the spontaneous energy of deep feeling or conviction' (Cockcroft and Cockcroft 1992: 129). It creates a rhythmic motion which, as Coleridge (1956: 206) remarked, creates the impression of someone striving 'to hold in check the workings of passion'. When overused, however, it 'produces banal and trivializing effects' (Cockcroft and Cockcroft 1992: 129). Below we shall see examples of both.

We will begin with a couple of apparently simple cases:

(3) I think the credibility comes from making *your own judgment about* **whether** or not things are better than they were, and **whether** they are headed in the right direction, and **whether** the achievement of a self-sustaining peace in Bosnia is possible. In my judgment, that is the case.

(4) So we're seeking sort of a rough parallelism, if you will, here between how the treaty handled the flanks before and how we need to handle Central Europe now. But *the* **exact** *numbers, the* **exact** *ceilings, the* **exact** *nature of that relationship* is one of the important details still to be finished.

At first sight these may appear to involve simple repetition of the words *whether* in example (3) and *exact* in example (4). However, the reiteration of *whether* actually signals the recurrence of the phrase *your own judgement about whether*, and *exact* is, in fact, part of a repeated pattern (or *schema*, see below) of the type '*the exact* + Noun'.

Note that the third member of the trio of noun phrases in example (4) introduces an element of variation, in that a prepositional phrase – 'of that relationship' – is appended to the noun head. A structure of three elements, the third of which introduces a degree of modification, is one of the classic forms of rhetorical parallelism (known as *tricolon*).[1]

Two occurrences of a phrase structure are sufficient to set up an expectation that there will be a third. The slight change renders the third item emphatic (and probably, more than incidentally, highlights the speaker's own rhetorical skill). The most successful example from these texts is undoubtedly:

(5) MR LOCKHART: Well, **you can use words like** 'punishment', **you can use words like** 'stole', and **you can be wrong**.

Here, the rhetorical purposes of emphasizing the error and simultaneously chastising the questioner are more than adequately achieved.

Having said this, however, this kind of parallelism is quite rare in these texts. More common is three-item parallelism with either no variation [also examples (2) and (3)]:

(6) Bosnia is a different place today **than it was** a year ago, **than it was** two years ago, certainly **than it was** two and a half years ago –

or seemingly random (that is, unordered) change:

(7) And **those who commit** them, **those who are responsible for** ordering them and **those who are responsible at** the political level will be held accountable in the International War Crimes Tribunal.

Most of the time the podium is thinking and speaking on his feet, whilst the elegance of third-item variation is a typical feature of pre-prepared rhetoric.

The President's speeches, on the other hand, are generally written in advance. One of the questioners draws attention to his use of the technique:

(8)   Q: The other question about that is that the President seemed to indicate yesterday that it was **in the hands of** *Congress* and **in the hands of** *the public* and **in the hands of** *God*.

Where *God*, though not syntactically different from the previous two items, is on a rather different semantic plane from Congress and the public. There is also an implied scale from the least to the most important – not uncommon in parallelisms (an example of the technique known as *incrementum*). The journalist, however, adds a fourth item:

(9) But part of it also seems to be **in his hands** [...]

Not only does this addition supply the syntactic variation which is 'missing' from the earlier parallels, but there is also an implied ironic question of whether the fourth element – the President – is more important than God. The device is, of course, classically known as *bathos*, definable as the deliberate deflation of grandiloquence, or fighting rhetoric with anti-rhetoric.

Although three is the most common number, there are sometimes more:

(10)   MR McCURRY: The economy is growing robustly, revenues are up. But **you lose** *so much* if you don't lock in this balanced budget agreement. **You lose**, first of all, *those savings* that we have to generate in Medicare to extend the solvency of the Medicare trust fund into the future. **You lose** *almost $900 billion worth of mandated reductions in federal spending over 10 years*. **You lose** *a lot of things* that we were just talking about a minute ago – the incentives for people to go and get educations that will raise their capacity to earn more money in the future. **You lose** *the provisions* that will protect legal immigrants from some of the consequences of the welfare reform bill.

This is a skilled piece of rhetoric. Although the phrase *you lose* experiences no internal modification, the complement of the verb phrase undergoes considerable development. The first item – 'so much' is very general, but we then proceed to a more detailed 'those savings' and thence to a still more detailed 'almost $900 billion worth of...'. Having dealt with money, the podium moves on to 'a lot of things' which things he then lists once more, ending on a high moral note, warning that 'you lose' protection for legal immigrants.

Very frequently the podium resorts to sequenced or interlocking parallelisms, that is, one parallelism on the heels of another:

(11)   MR LOCKHART: **I think we** need to find a way to get to the end of this process as quickly as possible. **I think** what **we**'ve seen today is we've now got a new creation of let's take another day and have a new process, presenting evidence. **I think** that's what the last part of this process was about. **I think we want to get this done. We want to get it done** *fairly*. **We want to get it done** *quickly*.

Or one occurring simultaneously or within another:

(12)   MR LOCKHART: I'm not going to get into speculating about what President Milosevic might or might not do. I will say that we've reached a decisive point in this process and **he clearly knows the choices** he faces, and **he clearly knows** that he can **choose** one of two **paths**. And it's very much in his interest to **choose** the **path** of peace.

This may well remind us of the warning above about overuse of parallelism producing banal effects. Once again:

(13)   MR LOCKHART: Scott, as I've told you, the Committee isn't here this weekend. **We're going to** go up early next week because the President has expressed that he wants to cooperate with what they're doing. **We are going to** sit down with them. **We're going to** discuss – **we're going to** listen to how they plan to **move forward**, and **we're going to** work with them on how we can **move forward** and how we can take this process and **move** it **along**.

If anything, these would seem to be the words of a man confused and under pressure. This is proof, if any were needed, that the use of rhetorical devices, especially in on-line speech production, is not necessary the sign of a speaker in control of the situation.

A still more revealing example is the following:

(14)   MR McCURRY: [...] But personality and who stands here is not a part of it. **That's why** when Joe walks in here and starts on Monday, it will be sort of a seamless transition, because there is only one person that got elected to do the job that we all do here, **and that's** Bill Clinton. **And that's who** you all are covering, **and that's who** we work for. **And that's who** *the American people* **want to know about** it – they **want to know about** his thinking and his decision-making. **And that's why** you legitimately **want to see** more of him.

Here we see not only a loss of clear-thinking, but also a slip of judgement. The podium is carried away by the grandiloquence of a series of parallelisms, allied to stock rhetorical expressions such as 'the American people' and fine thoughts about the President and the people knowing about 'his thinking'. He ends with a disastrous admission that the President is in fact being secretive and that the press's frequent complaints during this period that he is hiding from them are justified ('and that's why you legitimately want to see more of him').

The last example in this section, example (15) below, is probably the longest and one of the simplest series of parallels in these texts. The podium has been asked whether he believes President Clinton's evasiveness over his relationship with Ms Lewinsky bears comparison with that of a previous President, Nixon, over the Watergate scandal. Mr McCurry chooses attack as the best from of defence:

(15)   MR McCURRY: *What Richard Nixon did*, as the House Judiciary Committee looked at it, *was* **he used** the powers of his office to delay, impede, obstruct the investigation of an unlawful entry into the opposition party's political headquarters. **He covered up** and **concealed** the scope of the unlawful entry by those who did it. **He misused** government agencies to conceal the extent of the crimes that had been committed. **He obstructed** the investigations that were then undertaken to determine what the facts were. **He abused** his authority by obtaining confidential information from the Internal Revenue Service, which he then misused in violation of the constitutional rights of American citizens. **He misused** the FBI, the Secret Service to conduct unlawful wiretapping of American citizens. **He maintained** a secret unit in the White House to violate the constitutional rights of citizens and refused to provide information in a timely way to Congress, in contempt of Congress. So there's no parallel whatsoever.

The parallelism consists, on the surface, of a simple repetition of '*he* + past tense Verb'. There is no internal variation nor does there seem to be any particular crescendo or *incrementum* in the meaning of the verbs. In fact, though, the phrases 'he used', 'he covered up', 'he obstructed' and so on, all depend upon the introductory words 'what Richard Nixon did was ...', which seems to have a disapproving, accusatory connotation. Thus, even those verbs which are not in themselves sinister – *used, maintained* are rendered so. The (apparent) very simplicity of the structure '*he* + Verb' is what allows it to be repeated so extensively, allows the listing of malpractices to go on for so long without becoming rhetorically ineffective or rebarbative.

11.3.2 Parallelism and theories of lexical patterning

The use of parallelism can be seen in part as a special case of the tactical employment of what Pawley and Syder (1983) call *lexicalized sentence stems* or what Barlow and Kemmer (1994) call *schemas* (or *schemata*). A schema is a kind of phrase template in which some parts are fixed and others can be subject to variation. Barlow (1996: 5) gives the example *to let oneself go*, which contains the fixed element *go* and two variables: the verb *let*, which changes in agreement with its subject, and the following element in the phrase which will be chosen from the closed set of reflexives, depending on context, allowing possibilities such as *he let himself go, letting themselves go*, and so on. Among the examples cited earlier, in example (14) we find the template '*(and) that's wh**' where there is an optional opening item *and*, the fixed part *that's* and the final element chosen from the set of *wh-* question adverbs, which produces 'that's why', 'and that's why' and 'and that's who'.

There are two insights which can be obtained from an analysis of these occurrences of parallelism. Most writers on lexical patterning have concentrated on idiom, that is, those language expressions traditionally regarded and analysed, at least in part, as blocks. The occurrences of parallelism seen here however show that all sorts of non-idiomatic, 'normal' language can be involved in repeated patterning: *you lose* [example (10)], *I think (we), we want to get it done* [example (11)], *we're going to ...* [example (13)].[2] The technique of parallelism is a means to harness even the plainest of language to rhetorical effect.

The second insight is that the repeated expression can be very short. Parallelism is often exemplified with lengthy templates as in 'Teach us, Good Lord, to give and not to count the cost, to fight and not to heed the wounds, to toil and not to seek for rest ...' [quoted in Cook (1989: 15)], that is, '*to* (Verb) *and not to* (Verb phrase)'. But two items are, in fact, sufficient. The two items can be fixed and identical as in example (12), where *choose* and *path* are repeated, but at other times only one of the items is fixed and the other item is a variable deriving from a particular lexical class, as in example (14) with *that's why, that's who*. In extreme cases, *neither* item in the parallelism is entirely fixed, as in this (invented) example:

(16) he wins, you lose

a realization of the simplest of templates: 'Pronoun + Verb' in which both items are variable according to context. Note, though, that there is a semantic connection between the verbs, their meanings are linked by antonymy. Otherwise the parallelism in such extreme cases would either be obscure or seen as a joke.

Finally, links in meaning among the various occurrences of a parallel phrase undoubtedly help to make a particularly effective, rhetorically successful *trope*. One example from these texts is:

(17) **It looks like it's** politics; **it doesn't look like it's** doing the constitutional business of the American people.

where the second part is the negative image of the first: a *contrastive pair* or *anti-thesis*. Another example of semantically cohesive parallelism was seen in example (8) where there is a crescendo in meaning of the noun phrases following *in the hands of*: 'Congress', 'the Public', 'God'. But this is rare in the kind of on-line language we are dealing with here: it is more likely to be found where speakers have more time to prepare.[3]

11.3.3   The safety or 'default' mode

Finally, lexical parallelism is a major feature of what we might call the podium's 'rhetorical mode', a style he slips into when in difficulty or doubt over what to do or say next. A good example of this transition occurs when Mr McCurry is asked an unexpected question about the White House's response to the death of Nigeria's military leader:

(18)   Q: Abacha's death?

    MR McCURRY: Have we put out any formal statement? I'm asking you. (Laughter.) I haven't had a chance to – let me say **the United States government** acknowledges the death of General Sani Abacha. **The United States government** is interested in what type of opportunities exist for transition to civilian rule in Nigeria. A long-sought goal of U.S. policy has been to restore to **the people of Nigeria** a freely-elected democratic government that is consistent with **the great aspirations** of **the Nigerian people** and reflective of **the great potential** Nigeria has in the world community.

In the following, he is asked a question so apparently anodyne that he is again taken off guard:

(19)   Q: When the President was seeking office, he talked about making change his friend, and over the weekend he was talking about making adversity his friend. How does he intend to make adversity his friend?

His reply is guarded, in this 'default' rhetorical mode, just in case there is some hidden agenda he has not yet spotted:

(20)   MR McCURRY: I think you see him doing it each and every day as he addresses the questions that we face in the final budget deliberations with Congress and as he continues to do his work. He is addressing those priorities he believes he was elected by the American people to attend to, and he's been doing so steadfastly and will continue to do so.

Note the reference to 'the American people' and in example (18) to 'the Nigerian people'. Mention of a *people* in this way is a sure sign of rhetorical mode.

Another component of this style are slogans:

(21)   The price of inaction is much higher than the price of action

(on the bombing of Serbia) which occurs four times, and is in echo of a phrase originally uttered by the President. It is, of course, another example of antithetical parallelism. The following repeated slogan refers to Mr Milosevic:

(22)   He knows what he needs to do and he needs to do it.

Slogans however, when used without careful aforethought, can lead to trouble:

(23)   MR LOCKHART: David, I think that's an overly simplistic view, trying to put a scorecard on important and complicated relationships. We will take the steps that *we believe that we need to take in our national interest* and that *NATO believes that we need to take in our national interest.*

Taking steps *in our national interest* is a stock saying, an age-old catch-all to excuse politicians from having to justify their actions. Too late the podium remembers that action in the Balkans is supposed to be in conjunction with NATO, and *not* to further US policy alone. His self-correction does little to repair the gaffe.

Example (22) is also one of many examples in the podium's talk of tautology, itself a kind of lexical parallelism. It too can be used tactically (Partington 1995: 34–5)

(24)   Q: One week into this military operation, are we so far winning or losing?
       MR LOCKHART: I think it's impossible to answer that question […] And I've run out of ways to try to caution and urge this group to try to rush to judgment. *You all will need to do what you need to do.*

This seems to be a reproof. It is also a call to duty, reminiscent more than anything of the stock, even comic *a man's gotta do what a man's gotta do*. If the press write something that is judgmental about the administration, they are disloyal and failing in their duty. The podium even employs tautology to camouflage false propositions. More than once he stresses the idea that:

(25)   you don't have a deal until you have a deal

which nobody can deny. From here it is a short step to another of his affirmations:

(26)   you don't have an agreement until everything is agreed on

which is a little more controversial, though it maintains the form of a (pseudo-) tautology. But then we hear (my italics):

(27)   Like I said, I think it's impossible to predict with any certainty in a negotiation *when nothing is agreed to until everything is agreed to.*

which is far from being necessarily true or even generally the case in negotiation. By degrees of stealth the podium attempts to pass off as true what by itself would stand out as absurd.

However, not all tautology is tactical or deliberate. We have several examples of accidental or fatuous use:

(28)   And the President believes Secretary Christopher [and] Ambassador Holbrooke [...] are making *forward progress* towards the destination

(29)   But clearly, because we cooperate so *closely* with our *close* friend and ally, the Republic of Korea [...]

Progress should always, of course, be *forward*, and close *alliance* presupposes close *cooperation*. In both cases, these accidental tautologies are the unfortunate result of the pressure to keep talking. The final example below is undoubtedly the most peculiar and, were it not for the subject matter, it would be positively comic:

(30)   [...] and, as you watch the pictures every night, you'll understand what it's like for hundreds of thousands of people who have been driven from their home and *the unseen that we don't see* who have been brutally murdered.

11.4   'Borrowing' rhetoric: of war, of civil rights

There are times, too, when the podium seems to borrow rhetorical phrases from other spheres of experience. There are, for instance, left-overs from a previous conflict, the Gulf War, where the campaign aim was often said to be to 'degrade' Saddam Hussein's forces. In the early part of the Kosovo crisis too we find 'to degrade his forces' (*he* being President Milosevic). This develops into 'degrade his ability to make war', and finally becomes, more metaphorical and more rhetorical still, 'to degrade his ability to repress the Kosovar people'.

The most striking rhetorical borrowing, however, is the adoption of the language of social justice and civil rights by the podium (and probably by the administration in general) during the Kosovo crisis. The President is said to 'speak out':

(31)   MR LOCKHART: I think the President feels very strongly it's important to communicate with the American people. He has *spoken out* every day since this operation began [...]

and 'we' follow his lead:

(32)   But we will continue to *speak out*.

when, in both cases, all that is really meant is that we are speaking *to* the press. *Speak out* belongs to the rhetoric of denouncing injustice, for which you need plenty of courage, as the following edited corpus lines from the *BNC* demonstrate:

1   [...] and said people should **speak out** against prejudice and bigotry and on behalf of reconciliation and peace.

2 Should I then **speak out** and invite martyrdom?

3 We black Catholics must **speak out** in our schools for equality for our children [...]

(BNC)

The use of the expression lends the President a glowingly noble connotation.

This is also a process which can develop over time, as the following sentence concordance of *prevail* – another item reminiscent of the language of civil rights and justice – illustrates:

1 We continue to grind down, as the President said last week, the military machine of Milosevic and we will *continue* to do that until we **prevail** in this conflict.

2 But let me say that we have said all along that we need to persist with this air campaign, that this is the option that we believe as we are highly confident will get us to our military objectives. And if we *persist*, we will **prevail**.

3 Listen, I think you've heard the President say that we will *persist* and we will **prevail**.

4 The United States is not standing alone here – the United States is standing with 18 other countries in the NATO Alliance, all unified in this position – that we need to move forward, we need to be determined, we need to *persevere* until we **prevail**.

5 But the policy, and NATO's policy, now, is the President believes that the air campaign will succeed, will meet our military objectives, and we need to *persevere* until we **prevail**.

6 We are very confident General Clark, the President are very confident that with *perseverance* and as we stay with this, we will **prevail**.

These lines have been placed in chronological order. Each occurrence expresses the same concept: that if the allies *insist*, they will *'prevail'*. The verb used to express the insistence however, undergoes transition. At the beginning it is simply *continue* (line 1), it then becomes *persist* (lines 2 and 3), until finally it turns into *persevere* (line 5) or, alternatively, *perseverance* (line 6). Evidence from other concordances shows that *persevere* has a much more positive connotation or semantic prosody than does *persist*. *Rumours*, *doubts* and *worries* can persist. One can *persist* in something fairly stupid or ignoble: in fact it can contain a suggestion of pig-headedness and lack of fine judgement.

(33) According to The New York Times, authorities thought of their hi-tech war against the Mob 'in terms of Agincourt': mobsters like the plumed French cavalrymen stubbornly charging into the crossbows of English archers, *persisting* in their imprudent habits out of habit and reckless pride.[4]

(Newspaper corpus)

One who *perseveres*, instead, does so out of a sense of justice and heroically against all odds:

1　Justice intends to **persevere**.
2　[…] therefore go thou on, and evermore **persevere** in doing good.

(BNC)

It is no surprise that the language experts in the White House finally settled for this term. All this is, of course, a reminder of how speakers can choose and adapt a metaphor to portray a certain favourable picture of the world (see Chapter 10).

11.5　Tension between grandiloquence and informality

We have already seen a moment in which the podium deflates his own grandiloquence (Section 7.5.2):

(34)　MR McCURRY:　Want a little bit more of that? (Laughter.)
　　　Q:　No, that's enough. (Laughter.)
　　　Q:　Maybe later.
　　　MR McCURRY:　I don't think they're going to ask that question again.

and also one where the press draws attention to that of the President [examples (8) and (9) of this chapter]. There is often a clear tension between the general informality of these proceedings and the occasional purple rhetorical and/or boastful passage. A further example:

(35)　Q:　No, I don't want you to write the deal, but if those trade-offs are really excellent and the benefits to children and the American people are really terrific, better than you can imagine – (laughter) – in exchange for that, would you be willing to accept a limit to the damages from tobacco?

The questioner here mimics the podium's employment of hyperbolic language – 'are really excellent', 'are really terrific', 'better than you can imagine'. The rest of the audience has no trouble in interpreting the reference, hence the complicitous laughter. All these are, of course, examples of bathos as mentioned earlier.

11.6　A reflection on what makes successful rhetoric

The question of what makes a successful piece of rhetoric was raised at the start of this section. One or two intermediate reflections arise from the ensuing analysis. Sensitivity to your audience is clearly paramount. Too much bragging or browbeating, for example, does not impress the press. The problem for the podium is that he has so many audiences: the immediate one composed of journalists, the television and Internet viewers, official observers around the world, including unfriendly states, his own employers. Who does he pitch his rhetoric to?

It is hardly surprising that he occasionally gets the register wrong. Another related point is that a successful orator, while exploiting and enjoying the poetic possibilities of language, nevertheless never loses sight of the fact that rhetoric has an aim, that of persuasion, and thus avoids self-indulgence for its own sake. The directive function ought never to be wholly subservient to the poetic; the two should work in tandem.

11.7 The other side of the rhetorical coin: colloquialism

11.7.1 Slang, jargon, neologism

The bouts of grandiloquence, successful or not, are all the more noticeable given the general informal register of the exchanges in these briefings. It may seem odd to discuss this kind of register in a chapter on rhetoric, but informalism is the other side of the coin to grandiloquence, and is itself a persuasive rhetorical technique.

The following are some of the colloquialisms used by both sides in the corpus of briefings (MC = Mr McCurry, JL = Mr Lockhart):

Podium	*Press*
unfettered lark (Berger)	a ballpark
you guys (MC)	game plan
my dime (MC)	knuckling under
quarterbacking (MC)	back-pedaling
gobblygook (MC)	you guys, you folks
muck around (MC)	a dollar figure
the President dropped by (MC)	a piece of paper (= *a statement*)
cronies (Crowley)	get nabbed
this is stump Mike time (MC)	singing from the same page
in the ballpark (MC)	kissed and made up
folks (several)	like mom and apple pie
handicap in advance (JL)	junior league Hitler
jump up (meaning *come to the podium*) (MC)	jump start some wheels turning
fed up (JL)	
smoke and mirrors (JL)	
you're comparing apples and oranges (JL)	
the mother of all … (Berger)	

My dime is my turn at talk, especially if a long one. To *quarterback* something is to mastermind it (the origin is in American football). If something is *in the ballpark* it is a feasible estimate (baseball). To *handicap* is to make a rough estimate. A *smoke and mirrors* proposal is one – made by one's rivals – that will prove to be illusory. *The mother of all …*, used by Mr Berger in 'U.N. Security Council Resolution 687, the mother of all Security Council resolutions on Iraq', means the greatest, the most important. Note the hidden sarcasm at Iraq's expense, since the expression from which this derives – 'the mother of all battles' – was originally attributed to Saddam Hussein. A *dollar figure* is an approximation. If the podium is asked whether two officials are *singing from the same page*, the press is looking for a 'dissension in the White House ranks' story. Whatever is *like mom and apple pie* is thoroughly patriotic and American.

Below are lists of some of the jargon used:

Podium	Press
soft money (JL)	pork, to pork up
an op-ed piece (MC)	negatively impacting
a build-down (MC)	collateral damage
downsize (-ing) (several)	
empowerment/empowering (several)	
the impacted people (JL)	
a what-if (= hypothetical question) (MC)	
degrade his ability (JL)	
collateral damage (JL)	

Soft money refers to corporate and private donations to political parties. Donations above $1,000 are not supposed to be legal but are increasingly common. An *op-ed piece* is a comment article. A *build-down of arms* means a *downsizing* of one's military arsenal. *Pork* originally referred to 'appropriations, appointments etc., made by the government for political reasons rather than for public benefit' (Webster's *Encyclopedic*). Today, however, to *pork up* a proposal, budget, etc., means to add in extraneous matter hoping to get it passed along with the main measures, a nefarious practice perpetrated by political groups in Congress.

The employment of sports slang and technical jargon in order to create the sense of an in-group has already been discussed (Section 7.5.1), as has the use of informal register by the various podiums to humanize the bureaucratic nature of the proceedings and to present themselves and their clients as friendly and down-to-earth. Some of the jargon, as noted elsewhere (G. Lakoff 1991; Zagrebelsky 1992), has the intention of, conversely, bureaucratizing the inhuman, the cruelty of war: *degrade his ability, collateral damage* and so on. Particularly interesting is the use – by both sides – of *impacting/impacted*. A concordance of *impact** shows that its use as a verb – originally a military euphemism for 'hit' or 'destroy' – is still new enough for its unfavourable connotation to be explicitly marked with adverbs such as *negatively, adversely*:

(36)   MR LOCKHART: [...] but I think the President wanted to make sure that the recent wave of mergers was something that was serving to make American companies more competitive globally and was not *negatively impacting* consumers through lack of competition here at home.

(37)   Q: [...] So our efforts in our number three category, Balkans, are clearly *adversely impacting* our relationship with our most important concern, Russia, right?

In the following it is used in the passive, and without the overt indication of unpleasantness:

(38)   MR LOCKHART: [...] – *children are impacted* by what they see, and the games they play [...]

Nevertheless, the connotation can be recovered from context: the topic of the exchange is the effect of video nasties on children. The following case, however, is very different:

(39)   MR LOCKHART: As I've expressed to you in previous days, I think the President would like to find an appropriate moment to travel to talk to some of *the impacted people.*

The 'impacted people' are those whose children were killed in the Littleton school shooting. The use of *impacted* with no unfavourable modifier is clearly both euphemistic and tactical: it excuses the podium from using more unpleasant or compromising terms.

11.7.2   *Colloquial grammar*

We have concentrated here on informality in register as evinced in *lexical* choices, but informality is also apparent in the grammar of briefings. In other words, we find a number of grammatical constructions which are normally associated by native speakers with colloquial style. Although concordance technology is certainly not able to automatically decide – or extract – examples of informal or 'conversational' constructions, if the user decides beforehand which structures they are interested in, they can use keywords to tell the concordancer what to search for. For example, the concordancer was asked to look for a template like '*get* the * done*', and the following passage was recovered:

(40)   MR LOCKHART: Well, the balanced budget amendment was around for 10 or 15 years, and that didn't do anything to reduce the deficit in this country; *getting the work done did*. And I think the same applies to Social Security. We can *get the work done* now [...]

Getting the work done did is almost comic in its informality. Using keywords to search for syntactic structures in this way emphasizes the symbiosis of lexis and grammar (Sinclair 1991; Francis 1993).

Cook (1989: 61–2) suggests that inversions and clefts are typical of colloquial language. There are various heuristic tactics one can use to look for such constructions: for example, by typing '*did was*' and '*does is*':

(41)   I think what the President *did was* he […]
        What the Joint Security Declaration *does is* […]
        What this basic elements agreement *does is* […]

or '*is what*':

(42)   keeping Kosovo as part of Serbia *is what* Milosevic wants the most
        and the most important question of sequencing *is what* Milosevic needs to do

or '*what * is to*':

(43)   *what* we're doing now *is to* work together with others
        what we need *is to* codify or provide details

Finally, by looking for *ain't*, we find the occasional overt attempt at conversational or dialectal imitation:

(44)   MR McCURRY: […] what the framers of our Constitution thought of as
        impeachable offences is covered very clearly in that, and *this ain't it.*
(45)   Q: Say *it ain't so*, Joe.

Other revealing searches would include those with keywords: *let's, why not, how about…?* and other indicators of informality such as prepositional groups, for example, *out of, away with* which often indicate colloquial phrasal verbs (these two groups threw up *get out of, get away with, run out of, thrown out of, storm out of, come away with*).

11.8   Plays on words

Both sides occasionally indulge in plays on words, even punning, itself a form of rhetorical trope [or set of tropes (Cockcroft and Cockcroft 1992: 127–8)]. The simplest example is:

(46)   Q: Can you assure us – just to wind this up, can you assure us that –
        MR LOCKHART: You are winding me up, here.

in which Mr Lockhart plays on the two meanings of *wind up*: to 'conclude' and to 'provoke'. In another example:

(47)   MR LOCKHART: I just can't get the word "bouquet" out of my mouth.
        (Laughter.) Sorry.

The podium plays on *bouquet*'s meaning of 'aroma', 'flavour'. The mock apology is for his own facetiousness. Not to be outdone, the questioner responds:

(48)   Q: Does the bouquet of proposals from Congressman Archer – (laughter) – MR LOCKHART: Well done. (Laughter.)

Using *bouquet* to mean 'bunch', 'set'. The podium compliments the speaker for their ingenuity.

On other occasions, one cannot be sure whether the play (in this case, *oxymoron*) is deliberate or accidental:

(49)   MR McCURRY: We stopped the war there. We *won a peace*.

The following, on the other hand, is definitely unintentional:

(50)   Q: What do you think about efforts from third parties, *like Ukraine*, for example, to try to intervene?
       MR LOCKHART: As far as I know, that is an effort undertaken *by the Ukrainians*.

He means that the proposal is unilateral and has nothing to do with the United States, but the exchange is absurdly comic in effect.

Undoubtedly, the most sophisticated play comes from a journalist:

(51)   Q: Joe, […] if there is a government shut down, do you expect the public will blame the Democrats or the Republicans or *a pox on both your houses*?

The reference is to Mercutio's dying words in Shakespeare's *Romeo and Juliet* (actually 'a *plague* o' both your houses'). The Democrats and Republicans are cast in the role of the feuding families and the 'both your houses' refers to them, but also to the two Houses of Congress where government business should be done.

11.9   A summary of the difficulties caused by on-line rhetoric: grammar, register and collocation

We have already seen several occasions when the lack of time to prepare what one says causes the machine of rhetoric to miss a stroke, where the grand language fails to persuade or where the desire to impress lets something slip. Here we pursue this theme and look at some of the effects of time pressures on grammatical, register and collocational choices.

11.9.1   Grammar

Though often 'corrected' by the transcribers, grammatical re-plannings abound in both the podium's and the questioner's language. This is no surprise since they are a typical feature of many types of informal talk. Re-planning occurs when an utterance begins following one grammatical structure and at some point switches to another:

(52)   Q: Let me follow that up, Joe. You talked yesterday about Senator Byrd had a valid point when he talked about [...]
(53)   Q: [...] he was fired because he wouldn't inject something that they didn't tell him what it was
(54)   MR McCURRY: No, but neither is he someone that's easy to control or to tell him what to say.

There can even, it seems, be multiple re-planning:

(55)   MR LOCKHART: I think I answered that by saying I don't think I can answer that now, based on what we don't know.

which, at least when written down, seems rather humorous. The following rather odd inversion was also uncovered:

(56)   MR LOCKHART: [...] And our position has been clear and consistent from the very first day that a non-permissive, a hostile environment, *we do not favor putting ground troops into.*

which reads like New York rather than Washington grammar. Other examples of unusual grammar:

(57)   Yugoslav forces are hurting
        the ability to support and resupply the troops in Kosovo is eroding.

where a more usual construction would be the passive *being hurt* and *being eroded*. Compared to the passive, the ergative construction which actually occurs in these examples forestalls the question 'being hurt/eroded *by whom?*'. Whereas the passive can hide the actor of an event or process, the ergative can make it disappear completely. Other strange uses of transitivity include 'an operation that's ongoing', 'the business of this country is ongoing', 'responses that are upcoming', 'a response to the filing on expedited'. See also the comments earlier (Section 11.7.1) on 'children are impacted' and 'impacted people'.

11.9.2   *Register*

The podium is occasionally guilty of unfortunate fumbles in choice of register. One clear example:

(58)   MR BERGER: But let me just give you a couple of details about our *escapade* to Bosnia – our mission to Bosnia.

Possibly infected by a certain hilarity in proceedings up to that point, Mr Berger makes a very unfortunate choice of term – *escapade*, a jocular word for a deadly serious affair.

Another example is the following:

(59) MR LOCKHART: I have a couple of announcements, and one to start on, a very sad note. The President was very sorry to learn this morning of the passing of Meg Greenfield, and we will put a statement out to that effect.

Meg Greenfield was a journalist with the *Washington Post*. The note struck seems a discordant one: 'we will put out a statement to that effect' belongs to a bureaucratic register which sits ill with the rhetoric of remembrance. The podium is undoubtedly sincere and in fact goes on to add his personal condolences, but force of habit, the routine use of certain language probably deafens him to its inappropriacy here.

Nor is the press immune:

(60) Q: Has the Chinese government *calmed down* […]?

They are, however, under less constraint to be respectful to foreign powers than the podium.

Play on register is frequently performed to positive effect (e.g. see example (34) for a movement from rhetorical to jocular mode). But it can misfire, get out of hand, as in the examples in this section. The pressures of time inherent in the briefings situation lead to the occasional lapse of judgement.

11.9.3 *Collocation*

Several examples of unusual collocation were discussed in the section on semantic prosody in Section 0.3.3. As a reminder of its effects, we might consider this additional example:

(61) MR LOCKHART: I think they accurately reflect that there are people in Belgrade, in Yugoslavia who understand what the truth here is, as opposed to those who seek to *perpetrate something other than the truth*.

Perpetrate is an odd word to use with *truth*. Concordance evidence from these briefings shows that items like *tell*, *spread* or *convey* might have been more normal. However, though unusual, this collocational choice is far from unsuccessful. The concordance also shows that *perpetrate* generally collocates with highly pernicious activities (e.g. *fraud*, *bullying*, *plan of terror*), a connotation which the podium wishes to convey, since he is referring to political enemies.

11.10   Conclusion

Re-reading this chapter, I fear I may have painted the podium as the very picture of a linguistic oaf. This is not the case. I have carefully selected examples of rhetorical breakdown but, in the main, both Mr McCurry and Mr Lockhart, along with their colleagues who occasionally take the stand, are highly skilled users of language. Their problem is that they can never win. The podium looks foolish when he uses language poorly, but appears dangerous when he uses it well. This is the unconscious message of Kurtz's *Spin Cycle*, which contrasts the 'clumsy' efforts of Clinton's staff to control their own message in his first term with the 'much-needed order' imposed in the second (Kurtz 1998: xiv). They are criticized in the media in both events; at first for ineptitude, then for manipulativeness, for being *spinmeisters* (see Foreword).

The concern in this chapter has been to look at the language and rhetorical techniques involved in so-called 'spin'. The current author is not in a position to judge any of the 'extra-linguistic' forms of manipulation – including selective leaking of stories to favoured journalists, bargaining behind the scenes, bullying of editors – that the various podiums are accused of (always, it should be remembered, by members of the press or political opponents). The linguistic evidence from the briefings in *this* corpus, however, does not support the picture of a Machiavellian McCurry or a Luciferan Lockhart, controlling and manipulating events, as found in some reports of White House press affairs.

The counterposing of *spin* and *truth* as mutually exclusive (from reviews of Kurtz's book):

> Perhaps an informed public should begin to demand the truth in place of the spin.
>
> (Sarah Reaves White)

> Unfortunately the only loser in this game is the truth.
>
> (Gary Kamiya)

is similarly unconvincing. As was argued earlier, what is often called 'spin', at least in these briefings, seems little more than the art of rhetoric brought up to date and employed by professionals for debate with other professionals.[5] It is one version of the truth put forward by the podium in an adversarial environment, and it has to be robust and well argued or it will not survive. Those press people who complain about spin and equate it with untruth have failed to understand the adversarial, inquisitorial nature of press–administration relations (see Chapter 6).

There is, however, some evidence of the two sides coming close to rhetorical breakdown – that is, of their not communicating in any real sense – over the Clinton–Lewinsky affair. But there were *real* lies at the bottom of that business and no amount of rhetoric, of grandiloquence, of spin can turn a falsehood into truth. It should perhaps be cause for celebrating the system if real mendacity can cause such a convulsion in it: the adversarial nature of press interrogation is a democratic safety valve.

Finally, a good deal has been made in this chapter of the effects of time constraints on the rhetoric of the two sides, especially the podium's. It might be objected that these pressures are no different from those acting normally on any day-to-day conversation. But there are special, complicating factors at play. The podium's role is often similar to that of an interrogation subject who has his story only half prepared. And what is certainly not typical of conversation is the professional hostility of the questioners, their instinct for *pursuit* – one half of the topic of the next chapter. This makes the podium try even harder to be persuasive, which results in the grandiloquence we have seen, and probably also aggravates his tendency to *evasiveness* – the other theme of the next chapter.

12 Evasion and pursuit

'Certainly', says Harris (1991: 80) in her work on UK political interviews 'the common-sense perception of the listening public is very much that the role of the interviewer is to ask questions and that of the interviewee is to answer them'. This down-to-earth view, as the reader will have noted, has been adopted in this work. Harris gives equally pragmatic definitions of question and answer. Questions are defined as 'requests to provide information' (Harris 1991: 80). Answers, in consequence, should be moves which ideally provide that information. Predictably, things in practice are not quite so straightforward. In this chapter, we will examine what is probably the single most striking feature of the discourse of these briefings – the interplay of podium evasiveness and press pursuit.

   We have already dwelt to quite a degree on the conflicting interests of the two sides in briefings/interview talk. Politicians (including podiums) wish to project themselves in the best possible light, to avoid topics, facts, suggestions that show them in a poor light. And, according to Harris's (1991: 94, 96) figures, there can be little doubt that, in Britain, politicians are more evasive than other institutional respondents. The press's natural and professional desire is to uncover as much as possible, which entails digging below the surface of the politician's account, suggesting other versions, highlighting the negative, pursuing any signs of weakness, doubt and duplicity. In this atmosphere, it is no surprise to discover that not all questions are straightforward requests for information and not every reply provides all that is requested.

12.1 Avoidance in responses

12.1.1 Directness–indirectness of responses

Without intending to prejudge the order – whether podium evasiveness induces press pursuit or whether questioner hostility leads to respondent avoidance, in other words, refraining from apportioning responsibility or blame – we begin with Harris's attempt to define 'evasiveness'. First of all, she makes a distinction between *response* and *answer*. A response is defined as whatever follows a question. Only when a response fully satisfies the questioner can we talk of an *answer*.

She then devises a scheme of *response* from complete answer to full-scale evasion of the question:

> ANSWERING: *Direct answer* contains explicitly expressed 'yes' or 'no', 'of course', 'right', etc. *or* some other explicit selection of polarity.
> *Direct answer* which supplies value for a missing variable in response to a 'wh' question.
> *Indirect answer* which involves inference (either selection of some intermediate position between 'yes' and 'no' *or* either 'yes' *or* 'no' can be inferred from the answer), *or* a value for a missing variable can be inferred.
> *Indirect answer* from which neither 'yes' nor 'no' can be inferred *or* a value for a missing variable but which maintains cohesion, topic coherence, presuppositional framework and illocutionary coherence.
> *Challenges* of one or more of the presuppositions of a question.
> EVADING: *Challenges* of the illocutionary force of a question.
>
> (Harris 1991: 87)

However, as Harris herself recognizes, this correlation of degree of evasiveness with the linguistic feature of directness–indirectness has its limitations. For instance, as regards the first definition of *direct answer* – 'contains explicitly expressed "yes" or "no", "of course", "right", etc.' – a response may well contain an explicit assent/dissent item without going on to supply the information requested. There may even be occasions where a *yes* or *no* is given but the rest of the response gives the opposite answer, as in this example:

(1)   Q: That essentially means that we didn't go in Kosovo earlier because we were worried about casualties.
      MR LOCKHART: No. I think any military planner will tell you that in a situation like this, in a campaign like this, you want to approach this systematically. You want to reduce the risk as much as you can to Allied pilots and to those involved in this […]

He opens with 'no' but then confirms the question's import. Does this count as a direct answer?

Conversely, indirectness, an *apparent* unwillingness to answer the question, can even be used to respond *more effectively*, as in the following example:

(2)   Q: Right. But are you saying you want Gingrich to exert leadership now?
      MR LOCKHART: I'm saying it's not our position to dictate who does, but we accept the wisdom and the judgment of Representative Gephardt when he says the Hill is in chaos right now.

There exists, in fact, an *agreement reformulation*, which is used by the podium with precisely this function:

(3)   Q: So are you saying there's hope?
      MR LOCKHART: I'm saying that we wouldn't be involved in the process if we didn't think there was hope of moving this forward to a peaceful settlement.

This is clearly less direct than a simple *yes*, but situationally more appropriate and rhetorically more compelling.

Even '*challenges* of one or more of the presuppositions of a question' are not necessarily pragmatically evasive. The challenge might actually be a reinforcement, an intensification of the question polarity, for example, (invented example):

(4)   Q: So, having lost his political touch, Mr Patterson is out of the running?
      A: Well, he never really had any political touch.

12.1.2   *Speaker's intentions*

What is missing, what is needed in addition to linguistic indirectness, is some more pragmatic consideration of speaker *intention*, of whether or not the interviewee intends to supply the requested data, and whether indeed, they are in a position to supply it. Thus, we can make a distinction between *open* avoidance, when a respondent fails to give an answer because they do not know it, or cannot give it for contextual, contingent reasons (like national security or legal injunction) and *strategic* (or disingenuous, even deceitful) evasiveness, which can fall into two categories. The first is not giving the answer when you know it (attempt to hide). The second is pretending to answer but not doing so (attempt to mislead or beguile). Clayman (1993) gives a variety of examples of the latter, of speakers expressing agreement with the question but failing to answer, of respondents summarizing the question in order to alter its emphasis (see Section 9.2 on generalizing reformulations) and of the tactic of 'reaching back' into the question to answer an earlier part but conveniently overlooking the later ones. We will investigate several kinds of avoidance as practised by the podium in Section 12.2.

Unfortunately, it is not usually possible to investigate intention directly (i.e. by interrogating the speakers), but we can gain some insight by examining textual and contextual clues. Misleading claims and actual intentions can sometimes be uncovered.

12.1.3   *The picture so far*

Mr McCurry and Mr Lockhart are hardly the first politicians ever to avoid answering a question:

> Only 50 years after the first question, the Earl of Grafton was led to comment: 'If called upon in Parliament for information, which every member in

either House has a right to expect, they either give no reply or evade the question'.

[*Parliamentary History*, vol 19 *c*.326 in Howarth (1956: 36)
and quoted by Wilson (1990: 144)]

But they are certainly recidivist offenders. We have examined many examples of question avoidance previously in this book. In Section 5.6.3, we saw the podium denying knowledge of reports, of statements attributed to third parties, particularly with the formula *I am not aware of/familiar with* and other such. In Chapter 9, we looked at how reformulation of questions could be used to sidestep them. In Chapters 3 and 4, we saw how the podium can use footing shift to dodge the issue and how the press adopts their own preventative strategies. In Chapter 7, the relationship between hedging and evasiveness was investigated. In this chapter, we hope to pull these strands together and give an overall view of the mechanisms of evasion.

12.2   Ways of evading

12.2.1   *Open refusal to answer*

There are numerous instances of what we might call *bald, on-record* avoidance, where the podium simply states his unwillingness to give an answer.

(5)   MR McCURRY: Basically, it involves a combination of incentives and disincentives for the parties to encourage them to reach a peace settlement.
   Q: What are the disincentives?
   Q: Bombing?
   MR McCURRY: I'm not going to get into the specifics. Asked and answered.

The phrase *asked and answered* is an open, formal, shorthand declaration that he will spend no more time on this topic. In the following, Mr McCurry admits his avoidance quite openly:

(6)   Q: Is Mr Deutch briefing the President on the situation in Iraq today and what you may have learned from the defectors?
   MR McCURRY: As I indicated to some of you earlier, he's getting together with the Director of Central Intelligence today [...] He'll also be seeing the Secretary of State later on today. And he may, depending on Mr Lake's travel schedule, see the National Security Advisor, as well.
   Q: I don't think you answered that question, Michael.
   MR McCURRY: I sure didn't. I don't talk about intelligence briefings the President gets.

The evasion is clearly more likely to succeed if a valid justification is given, as here. 'Intelligence briefings' and 'security' in general are often invoked, as is the related excuse of not giving 'operational details' or 'specifics' [see example (5)], particularly on military matters. Another justification, as we have seen [Chapter 4, example (38)], is that lips are sealed for legal reasons, that matters are *sub judice*, as in the next example, where the topic is the provenance of election campaign funding:

(7)   Q: Joe, could you comment on the story in the Los Angeles Times this
           weekend about Johnny Chung admitting that, yes, he got money from
           a Chinese –
       MR LOCKHART: That story is, the facts in that story are the subject of an
           ongoing investigation of the Justice Department, and I don't think it
           would be appropriate for me to comment.

Mr McCurry is even able to joke about his supposed impotence:

(8)   Q: Why won't they talk to you?
       MR McCURRY: Because, Helen, this is a very important thing. The lawyers
           are bound by the canon of ethics and by the law not to
           discuss outside of the court room proceedings that have occurred under
           seal. The lawyers here at the White House take that so seriously that
           they make me go through the kind of torture I'm going through right
           now […]
       Q: Do they understand the position it puts you in?
       MR McCURRY: Absolutely, and they feel my pain. (Laughter.)

Every now and again, however, no reason is given for his silence:

(9)   Q: Back on the contempt order, how do you answer those who say that this
           vindicates the House Judiciary Committee and Ken Starr?
       MR LOCKHART: I don't. Next question.
       Q: Why not?
       MR LOCKHART: Because I don't.

The effect clearly is to imply that the question – on the Clinton–Lewinsky case, a constant trial of the podium's patience – is beneath contempt.

12.2.2 Claims of ignorance

Perhaps the most frequent podium justification for not answering, however, is ignorance, that he simply does not know the answer:

(10)   MR LOCKHART: I don't know the answer to that question. Let me – we'll
           take that one.

Note the expression *take the question* (see Section 4.3.2), meaning that he does not know the answer but will try to find out. Similar are phrases like *we can check on that, I'll come back to you on that*, etc., which conveniently defer an answer to some unspecified time in the future. Sometimes an ignorance claim can be combined with a footing statement:

(11)   MR McCURRY: I'm not a lawyer. I wouldn't know how to speculate an answer to that question.

The podium is saying that it is not part of his job or role as simple spokesperson to know such things.

At times, however, his denials of knowledge are unconvincing. It seems almost inconceivable that he did not know about various very important issues such as independence for East Timor:

(12)   Q: Does the U.S. support independence for East Timor?
       MR LOCKHART: Pardon?
       Q: Does the U.S. support independence for East Timor?
       MR LOCKHART: Not that I'm aware of.

Perhaps he is torn between the 'no' which would probably reflect the truth and the 'yes' which many of his audience might feel was the proper policy given the massacres that were being committed by occupying forces and their clients in the area.

His disavowal of knowledge of Italian disaffection with NATO bombing is similarly implausible.

(13)   Q: The Italian foreign minister has said that his nation opposed the bombing of Serbian TV and that, furthermore, it was not their understanding that NATO would go to that level. Could you comment on that, please?
       MR LOCKHART: Well, I'm not familiar with those statements [...]

He then switches immediately to 'rhetorical mode':

(14)   [...] but I can say and echo the words that have come from the NATO spokespeople and military, that we view the Milosevic regime as a typical authoritarian regime that uses instruments of oppression [...]

which is the default style the podium frequently resorts to, as we have already noted (Section 11.3.3), to get himself out of trouble. More of this tactic below. The questioner, however, is not so easily denied:

(15)   Q: As far as you understand the Italian – as far as the United States understands, the Italian government was behind the bombing of the –
       MR LOCKHART: Well, again, I'm not – I'm not familiar with any statement to the contrary.

But a claim of unfamiliarity with any statement to the contrary is not the same as an outright *yes*. The journalist has probably got what they wanted.

12.2.3   *Referring the question*

Similar to the footing statement (in that the podium pleads his non-competence) is avoidance by referring the question, by telling the questioner to ask someone else. On military matters that 'someone else' is usually the Pentagon, as in the following rather testy example:

(16)   MR LOCKHART: You very confidently sit there and tell us what we're doing and we're not doing. I'm telling you that the place to discuss operational detail, to the extent that it can be done, is at the Pentagon and not here.

Or the matter can be left to another podium:

(17)   Q: On Social Security, however, Joe, Chairman Archer is again urging the President to come up with a specific plan for saving the system now. Will he do that?
MR LOCKHART: Well, I have nothing new to add. Maybe Gene will have something more prophetic for you at 3:00 p.m.

The frequent phrase *let* someone *speak for themselves* is used for this purpose

(18)   Q: Do you see that – does the U.S. see that the Secretary General's reputation is at stake in this confrontation?
COLONEL CROWLEY: I think I'll let the Secretary General speak for himself on that.
(19)   Q: [...] what have the Russians told you? That they accept it, or no?
MR LOCKHART: I'll let the Russians speak for themselves on the subject.

The referral is not necessarily to people. It can also be to previous communiqués to the press (the pool reports), as in the following good-humoured example:

(20)   Q: What was the President's reaction to the big movement in California for Hillary for president? (Laughter.)
MR LOCKHART: Check the pool report. I think he said, whatever she wants to do, he supports [...]
Q: Good. Just check the pool report, which gets you off the hook.
MR LOCKHART: Yes, exactly.

12.2.4   *Speculation and hypotheticals*

The plea of non-competence is also the basis of recurrent refusals to 'speculate':

(21)   MR LOCKHART: I'm just not going to walk down a speculative road here today.

or to interpret (see Section 9.1):

(22) MR LOCKHART: Well, I am not going to interpret.

or to get into what Mr Lockhart calls 'hypotheticals':

(23) MR LOCKHART: [...] and I'm not going to get into a situation of answer-
      ing complex hypotheticals about what if this happens, what if that hap-
      pens. I think we've been clear.
(24) MR LOCKHART: We are well into double, if not triple, hypotheticals.
      So let's deal with what we know.

or any combination of the above:

(25) MR LOCKHART: I'm not going to speculate on a hypothetical.

This does not go unnoticed. One question begins with a barbed aside on
Mr Lockhart's dislike for these hypotheticals:

(26) Q: Not to ask a hypothetical question, because I know your aversion to that –
      (laughter) – what is it that NATO leaders [...]

and there are occasional good-humoured exchanges on the subject:

(27) MR LOCKHART: Okay, well, I'm choosing not to answer that hypothetical.
      (Laughter.)
      Q: As long as it's not a general principle, that's –
      MR LOCKHART: It should be. (Laughter.) I'm just not smart enough to
      remember it. (Laughter.)

Note the self-deprecating humour – another avoidance tactic, discussed in
Sections 7.5.3 and 12.2.7.

Perhaps surprisingly, this technique seems to be fairly effective in deflecting
questions. Generally, the press appear to accept that speculation is somehow out
of bounds or possibly unproductive, and aggressive follow-ups after the podium's
refusal to answer on these grounds are rare.

12.2.5   *Rhetorical mode, slogans and officialese*

As already pointed out, the podium can sometimes slip into 'rhetorical mode' in
the attempt to evade. This is at its most evident when vagueness is dressed up to
look like a more definite answer:

(28) MR BERGER: Now, [...] which is, what is the nature, shape, mission, dimen-
      sion of a follow-on force, [...] we will be discussing over the next

probably month and a half, among ourselves, with our NATO allies. There are a number of different options that NATO is studying for a different size force, different scope of mandate and mission and, therefore, some different costs. And we look at all those options and make a judgment on what we think makes the most sense.

Mr Berger enumerates various characteristics of the 'follow-up' force as if about to give precise details, but the details never come.

Elsewhere, Mr McCurry is asked whether the administration's stance towards the Sinn Fein politician Mr Adams has altered following his failure to condemn the IRA bombing of Canary Wharf (London, February 1996). He replies:

(29)   MR McCURRY: We continue to urge all parties to do what they can to use their office and to use their persuasive abilities to encourage those with whom they are in contact to honor the terms of the cease-fire and to return to peace.

This is obviously the language of diplomacy, the 'diplospeak' or 'diplobabble' that Mr McCurry was occasionally accused of. It reminds us again that the podium must take great care over some topics since his words may well have repercussions in the real world outside the briefings room.

In addition, shifting to rhetorical mode is probably also associated with the two related techniques of *raising safe topics*, discussed in Section 7.5.1, and of *generalization*. With the first of these, the podium avoids a difficult topic by moving to a less controversial one:

(30)   Q: Joe, a lot of people want to know what our exit strategy is. Can you shed any light on that?
        MR LOCKHART: Well, I think it may be the wrong way to look at this. Let me talk a little bit about what we believe the objectives to be. I think quite simply – and I'll talk in a little more detail – is that our objective is to stop the killing and achieve a durable peace [...]

With the second – generalization – a particular issue is sidestepped by invoking the larger picture, an appeal which often has the air of a slogan:

(31)   Q: Well, related to that, several senators said yesterday that their problem is that if the bombing does not work there does not appear to be any plan that they know of. Can you address that for us –
        MR LOCKHART: Let me address it this way: I think, as the President told the American public last Friday [...] the price of inaction here is higher than the potential price of action.

Alternatively, part of a question is generalized in order to ignore the rest, including its real illocution:

(32)   Q: Is the President grateful to Senator Mikulski because she has been so quiet about his problems in contrast to her ear-shattering, pre-vote denunciation of Judge Clarence Thomas?

MR LOCKHART: The President is always grateful for Senator Mikulski's service.

The question is not whether the President is grateful to the Senator but, by implying that his 'problems' are similar to those of Judge Thomas, contains an accusation both of the Senator (double standards) and of the President (philandering or molestation). By both generalizing and, at the same time, literalizing the question (i.e. paying attention only to its locutionary form 'Is the President grateful ...'), the podium avoids being embroiled in a difficult situation.

12.2.6   Challenging the question, questioner or source

The podium will occasionally explicitly challenge the 'premise' of a question [Chapter 9, example (98)] or sometimes the 'facts':

(33)   Q: The Israeli press is reporting today that Prime Minister Netanyahu has asked President Clinton to defer a decision on Pollard until after the impeachment trial. Is that why we haven't heard what the decision is, which had been expected last month?

MR LOCKHART: First off, there are several things wrong with the question. There was never expected to be a decision last month. Go back and look at the facts of this case.

and just occasionally the cohesion:

(34)   Q: I guess we're trying to find out whether the President is trying to keep this under seal, whether his position is to ask the court to keep it quiet.

MR McCURRY: Sam, there are a lot of problems there. I don't know what the 'this' is that you're referring to. I don't know what you think is under seal.

Other examples of challenges can be found in Chapter 5 where the podium challenges the authority (Section 5.6) or the neutrality (Section 5.7) of the source of criticism of his clients, and in Section 7.4.2 where threats to the questioner's face are discussed. In Chapter 9, we also saw how the podium has to keep his wits about him to detect and counter damaging question presuppositions like the ones in examples (33) and (34). Challenging the presupposition can also, however, entail not answering the rest of the question. The next example is more complex:

(35)   Q: Joe, the President was somewhat vague, perhaps deliberately, yesterday when he was asked about an exit strategy. Could you elaborate at all on that?

MR LOCKHART: I don't think he was vague. I think if you listened to what the President said […] – we are pursuing a military operation that will have one of two outcomes. One is President Milosevic will understand his need to embrace peace, or the second will be we will degrade his ability to make war.

The question contains a framing statement 'the President was somewhat vague …' preceding the question proper: 'Could you elaborate at all on that?'. The response challenges the frame. But since the damaging proposition in the frame is itself about presidential vagueness, evasiveness, the podium feels obliged to go on to give some sort of answer. An astute ploy on the journalist's part. Nevertheless, no real answer (addressing 'an exit strategy') is supplied.

12.2.7 Humour

As we have already seen, humour is commonly used in the hope of avoiding or escaping from a tough spot:

(36)   Q: How were you able to predict so long ago that the Clinton–Lewinsky relationship would turn out – could turn out to be very complicated, without a simple, innocent explanation?

MR McCURRY: Clairvoyance. (Laughter.)

The humour is very frequently self-deprecating (Section 7.5.3). Here, it is combined with the 'no hypotheticals' principle:

(37)   Q: Everybody understands the delay question, but it is awfully hard to envision the President vetoing a military pay raise while American forces are fighting overseas.

MR LOCKHART: That's one of the reasons why I'm not going to stand up here and answer that hypothetical. I'm not quite as dumb as I look, Jim. Close, but – (Laughter.)

In the same self-effacing vein:

(38)   Q: Is the General in the doghouse here?

MR LOCKHART: Here? There is no doghouse here; if there was, I'd live there. (Laughter.)

On both these occasions the humour is effective and the podium manages to avoid an answer. But it is not always so successful. In the following the questioner asks how Mr Clinton should behave towards Mr Gore, the Vice President, who is standing for presidential election:

(39)   Q: [...] but the President is a larger-than-life figure and he's somebody who gets attention every time he opens his mouth.
       MR LOCKHART: Well, we're going to put him on a diet. (Laughter.) He's going to be smaller, thinner, less noticeable.

The evasiveness is evident. The question is a difficult one for the podium to deal with. Should the President remain aloof, this might be taken as lack of support, should he take up arms in Mr Gore's favour, he could overshadow him or worse still, taint him with the air of scandal. Although the joke is well received, the questioner is not to be deflected ('he' is the President):

(40)   Q: Whenever he opens his mouth he gets a lot of attention. He doesn't have to do much.

Mr Lockhart tries once more:

(41)   MR LOCKHART: You need to stop me before I hurt again. (Laughter.)

But the questioner is relentless:

(42)   Q: If there's no – if you don't plan to make some kind of effort to put him off the stage, whatever he does he's going to potentially overshadow the Vice President.

The podium realizes that joking by itself will not work and he will have to address the question. He proceeds to do so, after a fashion:

(43)   MR LOCKHART: I don't think so. I think that the President fighting for a patients' bill of rights, minimum wage, prescription drugs through Medicare, gun safety legislation and a lot of other legislative priorities, where the Republicans and the special interests are standing in the way, and where the Governor of Texas is standing in the way or doing nothing to promote this – I don't see how that can negatively impact any Democrat in this country.

But this is no real answer. It is instead an employment of rhetorical mode both to evade and to indulge in a bout of pro-Democrat electioneering.

12.2.8 *Already answered*

The podium often refuses to reply on the grounds that he has already answered that particular question or already covered that ground:

(44)   MR McCURRY: I don't want to add to what I've already said; I think I've already addressed that question.

Or some other speaker has answered previously:

(45)   MR McCURRY: I don't have anything to add to what Mr Lindsey told your pool yesterday, and I think he addressed that.

At times he is clearly exasperated, as here, when someone breaks the flow of a serious debate on export contracts to ask 'how long does it take to find out if Mr Foley paid Social Security for nannies' (Section 6.2):

(46)   MR McCURRY: For the reasons that I expounded on at some great length a moment ago.

At other times he tries to appear amused by the question 'game':

(47)   MR LOCKHART: I think that's about the question you asked me a few minutes ago. I'll give you the same answer. Good try, though.

12.2.9 *'I think our position is well known' – 'Well, what is it?'*

Frequently, however, the podium's refusal on these grounds is challenged and there can be some debate about whether a question has been answered or not. Mr Lockhart is asked how he would view Ms Lewinsky's being called as a live witness or making a videotaped deposition. He replies:

(48)   MR LOCKHART: Well, I think our position is well-known on all of those issues.

But the questioner is not satisfied:

(49)   Q: Well, what is it?

and the podium is forced to be more precise:

(50)   MR LOCKHART: We don't believe there is any need for live witnesses; we don't believe there is any need to bring any of these videotapes to the floor.

The following longer extract illustrates the kind of debate that takes place over whether a question has been properly answered. It contains an array of evasive techniques on the part of the podium:

(51)   Q: Do you believe that settlement in the Jones case would change the President's exposure to questions like perjury, anything that's involved in the original case?

MR McCURRY: I'm not a lawyer. I wouldn't know how to speculate an answer to that question.

Q: No, I wasn't asking you personally. I was asking you if the White House believes –

MR McCURRY: I don't know that the White House has any corporate view on that question.

Q: Well, why does the White House believe it's a good thing for him to settle?

MR McCURRY: Mr Lindsey addressed that yesterday. I don't have anything to add to what he said.

Q: Well, he didn't really address that question.

MR McCURRY: He certainly did.

Q: What did he say?

MR McCURRY: It's in the pool report.

In his first reply, the podium employs a *footing statement* avoidance (Section 12.2.2): 'I'm not a lawyer'. The questioner then reminds him of his footing as White House representative: 'I wasn't asking you personally', but the podium resorts to the *ignorance ploy* (Section 12.2.2): 'I don't know ...'. The podium is being extremely literal-minded. The questioner insists, making the question more general ('Well, why does ...'). The podium claims another speaker (Mr Lindsey) has *already answered*, already 'addressed that' (Section 12.2.8). The journalist disputes this, the podium contradicts, the journalist then asks for the details to be repeated, only to be *referred elsewhere* (Section 12.2.3), to documentation, to 'the pool report'.

12.3   The press: hunting as a pack

The reverse of the coin to the podium's evasiveness is the press's aggressive and ingenious – and at times disingenuous – pursuit of a story. Chapter 6 contains several examples of pointed press sarcasm as well as their devil's advocacy and *agent provocateur* tactics. We saw too in Section 9.3 how embedded propositions can be used in the attempt to trap an unwary podium. This section summarizes some more of their hunting techniques.

12.3.1   Simple belligerence

The corpus contains several examples of simple belligerence, rudeness even, in seeking a satisfactory response:

(52)   Q: Well, how is that an answer?

(53)   Q: How could anybody really have believed that it would only take a year or a year and a half to reach a stage where they didn't need help?

We have already seen that this aggression is frequently the topic of comments, complaints and jokes on the part of the podium, as well as of commentators on the press (Section 6.1). They are liable to pounce on any word, at any time:

(54)   Q: Why don't they just move? What are they waiting for, NATO?
       MR McCURRY: NATO is – the use of military force as an option should
          come if we've exhausted the efforts to resolve this on diplomatically.
       Q: How much more exhaustive can they get?
       Q: – diplomatic efforts have failed?

The words 'exhausted' and 'diplomatically' in the podium's response prompt the
provocative, overly suspicious last question ('Diplomatic efforts have failed?').
There is a certain irony (and perhaps irresponsibility) in the press's call for action
('What are they waiting for, NATO?'), given their subsequent heavy criticism of
White House military operations.

12.3.2   *Impossible questions*

Podium evasiveness is not always culpable or even, as it were, avoidable. The press
very frequently ask questions that are, for various reasons, quite impossible for the
podium to answer. Consider (on Northern Ireland):

(55)   Q: Do you see any merit on either of those sides, or do you believe one
          more than the other?

This is a rather pointless question. The podium cannot for obvious diplomatic
reasons express preferences.

(56)   MR McCURRY: I think there is a lot of information. We'll evaluate it as best
          we can and make the proper decisions accordingly.

Equally unanswerable, though for different reasons, is the following:

(57)   Q: You said you checked. Does the President agree with his old friend,
          James Carville, on Mr Carville's new war against Newt Gingrich that he
          declared yesterday?

The question is in essence an attempt to embarrass the podium and the President.
Mr Carville is attempting to defend the President against political attacks from his
enemies, using some of their own rather dubious personal tactics. The President
and his representatives can neither defend nor condemn him in public:

(58)   MR McCURRY: I don't know that the President would state things in that
          fashion. What we have said to you, and would continue to say to you, is
          that we are now embarked on a constitutional process that requires
          solemnity and dignity.

This is unlikely to satisfy the press:

(59)   Q: You have said that, but does he endorse what Carville's doing, which has
       nothing to do with solemnity and dignity.
       MR McCURRY: I'll come back to you.

This delay evasion fails to deflect them:

(60)   Q: Does the White House approve of what Carville is saying, or not?
       MR McCURRY: I haven't heard people around here express those sentiments.
       Q: Why doesn't the President ask him to cut it out?
       MR McCURRY: I don't know.

This podium appeal to ignorance is equally unsuccessful and the pursuit goes on
until he is forced into open, bald on-record evasion:

(61)   Q: So you're saying, even if the President didn't want him to, he'd continue –
       MR McCURRY: Anything else?
       Q: What was the answer?
       MR McCURRY: Same one I gave now.
       Q: You wouldn't repeat it for us now, would you?
       MR McCURRY: Nope. (Laughter.)

All sides recognize this for what it is – an attempt to embarrass the podium rather
than a serious question. Hence, the final indulgent laughter at the concluding
refusal to answer.

12.3.3   Questions as accusations

As witnessed by the last series of exchanges, not all questions are simple requests
for information. In briefings they can also frequently be accusations:

(62)   Q: If I could follow up – claim that you're knuckling under to the alcohol
       industry. Is that true?

Generally, as we noted in Chapter 5, open accusations are couched in the language of reports, of attribution. In an example we have seen earlier (Section 5.3),
the attribution is to the podium himself:

(63)   Q: No, I'm quoting you. [...] 'The President is not under any medical
       treatment for any psychiatric or mental condition.'
       Now, that being the case, isn't the sole alternative what Reuters News
       Agency quoted Angie Dickinson saying in Hollywood: Clinton has
       a very horny appetite, and I find that quite reasonable.

The form of this move, this diatribe, is barely interrogative, it only just resembles a question. Nevertheless, since it functions as the first part of a question–answer adjacency pair, the podium is expected to respond in some way.

Sometimes even quite normal, fairly non-threatening questions can be phrased as accusation:

(64)   Q: The White House supposedly refuses to intervene to try to resolve the tobacco dispute. Is that true?

All the questioner is really asking is whether the White House intends to intervene or not.

12.3.4   *Ignoring the podium's reasons for not answering*

In Section 12.2.1, we have seen how the podium frequently gives a reason for his reticence – ignorance, legal complications and so on. These are routinely ignored by the press, if they have the scent of blood in their nostrils, even when they appear valid. An example is the following (the topic is the President's legal difficulties over his relationship with Ms Lewinsky):

(65)   Q: Mike, for today's record, has the President invoked executive privilege in this matter?
         MR McCURRY: In this matter, I am not aware that he has, but it's entirely conceivable he could have. I wouldn't know if the proceedings in which he would invoke such privilege were under seal, because the President's attorneys –
         Q: You're hinting that he has.
         MR McCURRY: I'm not hinting one way or another. I don't know.

The claim at this initial stage is of ignorance. The questioner challenges this appeal so the podium also patiently spells out the legal reasons why he cannot answer:

(66)   Q: Why wouldn't you know. I mean, you might say to us, I cannot tell you –
         MR McCURRY: Because, Sam, if a proceeding has happened in a court and it's under seal, lawyers are restricted and bound by the decision of the court not to discuss it with people who are not participating – me included.

But the press still insist:

(67)   Q: Okay, but has the judge given the parties a deadline, or is this just open ended?
         MR McCURRY: I can't answer that.

Q: What's the reason?

MR McCURRY: I'm not going to be able to say here. You're wasting time.

Q: You clearly do know, but maybe you can't tell us. First, you say you don't know –

Q: Sam has a point. Which is it? I mean, do you not know or can you not tell us?

There is little he can do to stem the tide:

(68) Q: Well this is extraordinary –

MR McCURRY: It won't be extraordinary as soon as you're in a position to learn more.

Q: Well, when will that be?

MR McCURRY: As soon as I'm in a position to learn more.

Q: Do you know when that will be?

MR McCURRY: I can't predict.

He probably knows more than he is in a position to reveal. In any case, it must be clear to an experienced press that no more information will be forthcoming. The point of the cross-examination would appear to be for the journalists to express their indignation at being kept in the dark and, a useful by-product, to give the podium some grief.

Even when the podium gives a thoroughly convincing reason for reticence – in the following case, that of not endangering the peace process in Northern Ireland – the press do not relent:

(69) MR McCURRY: [...] You will see us refraining from comments on the positions that individual parties have taken because our work will be towards the effort of getting them back to [...] a cease-fire that holds and that protects the people of Northern Ireland.

Q: So you're not willing even to say that you disagree with Mr Adams' statement that John Major was to blame for the bombing?

The podium has effectively already said he cannot answer questions like the one that follows and also explained the reason why. There are occasions like this one where the fine line between investigative journalism and meaningless mistrust seems to be crossed. The refusal to accept any explanation under any circumstances can be perverse.

12.3.5 *Sheer insistence*

It is very difficult, for reasons of space, to give a proper idea of just how dogged press questioning frequently is. The quest for an answer to a particular question can go on for long periods of time, even the whole duration of a briefing.

The session held by Mr McCurry on 21 January 1998, lasting 36 minutes, consisted largely of the press attempting to induce the podium to comment, to enlarge upon the President's statement, delivered that morning, that he had not had 'an improper relationship' with Ms Lewinsky. The same question:

(70) Q: Mike, you said this morning the President did not have an improper relationship with this former intern. What do you mean by an improper relationship?

is asked over and over again in different guises. Eight times the podium repeats that he *will not parse the statement for you*. Five times he has to insist that it *speaks for itself*, three times that he will not *go beyond* what was said and four times that he cannot *amplify* or *interpret* or *characterize* the President's words. In particular, the press want to know why the word *sexual* does not appear:

(71) Q: What is puzzling to many of us is that we've invited you probably two dozen times today to say there was no sexual relationship with this woman and you have not done so.
(72) Q: Does that mean no sexual relationship? Why not put the word 'sexual' in? That's the problem.
(73) Q: Just one more stab at this. So is your interpretation of that statement that he meant to categorically deny that he had a sexual relationship –

He is held responsible not only for what his client has said but also for what he has not said. Perhaps nowhere else in this corpus of briefings is the podium 'grilled' so hard:

(74) Q: Do you smell anything, a rat or anything?
      MR McCURRY: I smell the lights in here cooking furiously everyone who is standing under them.

12.4   Conclusions

12.4.1   The whys and wherefores of evasion

As we have seen, the podium's evasiveness (real and supposed) does not go unnoticed and there are numerous occasions on which the audience let him know of their dissatisfaction:

(75) Q: That's not my question.
      Q: That wasn't the question.
      Q: You still haven't answered the question why.

The podium's perceived evasiveness is discussed with a mixture of humour and exasperation. A rare docile question, on the debatable behaviour of one of the President's opponents during the Lewinsky crisis:

(76) Q: Was that yet another indicator, as far as the White House is concerned, about the partisan environment surrounding the proceeding?

is interrupted by another journalist's quip:

(77)   Q: Say yes. (Laughter.)

Please, he wants to say, drop your defensive guard just this once. Even the podiums themselves occasionally seem to admit that their stonewalling might at times be tedious. Mr McCurry is said to have described his job as 'telling the truth – slowly' (*Washington Post*, 24 July 1998). Witness also the following exchange:

(78)   Q: Why so late?
       MR TOIV: I'm sorry, it is not easy getting up here and saying nothing. It takes a lot of preparation. (Laughter.)

Clayman (1993: 172) claims journalists recognize evasive ploys 'even as they are produced'. Greatbatch (1986) claims that modern audiences too can judge when an interviewee is being evasive. Why then do the various podiums resort to it so often? One simple explanation of course is that, often enough, they have no choice, and that giving a thorough answer to some questions would mean severe political embarrassment and the loss of one's job. But the picture is sometimes more complex. There are in truth other possibilities, for example, telling lies or saying more than one has evidence for. Both of these would probably bring short-term benefits – for example, in the extended example in Section 12.3.4, simply saying 'yes – "no improper relationship" includes no *sexual* relationship' would have spared Mr McCurry a great deal of harassment. However, in my judgement of this material at least, they are options which both the major podiums – Mr McCurry and Mr Lockhart – studiously avoid. In Gricean terms, the podium is often faced with the choice of flouting the cooperative principle in one of three ways:

(a)   saying what he knows to be untrue;
(b)   saying more than he has evidence for;
(c)   saying less than he has evidence for.

In the long term, the third is the safest option.

In any case, evasiveness might just work. The television audience might take pity on a hounded podium. Pleading ignorance and non-competence can sometimes deflect trouble. But only occasionally. In her study of political interviews, Harris (1991: 94) notes that 'attempts at agenda shifting by politicians are extremely frequent and often successful'. In the briefings under scrutiny here, in contrast, agenda-shifting on any important issue, though frequently attempted, is rarely successful. Even though there is a rapid change-over of questioners, when they sense the podium is dodging the issue, they will hunt as a pack.

12.4.2   *The functions of questioning in politics*

The converse of the question 'why is the podium so frequently evasive?' is 'why, when the question is obviously a delicate one, do the press often go on badgering him long after they have any reasonable expectation of a straight answer'. Harris (1991) notes that not all the questions in her corpus are simple, straightforward requests for information, whilst Wilson (1990: 148) too sees that they can perform 'a number of acts, only one of which may be that of questioning'. Here too, the move occupying the first position in the question–answer adjacency pair can have a number of functions: to accuse, to blame, to embarrass, to frighten, to belittle, to win a point, to make a joke (usually sarcastic), to express indignation, to lay a trap. When questions are repeated with no real hope of an answer, they are frequently doing business as one or more of these.

Levinson (1992) likewise notes that questions are not always simply information-seeking. He first of all criticizes Searle's division (1969: 66) of questions into the two categories of 'real' (*I don't know the answer and want to discover it*) and 'exam' (*I know the answer but want to find out if you know it*) as too simple. He goes on to give examples of two macro-functions of questions, of how speakers employ questions to fulfil two major strategies in the design of their discourse – to organize knowledge and ideas, and to organize argument.

To illustrate the first of these – the organization of knowledge – he shows how teachers use questions in an almost ritualistic fashion to bring their pupils to a realization of how certain known ideas can relate to each other (in the particular instance he reports, of the analogy: food is to the body as petrol is to the car). We might add to this that speakers can also use questions – rhetorical questions and confirmation questions especially – to organize *their own* knowledge.

The second of these strategic macro-functions, and one highly relevant to these briefings, is in the organization of an argument. Levinson argues that, in court-room cross-examination:

> the question–answer format [...] together with an assignment of questioner/ answerer roles constructs a turn-taking organization that gives control of topical organization entirely to the questioner, thus making the format a possible vehicle for the expression of an argument.
>
> (Levinson 1992: 86)

The questioner, in other words, designs their questions, usually a series of related questions, in order to elicit a response 'that will advance and make explicit his argument' (Levinson 1992: 95). In Levinson's particular example, the defendant's lawyer asks a rape victim a series of questions about her personal habits, way of dressing and so on, not to discover the answers (which he already knows), but in order to make explicit to the audience (the jury) the proposition that she is 'a woman of dubious virtue'.

We have seen numerous examples in these briefings where journalists too use questions to organize an argument, usually a hostile one for the podium [examples (57)–(61); Section 6.5 on the *agent provocateur* technique]. But respondents are not totally passive or powerless. Whilst 'the questioner hopes to elicit a response that will count as part of an implicit argument, the answerer will try to avoid such a response' (Levinson 1992: 86). In other words, they will adopt a counter-strategy of resisting the argument in their responses. The podiums, of course, command many more discourse resources than the average court witness and have their own topic management strategies and skills. The competitive interplay of strategic argument-building by questioners and argument-resistance by respondents is especially well illustrated in these briefings.

13 General conclusions

13.1 The third age of corpus linguistics

We are currently in the third age of computerized corpus linguistics. The first, the Age of Pioneers was characterized by the pathfinding work conducted, mainly in the 1960s and 1970s, by such scholars as Francis (*Brown* corpus) and Carroll (*American Heritage*) in the United States and by Leech (*LOB*) and Svartvik (*London–Lund*) in Europe, in compiling and computerizing the first corpora in difficult intellectual and technological circumstances. The second, the Age of Expansion, which began in the 1980s, was marked by ambitious and expensive projects to build what Kennedy (1998: vi) calls the 'second generation megacorpora', very large heterogeneric corpora containing tens or in some cases hundreds of millions of words of text. They are mostly based at universities in the United Kingdom and include *Cobuild* (*Bank of English*), the *British National Corpus*, the *Longman* corpus network and the *International Corpus of English* (ICE) (Greenbaum 1996). These projects are ongoing and are invaluable to linguists all over the globe.

But some time in the 1990s, given the steady expansion of PC speed and memory capacity, it became possible to hold and access quite large collections of text on a home computer. Then, with the advent of, firstly the CD-ROM and then the Internet, it also became possible for individual researchers with limited finance (such as myself) to have access to almost unlimited amounts of texts of a wide variety of types. It was a (relatively) simple matter to design, download, compile and tailor a corpus to suit one's own particular studies. The third age, the Age of Specialization had begun.

McEnery and Wilson (1996: 172) predicted both these developments back in 1996: that the mega-corpora would continue to grow but also that 'small scale corpus collection initiatives will be undertaken over the next few decades related to a need of certain researchers and teachers to develop certain types of corpora not currently available' People's research needs and tastes differ and 'in short, there is, and will be for the foreseeable future, a pressure for the types of corpora available to expand as people want to study different things using corpora' (McEnery and Wilson 1996: 172). In Section 0.4, I have already recounted some of my experiences in collecting and adapting corpora to suit the purposes of the current research.

All this means there is a whole new generation of researchers who use corpora as one of their research tools: if we like, 'linguists who use corpora' rather than out-and-out 'corpus linguists'. We might even say that this spread of the use of specialized corpora is currently narrowing the distance between corpus linguists and most other kinds of linguist (with the exception of the irreducible rationalists):

> The boundaries, therefore, between corpus-based description and argumentation and other approaches to language description are not rigid, and linguists of varied theoretical persuasions now use corpora for evidence which is complementary to evidence obtained from other sources.
>
> (Kennedy 1998: 8)

We might go still further and note that it is not only *linguists* who compile and use their own corpora. Almost all the language-based sciences – philosophy, literary studies, psychology, sociology, etc. – have people working in them using corpora. As Atkins (1992) notes, potential users of corpora are not necessarily interested only in the language of texts, but in their content too. But corpus use encourages even non-linguists to look at and evaluate the language patterns this content is expressed in. Although language is often widely debated outside linguistics, linguistics itself has not always imposed itself in these debates (Stubbs 1996: 236). Ideally, in the Age of Specialization the merits of the systematic study of language – of linguistics – will be reappraised.

13.2   Designing the contents of a specialized corpus

Returning to corpus linguistics, *specialized* can have two meanings: (i) for special purposes; or (ii) containing a specialized sub-variety of the language. In the case of (i), how do we best match our corpus to our purpose, in other words how do we decide what to put in it? The best way is to start from what one wishes to study, the object(s) of the research which, in the present case were the rhetorical strategies in spoken political discourse. I currently teach in a faculty of Political Science and more specifically, I teach two courses, one on the language of politics, the other the language of newspapers, and so press briefings were relevant to both. I chose briefings rather than news interviews because more work has been done in linguistics on the latter, and I chose US material because my students preferred it, partly because of the attention paid to the Kosovo crisis and, especially, the Clinton–Lewinsky affair.

In the case where we take 'specialized' to mean sub-variety, equally methodologically valid is a more 'black box' style approach, in which one simply chooses the type of text one is interested in and sees what comes out of the study. There can be little doubt that the technical ease of procuring specialized corpora is currently promoting great interest in language variety, much of which follows Biber's pioneering work. In fact, the current author believes that all corpus language work is properly comparative and the more comparable corpora of specialized varieties that are made, the more work can proceed.

Another factor in choice of corpus contents is the technical quality of the texts. I have already mentioned quality and level of transcription (Section 0.1.2). In the present case, it was slightly disappointing that more hesitation phenomena were not included in the White House transcripts but, say, a close phonetic transcription of the debates would have been a distraction to myself and I dare say to many of the readers. A further consideration is completeness: in studying discourse complete texts may often be preferable to incomplete ones. For some purposes length of text may be a parameter. Text transcripts which have a corresponding audio and even video version will become increasingly available.

Finally, the actual availability of texts is, of course, of paramount concern. At the time of writing, for example, it is generally more difficult and expensive to obtain material from US media sources than from British or some others. Most US newspapers make users pay for access to Internet archives, most UK papers do not (as yet). Both the BBC and ITV make many current affairs programme transcripts available over the Web. This, of course, leads to the final factor in corpus choice – availability and copyright protection.

13.3   Linguists who use corpora

Corpus linguistics is not a separate school or branch of linguistics in the same way as systemic or generative linguistics. It is rather a methodology which is still trying to find the best ways of exploiting new computer technology to improve our knowledge of language. But the linguist-who-uses-corpora *is* a different kind of linguist, and in two separate but related ways. First, the corpus opens up new avenues of research, and provides new facts, often unexpected ones, for consideration. And the wealth of data that corpus study makes available is not just 'more of the same' but, since theory is never independent from observation, more information leads to refinements in theoretical knowledge.

Second, the tools and methodology used by the researcher inevitably influence the object of research, in linguistics as in all other observational sciences. What the linguist studies is not language itself – for that is impossible – but the linguistic *record*, and the corpus is an entirely new kind of record from other more traditional ones – recordings, transcripts, remembered conversations, intuited sentences and so on.

The third age linguist-who-uses-corpora uses them in harmony with other kinds of linguistic records and with other analytical techniques. 'Gone is the concept of the corpus as the sole *explicandum* of language use. Present instead is the concept of a balanced corpus being used to *aid* the investigation of a language' (McEnery and Wilson 1996: 169). Precisely because corpus linguistics is a methodology and not a school of thought, it can be combined with as many other instruments as deemed fit. To whoever this appears serendipitous, haphazard even, I recommend reading a history of scientific endeavour such as those by Koestler (1964), White (2001) or Bragg (1998), which show just how non-linear and unsystematic it often is. The present work is a record of heuristic trial and error with corpus research at its core but I have never hesitated to employ introspection and intuition (which, by the way, I find is always greatly improved by reading up as much as possible on the topic)[1] and direct observation of the texts, including watching and listening to briefings on the net and reading the transcripts: employing corpus technology to study discourse 'does not mean that the analyst starts off with a *tabula rasa*' (Hardt-Mautner 1995: 8).

These studies, then, are offered in a spirit of demonstration, to show how an integrated methodology can function. The linguistic record does not always surrender its secrets easily and needs to be cajoled, seduced and bullied in as many ways as we can imagine.

13.4   Podium and press: an adversarial *modus vivendi*

The picture of the relationship between the two sides which emerges from this analysis of their use of language is a complex one. It is undoubtedly regulated on a professional level by rules of engagement (Chapter 6) which are adversarial, at times belligerently so. This belligerence is what strikes many White House watchers, even insiders, who describe the relationship as 'relentless and unseemly' (Keith Schneider, *Detroit Free Press*), 'highly dysfunctional' (Gary Kamiya, *Salon* magazine), even 'sick':

> [...] the sick little world of obsessed, self-important, prosecutorial journalists and their opposing cadre of self-important, image-mongering White House flacks.
>
> (Pete Hamill, *New York Daily News*)

Such comments, however, seem to ignore the fact that the contest is, as we have seen, governed by a set of particular discourse conventions, even if there is much debate about what is admissible and occasional attempts to test them.

Perhaps the key word in Hamill's appraisal is 'prosecutorial'. There is indeed an analogy between the interrogation the podium is subjected to and the legal process. He states his version of events, while the press, like an opposing lawyer, try to find faults with it. Nor is the procedure, in the larger picture, a deleterious one. First of all, the need to justify itself to a testing audience guides the administration's hand and thought:

> The need for Mr McCurry to field questions in the briefing room forced the administration to decide just what the hell its policy was. The very act of dealing with the press compelled a sluggish bureaucracy to resolve its interminable disputes.
>
> (Kurtz 1998: 2)

And second, the democratic process cannot but be served by the subjection of power to such close scrutiny. The fact that the behaviour of the press has hardened over the last few decades, along with the kind of questioning a politician can expect, is a result of a desire on the part of a more sceptical, disillusioned and demanding electorate to keep the workings of power under close watch.

A further criticism is that everything that goes on in these briefings is mere tactic, they are simply a:

> formulaic dance between state-of-the-art spinners and an elite journalistic establishment whose determination not to be spun imparts its own distortion [...] Both sides know the other's moves in advance, both sides view everything the other side does as a mere tactic, and both sides are determined to beat their enemy to the punch.
>
> (Gary Kamiya: *Salon* Magazine 1998)

The philosophy behind such criticism is that 'tactic' is anti-thetical to 'sincerity', as 'spin' is to 'truth'. There is further misapprehension here. It is entirely normal and expected that the podium, just like any defence counsel, put its client's case in the best possible light (whilst at the same time claiming to be doing nothing more than 'telling the truth', as the podium does so frequently: Section 9.1). Conversely, as we have seen, it is the very essence of the press's job to act as devil's advocate, to offer alternative probatory versions of what may have happened, without necessarily sincerely believing in them. 'Mere tactic' is better described as *negotiation* between the two sides in attempting to reach a version of events satisfactory to both sides (Section 9.4).[2]

Comments which see only belligerence in the relationship also fail to contemplate the substratum of informality and interpersonal affect that underlies what goes on, even when the stresses and strains of conflicts of interest take their toll at the professional level. It is this interplay between the professionally adversarial and the peer-group mundane which makes these briefings a particularly interesting genre of talk and distinguishes them from other types of conflict talk which are, on the one hand, almost entirely institutional, such as courtroom or police interrogation, or trade union–management meetings or, on the other hand, totally familiar, for example, parent–child or peer-group disputes, all of which have been the object of previous studies.

Finally, these criticisms do not take account of the symbiotic relationship between podium and press, and the fundamental underlying cooperation this implies. As Kurtz puts it in rather sensational fashion:

> For all the animosity, the White House spinners and their cynical chroniclers were ultimately joined at the hip in a strangely symbiotic relationship [...] McCurry and company needed the press to peddle their message to the public, and the journalists needed an action-packed presidency on which to build their reputations and name recognition.
>
> (Kurtz 1998: xxii)

For a competitive and copy-hungry press, the podium is an invaluable source of stories, even if, in the worst cases, the story is that the White House is being uncommunicative on some event. In the very worst case, you can write an article about the podium: even the man giving you the news can become the news.

For the White House, a conduit through which to pass its account of events to the public is invaluable. Even if the press are ready to savage your every move, it is better they savage you after having heard your side of the tale.

Notes

Foreword

1 References to Kurtz are from Kurtz (1998). All other references in these three paragraphs are from various websites. Baker, P. and Kurtz, H. for the *Washington Post*; Dunham, R. for *Business Week*; Irvine, R. and Kincaid, C. for *Media Monitor*; Jurkowitz, M. for the *Boston Globe*; Kamiya, G. in *Salon*, Internet magazine; Reaves White, S. for the *Amazon* website; Warren, J. for the *Chicago Tribune*; Zweifel, D. in the *Capital Times*.

2 I use the term *podium* in this work because *spokesperson* has a strict technical meaning in Levinson's analysis of *footing* (Chapter 2) indicating someone who delivers a message from a third party in their own words but has no responsibility for the content (Levinson 1988: 170). This is very rarely the role of the White House press secretary. Levinson too speaks of 'podium talk'.

3 I refer to the podium with the masculine pronoun *he*. This is because, in the period under study, all the podiums were male.

4 The CNN White House correspondent at the time just happened to be called *Wolf* Blitzer.

5 They are 'joined at the hip in a strangely symbiotic relationship' (Kurtz 1998: xxi–xxii).

0 Introduction: corpora, discourse, politics and the press

1 Respective sites: www.whitehouse.gov/news/briefings/ and www.C-Span.org.

2 These are all available on CD-ROM from ICAME, who can be contacted at the HIT Centre, University of Bergen, Norway, http://www.hit.uib.no/icame or icame@hit.uib.no.

3 There is a certain amount of confusion in linguistics over what is meant by *discourse*. Some writers, like Kennedy, use it to mean, more or less, 'language in its spoken form'. Others intend any stretch of language seen in its authentic context. My use is close to the second, but I also happen to be concentrating on *spoken* discourse in this work.

4 A drafting committee consisting of Thomas Jefferson, Benjamin Franklin, John Adams, Roger Sherman and Robert Livingston was appointed to draw up the document, but the man who actually put pen to paper (using as he said 'neither book nor pamphlet') was Thomas Jefferson.

5 In the final paragraph of the document, *we* are defined as follows: 'We, therefore, the Representatives of the United States of America …'.

6 Debate has raged over the question of the representativity or otherwise of corpora. My (practical) view in this book is that a collection of texts (of one circumscribed genre gathered over a limited period of time) is likely to be more representative of the genre than a single text met and studied at random.

7 Although *must* is found once in a declarative question form, for example, 'So he must act before Kofi Annan gives his report next week?'.

8 With the obvious exception of corpora that are co-extensive with their universe of discourse, for example, a corpus containing the complete works of Shakespeare (Spevack 1970).

9 See, for example, Leech and Fallon (1992).

10 *Perfectly* is found 38 times in the British material, but only three times in *WHB* and six times in the larger USPR. It would seem to be very much a Britishism. Few dictionaries include this kind of information.

11 These last two are, of course, used with more than one function. Taking examples from their concordances, *really* is used relatively frequently in *INTS* as an intensifier: 'these are *really* big positives', but its predominant function is probably another – that of distinguishing between one item or proposition and another (often unnamed) one: 'this was *really* about animal welfare'. *Quite* can be an intensifier ('that's *quite* a separate matter', typically in the *INTS* texts: *quite clear/different/frankly/sure*), or a downtoner ('that seemed to work *quite* well') [Quirk *et al.* 1985: 446 (Note (a))]. None of this affects the main argument.

12 In other words, the personal, temporal or locational characteristics of the situation within which an utterance takes place' (Crystal 1997: 107), that is, elements of the context. The term *deixis* is from the Greek, meaning 'pointing to'.

13 The item *that* also appears in the lists. It is, in fact, the single relatively most frequent item in the WBS – USPR list. Although the majority of occurrences of *that* are in reporting or locutionary phrases – *say that, believe that, sure that, etc.* – its deictic function also contributes to its extreme 'key-ness'.

14 The principle of complementarity 'implies the impossibility of any sharp separation between the behaviour of atomic objects and the interaction with the measuring instruments which serve to define the conditions under which the phenomena appear' (Encyclopedia Britannica).

1 Briefings as a type of discourse

1 The term *turn* is used in CA, whereas *move* is more common in pragmatics generally. I make use of both.

2 Footing: who says what to whom

1 In a later work, Levinson (1992: 70–1) describes an element which he calls 'episode', the subdivision of a 'speech activity'. Although this seems to more-or-less correspond to my 'routine', I prefer the latter since the term 'episode' suggests to me an entire session which could stand alone, whereas this is not generally the case for elements at this level of analysis.

2 Levinson himself notes that the many examples of collaboration 'raise the fundamental question whether the collaborative nature of verbal interaction does not make inherently problematic the attribution of participant role'.

3 Wolf Blitzer, White House correspondent for CNN.

4 With the important provision that voice quality, intonation, etc. are part of the form.

5 As Scannell (1991: 11) remarks: 'Studio-based programmes with live audiences have at least three and often four communicative circuits of interaction simultaneously in play: host and participants, host and studio audience, participants and audience, host and listeners or viewers'.

3 Voices of the press

1 This is the most frequent use when the first person plural pronoun is in object position, that is, *us*, since the subject is often *you* the podium, or another interlocutor of the press.

Typical phrases involving *us* include: 'Can you tell us ...', 'Can you give us an assessment ...', 'One of the Attorneys General told us today that ...'.
2 He points out, for example, how Churchill's famous 'We shall fight them on the beaches' really meant '*You* shall fight them on the beaches'.

4 Voices of the podium

1 This is of course a long-standing motif in US culture. It is the theme of the classic film *Mr Smith Goes to Washington* made by Frank Capra as long ago as 1939. It has lost none of its popularity.
2 The strategy of accusing one's opponents of 'politicizing the issue' is openly discussed on one occasion. On the subject of information gathering, the podium says:

> MR TOIV: [...] the administration supports a census that is fair and accurate and that is done by the most modern, scientific means. Unfortunately, there are those on the Hill who are trying to politicize the issue.

One of the journalists however wants to know why this accusation is made every time someone disagrees with the administration stance:

> Q: Why are Republicans politicizing the issue? Why is anyone who opposes the President's point of view on something politicizing it? Why can't you just accept that they have a different point of view on it?

3 Inevitably, given the number of questioners (not all of whom will be present at all briefings), the podium has to cater for different levels of background knowledge.
4 Expansion is, of course, one of the principal logico-semantic relations between clauses identified by Halliday (1985: 202–26).
5 I am grateful to Peter Levy (personal communication) for this observation.
6 There is just one exception in the 28 occurrences: 'Right now, what I'm aware of is ...', which echoes 'are you aware of ...' in the preceding question (concordance line 6).

5 Footing shift for attribution: 'according to the *New York Times* this morning ...'

1 '[...] in Goffman's terms, "authorship" is overtly deflected.' (Clayman 1992: 173).
2 According to Cockcroft and Cockcroft (1992: 69), the appeal to authority, or 'the model of testimony', 'was always regarded as the weakest of the *topoi* (the models of argument), because it depended on the reliability of a witness and was therefore not *inherently* reliable'. It would appear that in the modern world things are very different. Today's culture:

> elevates the 'expert' (especially in the media), testimony is endlessly sought and provided, whether we are listening to interviews with 'ordinary people', or to world-wide reporting, or reading accounts of a new 'miracle cure'.
>
> (Cockcroft and Cockcroft 1992: 69)

3 US tabloids have quite a propensity for inventing stories. Given the topic, here, the 'discovery' of Mr Clinton's love-child, the briefing predictably slips into the comic:

> Q: The picture on the Internet – he looks exactly like the President.
> MR LOCKHART: That's good. And I'm an alien space baby, Lester. (Laughter.) And we're probably related – so, next.
> Q: Do we have some of your DNA?
> MR LOCKHART: Sam, that's personal and we'll talk afterwards. (Laughter.)

4 Hence complaints of the press attempting to manufacture news rather than just report it.

5 I also feel that he is challenging the journalist to come clean: is it 'some' who say this, or are *you* the principal of this idea? The façade of collaborative neutralism comes close to cracking for a moment here.

6 'Have you stopped beating your wife?' is famously a trick question. A *yes* answer implies that you certainly used to; a *no*, even worse, that you still do.

6 'Rules of engagement': the interpersonal relationship between the podium and the press

1 Harris, writing from a UK perspective, lists the media interviewers Day (1961), Dimbleby (1975) and Walden (1985), and the academics Wedell (1968) and Whale (1977), who all make this point.

2 He is partly drawing on Palete and Entman (1981).

3 The asterisk functions as a wildcard meaning 'and any character string' – thus **n't* would find *can't, don't, didn't, isn't, wouldn't* and so on.

4 I borrow the term from Richard Dunham's review of Kurtz's *Spin Cycle* (1998): 'For those of us privy to the briefing-room jousting between Press Secretary Michael D. McCurry and press corps agents provocateurs […]'.

7 Politics, power and politeness

1 The word *polite* derives from the Latin *polire* meaning 'to smooth, polish'. Another term – *politic* talk – has been coined to describe 'socially sanctioned norms of interaction' (Kasper 1990: 208). It would be nice to think that this latter term derives at least in part from the Greek πόλις ('city', 'community'), which would comfort Brown and Levinson's vision of politeness as the art of living in community with others. At the same time it highlights the connection of *politeness* with *politics*: the first is the skill of getting the best out of relationships on a personal level, the second on a more general social plane.

2 *Act* in the sense of speech act (Section 1.1.2).

3 Interruption is defined as starting a turn at talk in a place that is not a transition-relevance site (Sacks *et al.* 1974). Hutchby (1996: 92) argues that the 'dominant' participant can use interruption 'to exercise power within the interaction by constraining the participation options' of the other.

4 My experience of a South European society, Italy, is that relationships at work are much more superficially formal and hierarchical. Honorifics such as *Dottore, Professore, Avvocato* are commonly used even among equals. Superiors frequently address males lower in the pecking order by last name alone. Young females may be addressed by first name, older ones generally by *la Signora* + Surname (maiden surname, husband's surnames are not generally adopted on marriage), which seems to be a honorific in its own right (*Signora* used to be reserved for married women but is now used regardless of marital status and is a term of considerable respect).

5 Although he/she 'never speaks as a private individual but as Prime Minister, Member of Parliament, union leader, spokesman for the police, financial expert, and so on […] it is always his personal interpretation and his personal opinion' (Jucker 1986: 10).

6 In very extreme and unusual circumstances, resignations have followed [see Chapter 1 of Jones (1996) on the Tim Yeo affair].

7 Beard (2000: 21) notices the abundance of sporting metaphor especially from baseball in US politics. See Semino and Masci (1996) for the use of sporting metaphor (football) in recent political language in Italy.

8 MFN = *Most Favoured Nation.*

9 *Blue Chip* = A financial journal; OMB = *Office of Management and Budget,* a government body; CBO = *Congressional Budget Office,* a non-partisan advisory body to Congress.

10 Care was taken to include only *what* in questions.

11 Including constructions introduced by *how many, how long, how close*.

12 Actually, rather more than two. Caffi (1999), for instance, extending G. Lakoff's (1973) metaphor, divides mitigating items into *hedges* (mitigation on the illocution), *bushes* (mitigation on propositional content) and *shields* (mitigation achieved by means which are not explicitly linguistic: dislocation, objectivization, etc.). For our more limited investigation I have wielded Occam's razor and kept to the single category of *hedges*.

8 Conflict talk

1 An often cited case of loser–loser scenario is the virus that kills its host too quickly and so is unable to propagate (Ryan 1996).

2 However, it may well be apparent to all, podium, journalist, the others present that the podium has won and the journalist lost. There are occasions on which questioners return later in a briefing in an attempt to get their own back.

3 Witness Kurtz's appraisal: ' "My next move is to get off this podium as quick as possible," McCurry said, provoking laughter from a press core determined to get answers and information but sympathetic to the position of a sympathetic man' (Kurtz 1998: *All Politics*: CNN).

4 Grimshaw (1990: 302) notes 'Americans may have a particular penchant for definitive outcomes, sports contests are carried into overtimes and extra innings and we [...] tend to see the world as one of "winners" and "losers" '. However, it may well be the lack of definitive, absolute winning and losing in everyday interaction (witness the low rates of winning and submission in conflict talk) which causes this penchant in symbolic activities like sport.

5 Watson, who studied police–suspect interrogations, warns us of the dangers of this. Power cannot be presupposed as a feature existing prior to and objectively within the discourse but 'must be firmly located in the systematic examination of features integral to the discourse itself' (Watson 1990: 280 discussed by Hutchby 1996: 114).

6 One of the most extreme must be courtroom interrogation of witnesses by attorneys (Atkinson and Drew 1979) or the accused by police (Harris 1995). But even here, how much of the asymmetry is due to institutional roles and how much to the superior discursive expertise of the professional interrogator, due to training and experience in the job, is a moot point. From the point of view of the respondent, of course, the situation is a tough one either way. See Harris (1995), however, for occasions when the accused or police suspects 'answer back' and challenge the validity (the 'unfairness') of the asymmetries inherent in courtroom and interrogation talk.

9 The form of words

1 Fowler quotes Andrew Neil, editor of the *Sunday Times*, who equates reporting with impartiality and feels that opinion and comment can be confined to the editorial page.

2 According to Tuchman (1978: 103), a fire is *the* classic news story and saying about a reporter 'he can't even cover a fire' is the ultimate expression of their incompetence.

3 Occurrences of the *Truth and Reconciliation Commission* have been omitted.

4 Common in news interviews: Jucker (1986: 130), Harris (1991: 91), but also in other forms of antagonistic talk.

5 I borrow this term from Halliday and Martin (1993). Halliday talks of the *systematic ambiguity* of *mean* in scientific texts. Morley (1999: 67–8) mentions the ambiguity of *mean* in political writings.

6 A *Continuing Resolution*, often referred to as a 'CR', continues funding for a programme if the fiscal year ends without a new appropriation in place: 'A CR provides temporary funding at current levels or less.' (C-Span Congressional glossary).

7 I found considerable corpus evidence to show that *say that* (when *that* is a demonstrative) tends to have an unfavourable semantic prosody. The *that* in question is frequently something that requires explaining or excusing. The same holds for *think that* and *do that*.

10 Metaphors of the world

1 One commentator has likened the White House briefings themselves to a game of chess: 'one hopes that an informed electorate can demand more than a political chess game. Stalemate leaves everyone disappointed'. Sarah Reaves White for *Amazon*.

11 Rhetoric, bluster and on-line gaffes

1 Plentiful in, for example, Jefferson's Declaration of Independence: '... Life, Liberty, and the pursuit of Happiness' ['Noun + Noun + (*the* Noun *of* Noun)'], 'we mutually pledge to each other our Lives, our Fortunes and our sacred Honor' ['*our* Noun + *our* Noun + *our* (Adjective + Noun)'].

2 This fact lends weight to Sinclair's (1991, 1992) approach, which 'extends the notion of phraseology to encompass a great deal more of language than it is commonly considered to encompass' (Hunston and Francis 1999: 21).

3 It abounds, for instance, in Lincoln's Gettysburg Address of 1863. The most interesting example is probably: 'The world will little note, nor long remember what we say here, but it can never forget what they did here'. The parallel phrases have the same subject (*The world*), though it is understood in the second and becomes *it* in the third. There is a connection in meaning between *little* and *long* and between *long* and *never* as referring to time (although between *little* and *never* any link is tenuous). There is also a connection in this particular context, between *note, remember* and *forget*, all verbs of perception, and a very strong contrastive link between *what we say here* and *what they did here*. This example shows just how complex and interwoven parallelism can become and that the semantic links can owe a great deal to individual context.

4 The *New York Times* doubtless means *longbows* (see Trevelyan 1952: 227–9).

5 One professional who was under no illusions about the relationship of news, spin and truth was President Reagan's spokesperson, Larry Speakes, who kept a sign on his desk: 'You don't tell us how to stage the news and we don't tell you how to cover it' (quoted in Kurtz 1998: xvii–xviii).

13 General conclusions

1 Reminiscent of the golfer Gary Player's famous remark: 'The more I practice, the luckier I get'.

2 It may be argued that the analogy with the courtroom breaks down at this point, since as Levinson (1992: 91) points out, in a courtroom 'cross-examination is more like a zero-sum game, where one party's losses are the other party's gains'. However, there is rather more negotiation in legal affairs than this would suggest, especially in the US system, where *plea-bargaining* is a very common phenomenon.

Bibliography

Aarts, J., de Haan, P. and Oostdijk, N. (eds) (1993). *English Language Corpus Design, Analysis and Exploitation*. Amsterdam: Rodopi.

Aitchison, J. (1999). *Linguistics: An Introduction*. London: Hodder and Stoughton.

Aston, G. (1999). Corpus use and learning to translate. *Textus*, 12, 289–314.

—(ed.) (2001). *Learning with Corpora*. Houston, TX: Athelstan.

Atkins, B. (1992). Tools for computer-aided corpus lexicography: the Hector project. *Acta Linguistica Hungarica*, 41, 1–4, 5–71.

Atkinson, J. and Drew, P. (1979). *Order in Court*. London: Macmillan.

Atkinson, J. and Heritage, J. (eds) (1984). *Structures of Social Action*. Cambridge: Cambridge University Press.

Austin, J. (1962). *How to Do Things with Words*. Oxford: Oxford University Press.

Baker, M., Francis, G. and Tognini-Bonelli, E. (eds) (1993). *Text and Technology. In Honour of John Sinclair*. Amsterdam, Philadelphia, PA: John Benjamins.

Baldry, A. (2000). Introduction, in: A. Baldry (ed.), *Multimodality and Multimediality in the Distance Learning Age*. Campobasso: Palladino, pp. 11–40.

Barlow, M. (1996). Corpora for theory and practice. *International Journal of Corpus Linguistics*. 1/1: 1–37.

Barlow, M. and Kemmer, S. (1994). A schema-based approach to grammatical description, in: S. Lima, R. Corrigan and G. Iverson (eds), *The Reality of Linguistic Rules*. Amsterdam, Philadelphia, PA: John Benjamins, pp. 19–42.

Barthes, R. (1977). The death of the author, in: S. Heath (ed.), *Image, Music, Text*. New York: Hill, pp. 142–148.

Beard, A. (2000). *The Language of Politics*. London: Routledge.

Bell, A. (1996). Time, text and technology in news English, in: S. Goodman and D. Graddol (eds), *Redesigning English: New Texts, New Identities*. London: Routledge, pp. 3–26.

Bell, A. and Garrett, P. (eds) (1998). *Approaches to Media Discourse*. Oxford: Blackwell.

Berger, P. and Luckmann, T. (1976). *The Social Construction of Reality*. Harmondsworth: Penguin.

Bergmann, J. (1992). Veiled morality: notes on discretion in psychiatry, in: P. Drew and J. Heritage (eds), *Talk at Work*. Cambridge: Cambridge University Press, pp. 137–162.

Best, A. (1996). *Political Interviewing on the BBC Radio Four 'Today' Programme: a pragmatic analysis of the controversial Anna Ford/Kenneth Clarke Interview*, MSC dissertation, Birmingham: University of Aston. Online, available at: http:www.les.aston.ac.uk/lsu/diss.

Biber, D. (1988). *Variation across Speech and Writing*. Cambridge: Cambridge University Press.

Biber, D. and Conrad, S. (1999). Lexical bundles in conversation and academic prose, in: H. Hasselgård and S. Oksefjell (eds), *Out of Corpora*. Amsterdam: Rodopi, pp. 181–190.

Biber, D., Conrad, S. and Reppen, R. (1994). Corpus-based approaches to issues in applied lingustics. *Applied Linguistics*, 15/2, 169–189.

——(1998). *Corpus Linguistics: Investigating Language Structure and Use*. Cambridge: Cambridge University Press.

Biber, D., Johansson, S., Leech, G., Conrad, S. and Finegan, E. (1999). *Longman Grammar of Spoken and Written English*. London: Longman.

Billig, M. (1987). *Arguing and Thinking: A Rhetorical Approach to Social Psychology*. Cambridge: Cambridge University Press.

Blum-Kulka, S. (1983). The dynamics of political interviews. *Text*, 3/2, 131–153.

Boden, D. and Zimmerman, D. (eds) (1991). *Talk and Social Structure*. Cambridge: Polity Press.

Bragg, M. (1998). *On Giants' Shoulders*. London: Sceptre.

Brazil, D. (1985). *The Communicative Value of Intonation*. Birmingham: University of Birmingham.

Brown, G. and Yule, G. (1983). *Discourse Analysis*. Cambridge: Cambridge University Press.

Brown, P. and Levinson, S. (1987). *Politeness: Some Universals in Language Use*. Cambridge: Cambridge University Press.

Brown, R. and Gilman, A. (1960). The pronouns of power and solidarity, in: T. Sebeok (ed.), *Style in Language*. Cambridge, MA: MIT Press, pp. 253–276.

Burke, K. (1969). *A Rhetoric of Motives*. Berkeley CA: California University Press.

Caffi, C. (1999). On mitigation. *Journal of Pragmatics*, 31/7, 881–910.

Chafe, W. (1982). Integration and involvement in speaking, writing, and oral literature, in: D. Tannen (ed.), *Spoken and Written Language: Exploring Orality and Literacy*. Norwood, NJ: Ablex, pp. 35–55.

Cherry, R. (1988). Politeness in written persuasion. *Journal of Pragmatics*, 12/1, 63–82.

Clayman, S. (1991). News interview openings, in: P. Scannell (ed.), *Broadcast Talk*. London: Sage, pp. 47–75.

——(1992). Footing in the achievement of neutrality: the case of news-interview discourse, in: P. Drew and J. Heritage (eds), *Talk at Work*. Cambridge: Cambridge University Press, pp. 163–198.

——(1993). Reformulating the question: a device for answering/not answering questions in news interviews and press conferences. *Text*, 13/2, 159–188.

Cockcroft, R. and Cockcroft, S. (1992). *Persuading People: An Introduction to Rhetoric*. London: Macmillan.

Cohen, S. and Young, J. (eds) (1981). *The Manufacture of News: Social Problems, Deviance and the Mass Media*, 2nd edn. London: Constable.

Coleridge, S. (1956). In: G. Watson (ed.), *Biographia Literaria*. London: Dent.

Cook, G. (1989). *Discourse*. Oxford: Oxford University Press.

——(1995). Theoretical issues: transcribing the untranscribable, in G. Leech, G. Myers and J. Thomas (eds), *Spoken English on Computer*. London: Longman, pp. 35–53.

Crystal, D. (1997). *A Dictionary of Linguistics and Phonetics*, 4th edn. Oxford: Blackwell.

Davies, M. and Ravelli, L. (eds) (1992). *Advances in Systemic Linguistics: Recent Theory and Practice*. London: Planter.

Davis, R. and Owen, D. (1998). *New Media and American Politics*. New York: Oxford University Press.

Day, R. (1961). *Television: A Personal Report*. London: Hutchinson.

Dimbleby, J. (1975). *Richard Dimbleby: A Biography*. London: Hodder and Stoughton.

Drew, P. and Heritage, J. (1992). Analyzing talk at work: an introduction, in: P. Drew and J. Heritage (eds), *Talk at Work*. Cambridge: Cambridge University Press, pp. 3–65.

Drew, P. and Wootton, A. (eds) (1988). *Erving Goffman: Exploring the Interaction Order.* Cambridge: Polity Press.

Eder, D. (1990), Serious and playful disputes: variation in conflict talk among female adolescents, in: A. Grimshaw (ed.), *Conflict Talk: Sociological Investigations of Arguments in Conversation.* Cambridge: Cambridge University Press, pp. 67–84.

Ensink, T. (1997). The footing of a royal address: an analysis of representativeness in political speech, exemplified in Queen Beatrix's Address to the Knesset on March 28, 1995, in: C. Schäffner (ed.), *Analysing Political Speeches.* Clevedon: Multilingual Matters, pp. 5–32.

Fairclough, N. (1989). *Language and Power.* London: Longman.

——(1992). *Critical Language Awareness.* London: Longman.

Firth, J. (1935). The technique of semantics. *Transactions of the Philological Society*, 36–72.

——(1957). *Papers in Linguistics.* London: Oxford University Press.

Fisher, S. and Todd, A. (eds) (1987). *The Social Organization of Doctor–Patient Communication*, Washington, DC: Center for Applied Linguistics.

Flowerdew, J. (1993). Concordancing as a tool in course design. *System*, 21, 231–244.

Foucault, M. (1977). *Power/knowledge.* Hemel Hempstead: Harvester.

Fowler, R. (1991). *Language in the News.* London: Routledge.

Francis, G. (1993). A corpus-driven approach to grammar – principles, methods and examples, in: M. Baker, G. Francis and E. Tognini-Bonelli (eds), *Text and Technology. In Honour of John Sinclair.* Amsterdam, Philadelphia, PA: John Benjamins, pp. 137–156.

Galtung, J. and Ruge, M. (1981). Structuring and selecting news, in: S. Cohen and J. Young (ed.), *The Manufacture of News: Social Problems, Deviance and the Mass Media*, 2nd edn. London: Constable, pp. 52–63.

Garton, G., Montgomery, M. and Tolson, A. (1991). Ideology, scripts and metaphors in the public sphere of a general election, in: P. Scannell (ed.), *Broadcast Talk.* London: Sage, 100–118.

Gellner, E. (1959). *Words and Things.* London: Gollancz.

Glasgow University Media Group (1976). *Bad News.* London: Routledge & Kegan Paul.

——(1980). *More Bad News.* London: Routledge and Kegan Paul.

Goffman, E. (1967). *Interaction Ritual: Essays on Face to Face behavior.* Garden City, NY: Doubleday.

——(1981). *Forms of Talk.* Oxford: Blackwell.

Goodman, S. and Graddol, D. (eds) (1996). *Redesigning English: New Texts, New Identities.* London: Routledge.

Goodwin, C. and Goodwin, M. (1990). Interstitial argument, in: A. Grimshaw (ed.), *Conflict Talk: Sociological Investigations of Arguments in Conversation.* Cambridge: Cambridge University Press, pp. 85–117.

Granger, S. (1993). International corpus of learner English, in: J. Aarts, P. de Haan and N. Oostdijk (eds), *English Language Corpus Design, Analysis and Exploitation.* Amsterdam: Rodopi, pp. 57–72.

Greatbatch, D. (1986). Aspects of topical organisation in news interviews: the use of agenda-shifting procedures by interviewers. *Media, Culture and Society*, 8/4, 441–455.

——(1988). A turn-taking system for British news interviews. *Language and Society*, 17/3, 401–430.

——(1998). Conversation analysis: neutralism in British news interviews, in: A. Bell and P. Garrett (eds), *Approaches to Media Discourse.* Oxford: Blackwell, pp. 163–185.

Greenbaum, S. (1996). *Comparing English Worldwide: The International Corpus of English.* Oxford: Clarendon Press.

Grimshaw, A. (1990). Research on conflict talk: antecedents, resources, findings, directions, in: A. Grimshaw (ed.), *Conflict Talk: Sociological Investigations of Arguments in Conversation*. Cambridge: Cambridge University Press, pp. 281–324.

Haarman, L., Morley, J. and Partington, A. (2002). Habeas corpus: methodological reflections on the creation and use of a specialised corpus, in: C. Gagliardi (ed.), *Quantity and Quality in English Linguistic Research: Some Issues*. Pescara: Libreria dell'Università Editrice, pp. 55–119.

Habermas, J. (1984). *The Theory of Communicative Action*. Vol. 1: Reason and the rationalisation of society. London: Heineman.

Halliday, M. (1973). *Explorations in the Functions of Language*. London: Edward Arnold.

——(1985). *An Introduction to Functional Grammar*. London: Edward Arnold.

——(1992). Language as system and language as instance: the corpus as a theoretical construct, in: J. Svartvik (ed.), *Directions in Corpus Linguistics*. Berlin: Mouton de Gruyter, pp. 61–77.

Halliday, M. and Martin, J. (1993). *Writing Science: Literacy and Discursive power*. London: Falmer Press.

Hardt-Mautner, G. (1995). '*Only Connect.*' Critical discourse analysis and corpus linguistics, University of Lancaster. Online, available at: http://www.comp.lancs.ac.uk/computing/research/ucrel/tech_papers.html.

Harris, S. (1991). Evasive action: how politicians respond to questions in political interviews, in: P. Scannell (ed.), *Broadcast Talk*. London: Sage, pp. 76–99.

——(1995). Pragmatics and power. *Journal of Pragmatics*, 23/2, 117–135.

——(2001). Being politically impolite: extending politeness theory to adversarial political discourse. *Discourse and Society*, 12/4, 451–472.

Heath, S. (ed.) (1977). *Image, Music, Text*. New York: Hill.

Henderson, W. (1982). Metaphor in economics. *Economics*, 18/4, 147–157; reprinted in M. Coulthard (ed.), (1986). *Talking about Text*, Discourse Monograph No. 13, University of Birmingham: English Language Research.

Heritage, J. (1985). Analysing news interviews: aspects of the production of talk for an overhearing audience, in: T. van Dijk (ed.), *Handbook of Discourse Analysis*, Vol. 3. London: Academic Press, pp. 95–117.

Heritage, J. and Greatbatch, D. (1991). On the institutional character of institutional talk: the case of news interviews, in: D. Boden and D. Zimmerman (eds), *Talk and Social Structure*. Cambridge: Polity Press, pp. 93–137.

Herman, E. and Chomsky, N. (1999). Manufacturing consent, in: H. Tumber (ed.), *News: A Reader*. Oxford: Oxford University Press, pp. 166–179.

Hoey, M. (1983). *On the Surface of Discourse*. London: George Allen and Unwin.

Holtgraves, T. (1997). Yes, but … positive politeness in conversation arguments, *Journal of Language and Social Psychology*, 16/2, 222–239.

Howarth, P. (1956). *Questions in the House: The History of a Unique British Institution*. Oxford: Bodley Head.

Hunston, S. and Francis, G. (1999). *Pattern Grammar*. Amsterdam, Philadelphia, PA: John Benjamins.

Hutchby, I. (1991). The organisation of talk on talk radio, in: P. Scannell (ed.), *Broadcast Talk*. London: Sage, pp. 119–137.

——(1996). *Confrontational Talk*. Mahwah, NJ: Lawrence Erlbaum Associates.

Hymes, D. (1964). Towards ethnographies of communicative events. *American Anthropologist*, 66, 12–25.

Hymes, D. (1971). *On Communicative Competence*. Philadelphia, PA: University of Pennsylvania Press; reprinted in J. Pride and J. Holmes (eds) (1972), *Sociolinguistics*. Harmondsworth: Penguin.

Jakobson, R. (1960). Concluding statements: linguistics and poetics, in: T. Sebeok (ed.), *Style in Language*. Cambridge, MA: MIT Press, pp. 350–377.

Jones, N. (1996). *Soundbites and Spin Doctors: How Politicians Manipulate the Media and Vice-Versa*. London: Cassell.

Jucker, A. (1986). *News Interviews: A Pragmalinguistic Analysis*. Amsterdam, Philadelphia, PA: John Benjamins.

Kasper, G. (1990). Linguistic politeness: current research issues. *Journal of Pragmatics*, 14/2, 193–218.

Kennedy, G. (1998). *An Introduction to Corpus Linguistics*. London: Longman.

Koestler, A. (1964). *The Sleepwalkers*. Harmondsworth: Penguin.

Kress, G. (1994). Text and grammar as explanation, in U. Meinhof and K. Richardson (eds), *Text, Discourse and Context*. London: Longman, pp. 24–46.

Kress, G. and Hodge G. (1979). *Language as Ideology*. London: Routledge.

Kurtz, H. (1998). *Spin Cycle: How the White House and the Media Manipulate the News*. New York: Touchstone.

Labov, T. (1990). Ideological themes in reports of interracial conflict, in: A. Grimshaw (ed.), *Conflict Talk: Sociological Investigations of Arguments in Conversation*. Cambridge: Cambridge University Press, pp. 139–159.

Labov, W. (1972). *Sociolinguistic Patterns*. Philadelphia, PA: University of Pennsylvania Press.

Labov, W. and Fanshel, D. (1977). *Therapeutic Discourse: Psychotherapy as Conversation*. New York: Academic Press.

Lakoff, G. (1973). Hedges: a study in meaning criteria and the logic of fuzzy concepts. *Journal of Philosophical Logic*, 2, 458–508.

——(1991). Metaphor and war: the metaphor system used to justify war in the Gulf. Online, available at: http://eserver.org/govt/gulf-war/metaphor-and-war-in-gulf.text.

Lakoff, G. and Johnson, J. (1980). *Metaphors We Live By*. Chicago, IL: University of Chicago.

Lakoff, R. (1973a). Questionable answers and answerable questions, in: B. Kashru, R. Lees, Y. Makiel, A. Pietrangeli and S. Saporta (eds), *Issues in Linguistics. Papers in Honor of Henry and Renée Kahane*. Urbana, IL: University of Illinois Press, pp. 453–467.

——(1973b). The logic of politeness: minding your p's and q's. Papers from the 9th Regional Meeting. Chicago Linguistics Society, 292–305.

——(1989). The limits of politeness: therapeutic and courtroom discourse. *Multilingua*, 8, 101–129.

Leech, G. (1983). *Principles of Pragmatics*. London: Longman.

Leech, G. and Fallon, R. (1992). Computer corpora – what do they tell us about culture? *ICAME Journal*, 16, 29–50.

Leech, G., Myers, G. and Thomas, J. (eds) (1995). *Spoken English on Computer*. London: Longman.

Levinson, S. (1983). *Pragmatics*. Cambridge: Cambridge University Press.

——(1988). Putting linguistics on a proper footing: explorations in Goffman's concepts of participation, in: P. Drew and A. Wootton (eds), *Erving Goffman: Exploring the Interaction Order*. Cambridge: Polity Press, pp. 161–227.

——(1992). Activity types and language, in: P. Drew and J. Heritage (eds), *Talk at Work*. Cambridge: Cambridge University Press, pp. 66–100.

Lewis, C. (1984). *Reporting for Television*. New York: Columbia University Press.

Linell, P. and Luckmann, T. (1991). Asymmetries in dialogue: some conceptual preliminaries, in: I. Markova and K. Foppa (eds), *Asymmetries in Dialogue*. Hemel Hempstead: Harvester Wheatsheaf, pp. 1–20.

Lombardo, L., Haarman, L., Morley, J. and Taylor, C. (1999). *Massed Medias: Linguistic Tools for Interpreting Media Discourse*. Milano: LED.

Louw, B. (1993). Irony in the text or insincerity in the writer? – The diagnostic potential of semantic prosodies, in: M. Baker, G. Francis and E. Tognini-Bonelli (eds), *Text and Technology. In Honour of John Sinclair*. Amsterdam, Philadelphia, PA: John Benjamins, pp. 157–176.

Maltese, J. (1992). *Spin Control: The White House Office of Communications and the Management of Presidential News*. Chapel Hill, NC, London: University of North Carolina Press.

Maynard, D. (1991). Interaction and asymmetry in clinical discourse. *American Journal of Sociology*, 97, 448–495.

McEnery, A. and Wilson, A. (1996). *Corpus Linguistics*. Edinburgh: Edinburgh University Press.

—— (2000). *Corpus Linguistics*, 2nd edn. Edinburgh: Edinburgh University Press.

Mehan, H. (1985). The structure of classroom discourse, in: T. van Dijk (ed.), *Handbook of Discourse Analysis*. London: Academic Press, pp. 120–132.

Meinhof, U. and Richardson, K. (eds) (1994). *Text, Discourse and Context*. London: Longman.

Minsky, M. (1975). A framework for representing knowledge, in: P. Winston (ed.), *The Psychology of Computer Vision*. New York: McGraw Hill, pp. 211–277.

Morley, J. (1998). *Truth to Tell: Form and Function in Newspaper Headlines*. Bologna: CLUEB.

——(1999). Sticky business: a case study of cohesion in the language of politics in the *Economist*, in: L. Lombardo, L. Haarman, J. Morley and C. Taylor (eds), *Massed Medias: Linguistic Tools for Interpreting Media Discourse*. Milano: LED, pp. 19–84.

O'Barr, W. (1982). *Linguistic Evidence*. New York: Academic Press.

O'Donnell, K. (1990). Difference and dominance: how labor and management talk conflict, in: A. Grimshaw (ed.), *Conflict Talk: Sociological Investigations of Arguments in Conversation*. Cambridge: Cambridge University Press, pp. 210–240.

Palete, D and Entman, R. (1981). *Media Power Politics*. New York: The Free Press.

Parsons, T. (1951). *The Social System*. Glencoe: The Free Press.

Partington, A. (1995). Kicking the habit: the exploitation of collocation in literature and humour, in: J. Payne (ed.), *Linguistic Approaches to Literature*, English Language Research Journal, 17. Birmingham: University of Birmingham, pp. 25–44.

——(1998). *Patterns and Meanings*. Amsterdam, Philadelphia, PA: John Benjamins.

——(2001). Corpora and their uses in language research, in: G. Aston (ed.), *Learning with Corpora*. Houston, TX: Athelstan, pp. 46–62.

Pawley, A. and Syder, H. (1983). Two puzzles for linguistic theory: nativelike selection and nativelike fluency, in: J. Richards and R. Schmidt (eds), *Language and Communication*. London: Longman, pp. 191–226.

Payne, J. (ed.) (1995). *Linguistic Approaches to Literature*, English Language Research Journal, 17. Birmingham: University of Birmingham.

Philips, S. (1990). The judge as third party in American trial-court conflict talk, in: A. Grimshaw (ed.), *Conflict Talk: Sociological Investigations of Arguments in Conversation*. Cambridge: Cambridge University Press, pp. 197–209.

Pomerantz, A. (1984). Agreeing and disagreeing with assessments: some features of preferred/dispreferred turn shapes, in: J. Atkinson and J. Heritage (eds), *Structures of Social Action*. Cambridge: Cambridge University Press, pp. 57–101.

Pride, J. and Holmes, J. (eds) (1972). *Sociolinguistics*. Harmondsworth: Penguin.

Psathas, G. (ed.) (1980). *Interaction Competence.* Washington, DC: University Press of America.

Quirk, R., Greenbaum, S., Leech, G. and Svartvik, J. (1985). *A Comprehensive Grammar of the English Language.* London: Longman.

Reah, D. (1998). *The Language of Newspapers.* London: Routledge.

Richards, J. and Schmidt, R. (eds) (1983). *Language and Communication.* London: Longman.

Roberts, C., Davies, E. and Jupp, T. (1992). *Language and Discrimination: A Study of Communication in Multi-ethnic Workplaces.* London: Longman.

Ryan, F. (1996). *Virus X.* London: HarperCollins.

Sacks, H. (1972). An initial investigation of the usability of conversational data for doing sociology, in: D. Sudnow (ed.), *Studies in Social Interaction.* New York: The Free Press, pp. 31–74.

——(1992). Repair after next turn: the last structurally provided defence of intersubjectivity in conversation. *American Journal of Sociology*, 97, 1295–1345.

Sacks, H., Schegloff, E. and Jefferson, G. (1974). A simplest systematics for the organization of turn taking for conversation. *Language*, 50, 696–735.

Saville-Troike, M. (1989). *The Ethnography of Communication.* Oxford: Blackwell.

Scannell, P. (1991). Introduction: the relevance of talk, in: P. Scannell (ed.), *Broadcast Talk.* London: Sage, pp. 1–13.

Schäffner, C. (1997). Editorial: political speeches and discourse analysis, in: C. Schäffner (ed.), *Analysing Political Speeches.* Clevedon: Multilingual Matters, pp. 1–4.

Schank, R. and Abelson, R. (1997). *Scripts, Plans, Goals and Understanding.* Hillsdale, NJ: Lawrence Erlbaum.

Schiffrin, D. (1985). Conversational coherence: the role of *well. Language*, 61/3, 640–667.

Scott, M. (1998). *WordSmith Tools.* Oxford: Oxford University Press.

Scott, M. and Johns, T. (1993). *MicroConcord.* Oxford: Oxford University Press.

Searle, J. (1969). *Speech Acts: An Essay in the Philosophy of Language.* Cambridge: Cambridge University Press.

Sebeok, T. (ed.) (1960). *Style in Language.* Cambridge, MA: MIT Press.

Semino, E. and Masci, M. (1996). Politics is football: metaphor in the discourse of Silvio Berlusconi in Italy. *Journal of Pragmatics*, 7/2, 243–270.

Sinclair, J. (1991). *Corpus, Concordance, Collocation.* Oxford: Oxford University Press.

——(1992). Trust the text: the implications are daunting, in: M. Davies and L. Ravelli (eds), *Advances in Systemic Linguistics: Recent Theory and Practice.* London: Planter, pp. 5–19.

Sinclair, J. and Coulthard, M. (1975). *Towards an Analysis of Discourse: The English Used by Teachers and Pupils.* Oxford: Oxford University Press.

Slugoski, B. (1985). *Grice's Theory of Conversation as a Social Psychological Model*, D. Phil. Oxford: University of Oxford.

Sperber, D. and Wilson, D. (1995). *Relevance*, 2nd edn. Oxford: Blackwell.

Spevack, M. (1970). *Complete and Systematic Concordance to the Works of Shakespeare.* Hildesheim: Olms.

Stubbs, M. (1996). *Text and Corpus Analysis.* Oxford: Blackwell.

Sudnow, D. (ed.) (1972). *Studies in Social Interaction.* New York: The Free Press.

Svartvik, J. (ed.) (1992). *Directions in Corpus Linguistics.* Berlin: Mouton de Gruyter.

Teubert, W. (1996). Comparable or parallel corpora? *International Journal of Lexicography*, 9/3, 238–264.

Trevelyan, G. (1952). *History of England*, 3rd edn. London: Longmans.

Thompson, G. (1997). *Introducing Functional Grammar.* London: Arnold.

Thompson, J. (1984). *Studies in the Theory of Ideology.* Cambridge: Polity Press.

Tuchman, G. (1978). *Making News: A Study in the Construction of Reality*. New York: The Free Press.

Tumber, H. (ed.) (1999). *News: A Reader*. Oxford: Oxford University Press.

Urban, G. (1986). Rhetoric of a war chief. *Working Papers and Proceedings of the Center for Psychosocial Studies*, Chicago, 5, pp. 1–27.

Van Dijk, T. (ed.) (1985). *Handbook of Discourse Analysis*. London: Academic Press.

——(1993). Critical discourse analysis. *Discourse & Society* (special issue), 4/2.

Vuchinich, S. (1990). The sequential organization of closing in verbal family conflict, in: A. Grimshaw (ed.), *Conflict Talk: Sociological Investigations of Arguments in Conversation*. Cambridge: Cambridge University Press, pp. 118–138.

Walden, B. (1985). Interview: Weekend Walden. *Communication and Media*, 1/4.

Watson, D. (1990). Some features of the elicitation of confessions in murder interrogations, in: G. Psathas (ed.), *Interaction Competence*. Washington, DC: University Press of America, pp. 263–295.

Wedell, E. (1968). *Broadcasting and Public Policy*. London: Michael Joseph.

Whale, J. (1977). *The Politics of the Media*. London: Fontana.

White, M. (2001). *Rivals: Conflict as the Fuel of Science*. London: Secker and Warburg.

Williams, R. (1976). *Keywords*, 2nd edn. London: Fontana.

Wilson, J. (1990). *Politically Speaking*. Oxford: Blackwell.

——(1991). The linguistic pragmatics of terrorist acts. *Discourse and Society*, 2/1, 29–46.

Woodbury, H. (1984). The strategic use of questions in court. *Semiotica*, 48/3–4, 197–228.

Wortham, S. (1996). Mapping participant deictics: a technique for discovering speaker's footing. *Journal of Pragmatics*, 25, 331–348.

Zagrebelsky, M.-T. (1992). Processes of lexical and semantic innovation in contemporary English: the case of the Gulf War. *Textus*, V, 111–122.

Zanettin, F. (1994). Parallel words: designing a bilingual database for translation activities, in: A. Wilson and A. McEnery (eds), *Corpora in Language Education and Research: A Selection of Papers from Talc94*, Unit for Computer Research on the English Language, Technical Papers 4 (special issue), Lancaster University, pp. 99–111.

Index

Printed in Great Britain
by Amazon